ACQUIRING PRAGMATICS

Social and cognitive perspectives

Sandrine Zufferey

LONDON AND NEW YORK

First published 2015
by Routledge
2 Park Square, Milton Park, Abingdon, Oxon OX14 4RN

and by Routledge
711 Third Avenue, New York, NY 10017

Routledge is an imprint of the Taylor & Francis Group, an informa business

British Library Cataloguing-in-Publication Data
A catalogue record for this book is available from the British Library

Library of Congress Cataloging-in-Publication Data
Zufferey, Sandrine, author.
Acquiring pragmatics: social and cognitive perspectives/Sandrine Zufferey.
pages cm
Includes bibliographical references and index.
1. Discourse analysis—Social aspects. 2. Pragmatics—Social aspects.
3. Speech acts (Linguistics) 4. Cognitive grammar. 5. Language acquisition.
I. Title.
P302.84.Z84 2015
401′.41—dc23
2014024433

ISBN: 978-0-415-74642-7 (hbk)
ISBN: 978-0-415-74644-1 (pbk)
ISBN: 978-1-315-74795-8 (ebk)

Typeset in Bembo Std
by Swales & Willis Ltd, Exeter, Devon, UK

Printed and bound in Great Britain by
TJ International Ltd, Padstow, Cornwall

ACQUIRING PRAGMATICS

'Sandrine Zufferey has done the fields of pragmatics, language acquisition, and cognitive science an invaluable service. Her book covers a remarkably broad range of results and ideas that she skillfully integrates into a beautifully structured, impeccably researched, and engaging synthesis. An authoritative and endlessly fascinating exposition of the state-of-the-art, *Acquiring Pragmatics* should be required reading for anyone interested in the study of pragmatics, its acquisition, and its place within the sciences of the mind.'

Julien Musolino, *Rutgers University, USA*

Acquiring Pragmatics offers a comprehensive synthesis of state-of-the-art research on the acquisition of pragmatics. It introduces the current topics of research in theoretical pragmatics, and explores the issues they raise for language acquisition research and the new experimental designs that have been developed to address them.

While each chapter covers one topic in depth, it also places a strong emphasis on the underlying methodological aspects of each issue, which will help the reader to develop their own experimental designs. Key topics covered include:

- the interfaces between pragmatics and language acquisition
- the social aspects of pragmatic competence
- the cognitive aspects of pragmatic competence
- the acquisition of pragmatics in autistic spectrum disorders and second language acquisition.

Acquiring Pragmatics is key reading for advanced undergraduate and graduate students studying pragmatics and language acquisition.

Sandrine Zufferey is a post-doctoral research fellow at the University of Fribourg in Switzerland. Her research focuses on the acquisition and processing of discourse connectives. Her work takes a cross-linguistic perspective in order to study the way linguistic encoding affects cognitive processes.

CONTENTS

ACKNOWLEDGMENTS

This book is based on the teaching material for the course on pragmatics and language acquisition that I taught at the University of Geneva between 2009 and 2011. I therefore first and foremost thank all my students for their numerous insights and stimulating contributions, as well as their useful feedback on the course material. I also thank the Linguistics Department at the University of Geneva, and especially professor Jacques Moeschler, for giving me the opportunity to create this course.

My warmest gratitude is also due to the colleagues who read and commented on portions of the book, namely Andrei Popescu-Belis, Jacques Moeschler, Anne Reboul, and Didier Maillat. I am also greatly indebted to the anonymous reviewers for their useful comments.

This book was written while I was working as a post-doctoral researcher at the Utrecht Institute of Linguistics (UiL OTS). I thank all my colleagues at UiL OTS, and especially the discourse group led by professor Ted Sanders, for sharing their expertise on language acquisition and processing. I felt privileged to grow professionally as a member of this excellent research group. My post-doctoral stay in Utrecht was supported by an ERC Marie Curie IEF grant for the DISCOM project (299185) and I gratefully acknowledge this financial support.

I also thank the team at Routledge, especially Nadia Seemungal for discussing the early stages of this project with me and helping me to give it its current format, and to Rachel Daw for her constant enthusiasm and support at every stage of the project. It was a great pleasure to work with you.

Finally, I thank my husband for his unfailing love and support in everything that I undertake, and my children for coping with a busy mum and giving me daily examples of their wonderful pragmatic skills.

INTRODUCTION

Pragmatics is one of the core domains of linguistics. During the past decades, it has been a rapidly growing field of study, and considerable paradigm shifts have occurred. From the study of socially determined rules governing the production of speech acts, pragmatics has now also become part of the cognitive sciences and aims at understanding how listeners bridge the gap between the under-determined linguistic meaning of utterances and the full-blown speaker's meaning. The multifaceted nature of research in pragmatics has been matched in the developmental literature by a growing number of studies covering many different aspects of verbal communication, ranging from the acquisition of speech acts to the development of theory of mind abilities and the reasoning skills involved in the derivation of scalar implicatures.

The main objective of this book is to offer a synthesis of state-of-the-art research on the acquisition of pragmatic competencies, focusing on a selection of the most thoroughly researched topics (see also Matthews, 2014 for an up-to-date review of additional topics). From a social perspective, the acquisition of pragmatic competencies encompasses the ability to interact with others in an appropriate manner in conversations and to adapt to different addressees, to be polite, and to follow the conventional rules governing the production of speech acts. It also includes the study of the social contexts in which children develop these competencies: peer interactions, family conversations, school, and so on. From a cognitive perspective, acquiring pragmatic competencies means developing the necessary cognitive abilities to enrich the linguistic meaning of utterances. These competencies include the ability to draw inferences, to reason about mental states, and to integrate contextual information from various sources. A major recent development of the field since classical reference books were published (e.g. Bates, 1976; Ninio & Snow, 1996) has been the change of focus from almost exclusively social approaches in developmental pragmatics to new research aiming at empirical testing of the theoretical models stemming from cognitive approaches to pragmatics.

The separation between social and cognitive approaches is a classic one in pragmatics. For Escandell-Vidal (2004: 2), social pragmatics encompasses the study of 'external' factors determined by social and cultural norms, while cognitive pragmatics includes the study of 'internal' processes, such as the cognitive bases of linguistic performance. In her model of pragmatic knowledge, O'Neill (2012) separated pragmatic skills into three interrelated categories: social knowledge, encompassing social stereotyped knowledge and etiquette rules; social-cognitive knowledge, including the recognition of facial expressions and mental state concepts; and cognitive knowledge, including script knowledge and understanding of time. This classification has the merit of showing that social and cognitive topics in pragmatics form a continuum rather than well-separated domains, though in fact they may be more accurately conceived as different views on the same topics. For example, the acquisition of metaphors is a central topic for both the social and cognitive approaches to pragmatics. Social studies have investigated the impact of social contexts on children's production and understanding of metaphors (Cameron, 1997), whereas cognitive studies aim at understanding the processes enabling children to understand them (e.g. Pouscoulous, 2011; Cacciari & Padovani, 2012). Zufferey (2010: 40) argued that many of the topics traditionally included in the social studies of developmental pragmatics are also relevant from a cognitive perspective.

In this book, social and cognitive perspectives are covered in separate parts, in order to reflect the distinct theoretical background from which studies are conducted, without assuming a total separation between them, as cross-references are regularly made between them. The book is structured as follows.

The first part, including Chapters 1 and 2, is dedicated to introducing background knowledge about pragmatics and language acquisition. Chapter 1 is more specifically devoted to introducing the field of pragmatics, defined as the study of language in use. The social and cognitive sides of pragmatic competencies and their relation to acquisition studies are also discussed.

Chapter 2 includes a succinct overview of the main milestones of language acquisition. It also demonstrates that the acquisition of pragmatics and of the functional aspects of language such as syntax and the lexicon are in many ways related. Key concepts for language acquisition research such as the distinction between competencies in comprehension versus production are discussed, as well as the most common empirical methods used to study the acquisition of pragmatics such as corpus studies, constrained elicitation, metalinguistic judgments, truth value judgments, and preferential looking time (eye-tracking), assessing their main advantages and limitations.

The second part of the book is devoted to social approaches to the acquisition of pragmatics, and includes Chapters 3 and 4. Chapter 3 focuses on speech act theory and presents data on the acquisition of two speech acts (requesting and promising), addressing the following questions: When do children start to understand and produce direct and indirect speech acts? What is the role of conventionalization for the acquisition of indirect speech acts? Why is there an order of emergence between speech acts such as requests and promises? The conventional rules of speech act theory are discussed from a cognitive perspective, with the conclusion that acquisition data can be accounted for by an inferential model of communication without the need to add a theory of speech acts.

Chapter 4 focuses on the acquisition of social skills associated with pragmatic competencies, focusing on the following questions: When do children become able to adapt their speech acts to reflect relations of power with their addressee, and to use social indicators such as discourse markers and politeness makers? What is the role of family and peer interactions for the development of social pragmatic competencies? How do variations of pragmatic norms across languages and cultures affect children's development of these competencies? We conclude that children are already able to use social cues and adapt their use of language accordingly around their third birthday, and that the range of cross-cultural variations in pragmatic norms is limited by universal cognitive biases.

The third part of the book is dedicated to cognitive approaches to pragmatics and includes Chapters 5 to 8. Chapter 5 explores the relationship between the acquisition of pragmatic competencies and the development of theory of mind abilities, an active research area in cognitive psychology for the past 30 years. The importance of the ability to reason about other peoples' mental states for understanding utterances, in other words of having theory of mind abilities, is addressed through the following questions: What is the timeline of children's development of theory of mind abilities? How is this development matched with the acquisition of specific aspects of pragmatics competencies? The notion of theory of mind has generated an important body of literature and many recent controversies have emerged regarding the factors influencing its development and the best ways to measure it. The most recent results on these issues will be synthetically presented, emphasizing their consequences for the relation between theory of mind and pragmatics. We conclude that children's possession of implicit theory of mind abilities around their first birthday, evidenced in a recent body of literature, accounts for children's early successes at verbal communication.

An important dimension of pragmatic competencies from a cognitive perspective is the ability of listeners to understand a different meaning than the one literally expressed by some utterances, for instance in the case of metaphor and irony. In Chapter 6, we first explain how current pragmatic models have accounted for the functioning of metaphor and irony, stressing the implications for the way these forms of non-literal language are acquired. The developmental literature on these questions is surveyed with the following questions in mind: When do children acquire metaphor and irony? What are the similarities and differences in the cognitive processes underlying these acquisitions? What are the factors accounting for children's late acquisition of irony? This chapter also illustrates that developmental data can contribute to empirically assess the validity of theoretical pragmatic concepts.

Chapter 7 is devoted to the notion of scalar implicature, the most thoroughly studied aspect of pragmatics in the acquisition literature from the last decade. We introduce the notion of scalar implicature in the context of the Gricean notion of conversational implicature and the distinction between generalized and particularized implicatures. The following questions are addressed: When are children able to derive scalar implicatures? Are some scales more difficult than others? Does the nature of the task that children are asked to perform influence their ability to derive scalar implicatures? We conclude that children's late ability to derive scalar implicatures, evidenced in a number of early experiments, does not reflect a genuine pragmatic incompetence but is due to the necessity to learn that words can be related on a scale, and are also partly due to difficulties inherent to some experimental designs. The derivation of other types of implicatures, namely relevance implicatures, is discussed in Chapter 3 in the context of indirect speech acts.

Chapter 8 addresses the relations between pragmatics and discourse, through the acquisition of the relational devices used to make texts and discourses cohesive and coherent. The chapter will more specifically focus on the acquisition of referring expressions and discourse connectives, addressing the following questions: When do children start to modulate their use of referring expressions to reflect the degree of accessibility of a referent for their addressee? Is there a difference between children's ability to integrate perceptual and linguistic contextual information about accessibility? What is the order of acquisition between discourse connectives conveying various discourse relations? To what extent do cross-linguistic differences in the encoding of discourse relations influence their acquisition? We argue that children are able to assess accessibility even before they can use language and that they show evidence of relating sentences coherently as soon as they produce multi-clause sentences. In striking contrast, children acquire pronouns and discourse connectives much later in development, due to the necessity to integrate the complex procedural instructions attached to them.

The last part of the book, including Chapters 9 and 10, is devoted to the acquisition of pragmatic competencies under specific constraints, as a way to shed additional light on the social and cognitive processes underlying their typical acquisition. Two specific cases are considered. First, some neurological conditions are characterized by a marked deficit in the development of pragmatic competencies. The best-known case of neurodevelopmental disorder characterized by a strong form of pragmatic impairment is autism spectrum disorder (ASD). In Chapter 9, the range of pragmatic competencies discussed in Chapters 3 to 8 is revisited in the light of the impairment observed in ASD children. We will focus on the following issues: What is the range of social and cognitive impairments evidenced in autism? To what extent are these impairments secondary manifestations of primary deficits in the structural components of the language faculty? Are the cognitive theories of autism able to account for these communication deficits? We argue that both social and cognitive pragmatic competencies are affected to some degree in autism, and that these impairments are related to deficits in implicit theory of mind abilities, but also caused by language impairments that were until recently overlooked in the literature.

Chapter 10 discusses the recent body of literature that has investigated interlanguage pragmatics—in other words, the way second language learners acquire, understand, and use pragmatic competencies in a new language. The various aspects of pragmatics that come into play during the acquisition of a second language are presented and discussed, answering the following questions: What are the similarities and differences between first and second language acquisition of pragmatic competencies? What are the universal and language specific aspects of pragmatics? To what extent are difficulties in second language pragmatic competencies caused by negative transfer from the speakers' first languages? The components of pragmatic competencies discussed in Chapters 3 to 8 are again reviewed in relation to second language acquisition. We argue that even though the cognitive mechanisms at work for pragmatic enrichment are universal, cognitive aspects of pragmatic competencies can be problematic for second language learners when there is a necessity to include culture-specific premises as input to inferential processes.

In the conclusion of this book, we present a synthetic timeline of children's development of pragmatic competencies. We argue that the core cognitive competencies underlying pragmatic development are already in place when children start producing language, and that children's gradual acquisition of pragmatic competencies during childhood relies on their developing linguistic, conceptual, and social competencies, as well as to the development of processing resources in working memory.

References

Bates, E. (1976). *Language and Context: The Acquisition of Pragmatics*. New York/San Francisco: Academic Press.

Cacciari, C. & Padovani, R. (2012). The development of figurative language. In M. Spivey, K. McRae, & M. Joanisse (eds), *The Cambridge Handbook of Psycholinguistics* (pp. 505–522). Cambridge: Cambridge University Press.

Cameron, L. (1997). Discourse context and the development of metaphor in children. In L. Thompson (ed), *Children Talking: The Development of Pragmatic Competence* (pp. 49–64). Clevedon: Multilingual Matters.

Escandell-Vidal, V. (2004). Norms and principles: Putting the social and cognitive pragmatics together. In R. Marquez-Reiter & M.E. Placencida (eds.), *Current Trends in the Pragmatics of Spanish* (pp. 347–371). Amsterdam: John Benjamins.

Matthews, D. (ed.) (2014). *Pragmatic Development in First Language Acquisition*. Amsterdam: John Benjamins.

Ninio, A. & Snow, C. (1996). *Pragmatic Development*. Boulder: Westview Press.

O'Neill, D. (2012). Components of pragmatic ability and children's pragmatic language development. In H.-J. Schmid (ed.), *Cognitive Pragmatics* (pp. 261–290). Berlin: de Gruyter.

Pouscoulous, N. (2011). Metaphor: For adults only? *Belgian Journal of Linguistics*, 25, 51–79.

Zufferey, S. (2010). *Lexical Pragmatics and Theory of Mind: The Acquisition of Connectives*. Amsterdam: John Benjamins.

PART I

Introduction

1

INTERFACES BETWEEN PRAGMATICS AND LANGUAGE ACQUISITION

The study of pragmatics traditionally encompasses a wide array of phenomena related to verbal communication such as speech acts, non-literal language, implicatures, and discourse structure. In this chapter, these essential concepts of pragmatics are briefly introduced, emphasizing the theoretical context in which they arose. In the second part of the chapter, we show how these topics can be integrated into the study of children's developing pragmatic competencies. The chapter thus presents a general panorama of pragmatics in its cognitive and social dimensions, with the objective to provide a global and coherent picture of the topics that will be covered in the book.

1.1. Pragmatics: from origins to current models

The first definitions of the term 'pragmatics' go back to the 1930s (e.g. Carnap, 1938; Morris, 1938). The main criterion used at the time to characterize pragmatics with respect to other fields of language study was that pragmatic phenomena have to be accounted for by referring to the language user. The importance of this criterion has remained unchanged ever since, and pragmatics is still often defined in general terms as the study of language in use (e.g. Huang, 2007; Mey, 1993; Sperber & Noveck, 2004). This definition is primarily meant to divide the study of linguistic meaning between pragmatics and semantics: While semantics focuses on the study of the context-invariant meaning of words and sentences, pragmatics addresses the meaning conveyed by utterances produced in a specific context by a given speaker who has an identifiable communicative aim. This definition has proved, however, to be underspecified to include a coherent set of topics in the field of pragmatics, because a wide array of loosely related phenomena are one way or another related to the use of language. Notwithstanding the theoretical implications of this lack of consensus, a practical consequence of this state of affairs is that the field lacks unity, as it includes studies ranging from the factors influencing the use of politeness markers (e.g. Brown & Levinson, 1987) to the cognitive processes underlying the derivation of implicatures (e.g. Noveck, 2001).

A number of more specific criteria are regularly called upon to refine the definition of pragmatics. Ariel (2010) listed 10 criteria often used in the literature, such as the fact that pragmatics is limited to the study of non-truth conditional meaning (vs. truth-conditional meaning in semantics), focuses on indirect and non-literal meaning (vs. the explicit meaning constituting what is said in semantics), rests on inference (vs. a conventional code in semantics), refers to units that are larger than the sentence (vs. a scope limited to the sentence for semantics), and so on. As several authors have pointed out (e.g. Ariel, 2010; Recanati, 2004) all these criteria are, however, not always compatible. For example, recent research has shown that a number of linguistic phenomena are both inferential and truth-conditional (e.g. Carston, 2002; Recanati, 2010), leading to a renegotiation of the semantics–pragmatics interface. Because of the difficulties of listing precise and compatible criteria leading to a coherent definition for the field of pragmatics, textbooks often simply determine the scope of the field by listing a range of topics that are considered to be its primary focus of investigation. For example, Huang (2007: 2) noted that: "the central topics of inquiry of pragmatics include implicature, presupposition, speech acts and deixis." Similarly, Levinson (1983) focused solely on deixis, conversational implicature, presupposition, speech acts, and conversational structure.

In this book, our aim is not to solve the question of which linguistic phenomena should or should not be included in the study of pragmatics. We will rather try to report on the most active areas of investigation related to acquisition of pragmatics. A broad distinction will be made between theories emphasizing the social aspects of verbal communication such as speech acts, politeness, and the role of interpersonal interactions and those focusing on cognitive processes such as the derivation of implicatures, theory of mind abilities, understanding of non-literal language, and discourse structure. More emphasis will be placed on the cognitive aspects of pragmatics (four chapters against only two for the social theories), as they reflect many of the most recent developments in theoretical and experimental pragmatics. But before turning to specific aspects of the acquisition of pragmatics in the next chapters, we will first go back to the origins of the field and outline its evolution toward the main current trends. This outline will enable us to briefly introduce the concepts that will be discussed throughout the book.

1.1.1. Speech act theory

Most scholars agree that pragmatics truly began with the work of John Austin, a philosopher who reacted against the dominant view of his time in the philosophy of language. During the first half of the twentieth century, language philosophers believed that the primary function of language was to describe the world. The starting point of Austin's speech act theory was to reject this view, which he called the 'descriptive fallacy'. According to Austin (1962), while it is true that some utterances like (1) and (2) do indeed aim at describing the world, others like (3) and (4) serve others functions altogether. They are not uttered to *describe* something but to *do* something: ask a question (3) or make a promise (4).

(1) It is raining.
(2) The cat is on the doormat.
(3) What time is it?
(4) I promise to come to see you.

Austin therefore started by separating utterances that are used to describe the world, called 'constatives', and those used to perform an action, called 'performatives'. The challenge for Austin was to find a rule enabling him to separate all utterances into one of these two categories. This has proved to be much more difficult than he had anticipated. To begin with, Austin defined the category of performatives as being limited to sentences containing a performative verb like *promising*, *saying*, or *asking* at the first person of the simple present tense, indicative mood and active voice. Following this definition, a sentence like (3) cannot be included in the category of performatives even though its function is clearly not descriptive. In order to solve this problem, Austin submitted that (3) is in fact an *implicit* performative that can be reformulated as an explicit performative by adding a performative verb as in (5).

(5) I am asking you what time it is.

The problem then was that all sentences could potentially be classified as implicit performatives. For example, (6) could be the explicit performative of (1).

(6) I state that it is raining.

Because of this problem and others (see Huang, 2007), Austin gave up the idea of separating utterances into constatives and performatives, and formulated instead a much more radical theory. In the second version of speech act theory, all utterances convey three types of speech acts: a locutionary act (the fact of producing a grammatical sentence with a meaning and a reference), an illocutionary act (for example, asking a question, making a promise, and thanking), and a perlocutionary act (for example, persuading and threatening). According to Austin, only illocutionary acts are an object of investigation for pragmatics, as locutionary acts bear on the structure of language and perlocutionary acts are not fully under the control of the speaker (an utterance may produce a different effect on some addressees than the one intended by the speaker).

Austin also formulated a set of conditions that must be fulfilled in order for a speech act to be successfully communicated, or in his words to be 'felicitous'. For example, one of the conditions enabling a speaker to give an order to someone is that he should have authority over this person. If one of the conditions is not met, the speech act misfires and the action is not fulfilled. These conditions anchor speech act theory into a study of socially and conventionally determined rules. In the words of Huang (2007: 93): "simply stated, the central tenet of speech act theory is that the uttering of a sentence is, or is part of, an action within the framework of social institutions and conventions."

After the early death of Austin, speech act theory has been further developed by John Searle (1969, 1979). In addition to his reformulation of taxonomy of speech acts, one of Searle's most crucial contributions to speech act theory was to observe that in many cases, speech acts are not transparently communicated in the language. For example, in order to ask someone to leave the room, a speaker may use several different formulations as in (7) to (10).

(7) Leave the room!
(8) I ask you to leave the room.
(9) Can you leave the room?
(10) You had better go now.

While (7) and (8) explicitly convey a request for leaving the room by the use of an imperative form (7) or a performative verb, (8), (9) and (10) convey this information indirectly through a question (9) and a statement (10). The crucial question is how can a hearer understand (7) when (9) is uttered? Searle solved this puzzle by submitting that each speech act comes with a set of conditions that must be fulfilled in order for it to be felicitous. For example, one of the conditions for performing a felicitous request is that the hearer should have the ability to perform it. In (9), the speaker is explicitly questioning the hearer's ability by the formulation 'Can you X?' Explicitly mentioning this condition is, according to Searle (1975), what triggers the inference leading to the interpretation of (9) as an indirect request. Another observation recurrently made in speech act theory is that indirect speech acts such as (9) are very commonly used for performing an indirect request, which led to the hypothesis that they are conventionalized or standardized (Bach & Harnich, 1979; Morgan, 1978; Searle, 1975). The hypothesis states that for such speech acts, the inferences necessary to compute the transition between direct and indirect speech acts, for which Searle appealed to Grice's principles of conversation described below, are not calculated. We will come back to the implications of the difference between direct and indirect speech acts for acquisition as well as the standardization hypothesis in Chapter 3 (Section 3.1).

Another question stemming from the observation that speech acts are often indirectly performed is why they should be favored over direct speech acts as means of communication. After all, direct speech acts are transparent and do not rely on inferences and a set of felicity conditions. Using them therefore implies fewer risks of being misunderstood. The explanation given by Searle (1975) for the prevalence of indirect speech acts in verbal communication is that they represent more polite ways to formulate a request than direct speech acts. Indeed, (9) would probably appear to most hearers as more polite than (7). Another related observation is that direct speech acts put the face of the hearer in jeopardy (e.g. Goffman, 1959; Brown & Levinson, 1987) because he is explicitly ordered to do something. An indirect request in the form of a question, for example, opens the possibility for the hearer to answer by 'yes' or 'no', hence the hearer can accept to perform the requested action without appearing to obey a command, or refuse to perform the requested action without putting the face of the speaker in jeopardy. This observation led scholars to include the study of politeness rules as one of the topics of interest for pragmatics (e.g. Brown & Levinson, 1987; Leech, 1983; Kádár & Haugh, 2013). However, indirect speech acts are not always more polite than direct ones (Blum-Kulka, 1987). For example, the indirect request in (12) would probably appear to more hearers to be more offensive than the direct one in (11).

(11) Leave us now please!
(12) Can't you see we don't want you here?

Politeness is therefore not the only factor motivating indirect communication. Later cognitive models of pragmatics, especially relevance theory, have explained this phenomenon in terms of cognitive efficiency, as we will see below.

In a nutshell, speech act theory and more specifically the felicity conditions formulated to explain the transition between indirect and direct speech acts as well as the conditions for the standardization of indirect speech acts anchor pragmatics into the study of socially determined rules governing verbal communication. The theory has also paved the way for the inclusion in the field of pragmatics of an important body of literature studying the social and conventional rules governing communication (see Section 1.1.4 and Chapter 4). But speech act theory also leads to a number of hypotheses about the way speech acts should be processed by adult speakers and acquired by children. We review these predictions in Chapter 3 and conclude that from a cognitive perspective, speech act theory is not corroborated by acquisition data.

1.1.2. The Gricean turn

It is not much of an overstatement to say that Grice has revolutionized pragmatics by proposing a radically different conception of verbal communication than the one put forward by speech act theory. Grice submitted that in order to be successful, an act of communication simply requires that the hearer recognize the speaker's intention. For example, let's imagine that Sarah utters (13) in order for Peter to leave.

(13) It is late.

The transition between Sarah's utterance and her informative intention is not coded in the language. Grice believes that for Peter to understand Sarah's meaning, he must simply identify her intention, in other words what she is asking him to do, without the need to refer to a set of felicity conditions governing speech acts. The main challenge for Grice was to explain how a hearer can recognize the speaker's intention and hence understand the meaning of the utterances. According to Grice, the hearer reasons by way of logical deductions and follows a number of principles governing conversations. The main idea defended by Grice is that communication is a cooperative activity, in the sense that all conversations have a goal toward which all participants are working. This hypothesis was formulated as a general Cooperative Principle (Grice, 1967/1989: 26–27): "Make your contribution such as it is required, at the stage at which it occurs, by the accepted purpose or direction of the talk exchange in which you are engaged." Grice spelled out this general principle into nine maxims of conversation, classified in four categories:

Maxim of quantity

1. Make your contribution as informative as is required (for the current purposes of the exchange).
2. Do not make your contribution more informative than is required.

Maxim of quality

Supermaxim: try to make your contribution one that is true.

1. Do not say what you believe to be false.
2. Do not say that for which you lack adequate evidence.

Maxim of relation

1. Be relevant.

Maxim of manner

Supermaxim: be perspicuous.

1. Avoid obscurity of expression.
2. Avoid ambiguity.
3. Be brief (avoid unnecessary prolixity).
4. Be orderly.

Even though the maxims are formulated as imperatives, Grice thought that they represented the way conversations usually work and not something that speakers have to learn. The application of the maxims or in some cases their obvious violation or flouting is directly related to the phenomenon of indirect or non-literal communication. More specifically, the observance of maxims trigger what Grice called 'conversational implicatures'. For example, by following the first maxim of quantity, the addressee of (14) will infer that Jane has exactly two sisters and not at least two sisters.

(14) Jane has two sisters.

Grice observes that is some cases a maxim has to be violated in order to comply with another maxim, deemed to be more important for the success of communication. For example, let's imagine that a speaker answers the question asked in (15) by (16). Here (16) violates the maxim of quantity, because the hearer requires more specific information in order to find the dean's office. But by so doing, the speaker who does not know more precisely where the dean's office is follows that maxim of quality, by not saying something for which he lacks adequate evidence.

(15) Where is the dean's office?
(16) Somewhere on this floor.

Grice also treats all cases of non-literal language uses like metaphor and irony as cases of blatant violations of the first maxim of quality (do not say what you believe to be false). Again, these violations trigger implicatures. We will discuss in Chapter 6 how current models of pragmatics and cognitive linguistics analyze metaphors and why Grice's account of metaphors as cases of conversational implicatures has been abandoned in these models.

Grice also made a distinction between particularized implicatures – that are triggered in a certain context but not every time a given utterance is produced – and generalized implicatures that are usually triggered by the use of an utterance. For instance, (18) represents a particularized implicature drawn on the basis of (17). In other contexts, the same utterance might have triggered other implicatures, such as (19) or (20) to name but a few.

(17) It is 5 pm.
(18) The class is over.
(19) Let's go out for a drink.
(20) We are going to miss the train.

By contrast, (22) is a generalized implicature derived from (21). The reason for this is that in most cases, when the word 'some' is used, the implicature 'not all' is triggered because of the maxim of quantity. We will discuss the difference between generalized and particularized implicatures in some depth in Chapter 7.

(21) Some of Alex's friends study psychology.
(22) Not all of Alex's friends study psychology.

Grice also considered another type of implicatures attached to specific words called 'conventional implicatures'. Grice did not elaborate much on this type of implicature and the few examples he gave concern words like 'therefore' in (23) that trigger implicatures such as (24).

(23) Laura is a girl. Therefore she is intelligent.
(24) Girls are intelligent.

We will come back to the role of discourse connectives like 'therefore' in Chapter 8 and insist on their role as procedural indicators of textual coherence.

To summarize, in Grice's pragmatics, utterances do not encode the meaning that speakers want to convey but merely pieces of evidence of the speaker's meaning. In order to reconstruct the full-blown speaker's meaning, the hearer must complement the linguistic pieces of evidence provided by the utterance with inferences drawn from the context. The notion of conversational implicatures is certainly one of the most important aspects of Grice's approach and contemporary cognitive pragmatic theories merely differ in how they developed and modified this notion.

1.1.3. Neo- and post-Gricean models

Following Grice's theory of implicatures, two different trends have emerged: the neo-Gricean model represented by Gazdar (1979), Levinson (1983, 2000), and Horn (1984, 2004) and the post-Gricean model represented by relevance theory, formulated by Sperber and Wilson (1986/1995, 2012).

The main goal of the neo-Gricean model of pragmatics has been to modify the Gricean maxims in such a way as to avoid some of the problems raised by Grice's formulation. For example, Horn (2004) replaced the maxims of quantity, relation, and manner by two interdependent principles:

- Q principle: Say as much as you can (given R).
- R pinciple: Say no more than you must (given Q).

Levinson (2000: 38–39) proposed an alternative formulation of these heuristics to which he added a third one (M), in order to deal with implicatures that are not related to what is said but to the way it is said (like Grice's maxim of manner).

- Q heuristic: What isn't said, isn't.
- I heuristic: What is said simply is stereotypically exemplified.
- M heuristic: What is said in an abnormal way isn't normal.

One of the main objections raised against Grice's maxims is that their application could in some cases provoke clashes in the derivation of implicatures. In order to address this issue, Levinson (2000) stated an order of precedence between the principles: Q > M > R. This order has, however, been contested by Huang

(2007: 40) who claimed that the R principle has precedence over the Q principle "until the use of a contrastive linguistic form induces a Q-implicature to the non-applicability of the pertinent R-implicature."

The important development of neo-Gricean pragmatics, which can be addressed by the three principles listed above, concerns the study of generalized implicatures. Levinson (2000: 16) gave the following definition of generalized and particular implicatures:

- An implicature i from utterance U is *particularized* if U implicates only by virtue of specific contextual assumptions that would not invariably or even normally obtain.
- An implicature i from utterance U is *generalized* if U implicates I *unless* there are unusual specific contextual assumptions that defeat it.

He proposed in addition a taxonomy of these implicatures as well as a system of rules of default inferences attached to some words like 'and', 'the', and 'some'. His theory aims at explaining the default interpretations that are triggered independently of context by the uses of these words. We will come back to the notion of generalized implicatures in Chapter 7, devoted to the notion of scalar implicatures.

In sum, neo-Gricean models propose ways to adapt Grice's inferential model of communication in order to apply it to some specific linguistic problems, regularly arising from the use of some words and triggering generalized implicatures. By doing so, they essentially limit the scope of pragmatics to a sub-type of Grice's implicatures. By contrast, relevance theory focuses on the cognitive mechanisms involved in the derivation of particularized implicatures and refutes the necessity of maintaining a separate category for generalized implicatures.

Relevance theory proposes a more radical reduction of the Gricean maxims to one single general principle governing human communication: the principle of relevance. Sperber and Wilson's aim is to keep Grice's intuitions about the role of intentions for verbal communication, while formalizing them in a complete and cognitively plausible theory. The principle of relevance implies both a cognitive and a communicative side.

The cognitive principle of relevance is formulated as follows: "Human cognition tends to be geared to the maximization of relevance" (Sperber & Wilson, 1995: 260). The idea behind this principle is that human perceptual mechanisms have evolved in such a way as to allocate its (limited) resources to the potentially most relevant input from the environment. In addition, the most relevant assumptions are automatically retrieved from the context and processed in the most efficient way. The cognitive notion of relevance is defined in terms of costs and benefits. The benefits are the correct interpretations of utterances and the costs represent the cognitive effort necessary to reach these interpretations. The more numerous the benefits are, the higher the relevance. The more costly the interpretation process is, the lower the relevance. Following this principle, an indirect answer to a question can be more relevant than a direct one. For example, let us assume that Mary answers either (26) or (27) to John's question (25).

(25) John: Are you coming to the lecture this afternoon?
(26) Mary: I have a dentist appointment at 4 pm.
(27) Mary: No.

In (26) Mary's answer is not literal: she does not explicitly say 'yes' or 'no', contrary to (27). However, her indirect reply is more relevant than her direct reply, because it conveys in one single utterance both an answer to John's question and a reason for her refusal. Mary's refusal, even though not explicit, is deduced by retrieving knowledge about dentist appointments and comparing the time of Mary's appointment with that of the lecture. Relevance theory thus provides a new answer for the prevalence of non-literal speech acts in verbal communication. They are not motivated by politeness but produced in contexts where they are optimally relevant.

The cognitive aspect of relevance has clear implications for communication as well. As Sperber and Wilson (2012: 6) explained: "in order to communicate, the communicator needs her audience attention. If attention tends automatically to go to what is most relevant at the time, then the success of communication depends on the audience taking the utterance to be relevant enough to be worthy of attention."

The communicative principle (Sperber & Wilson, 1995: 260) states that: "Every act of ostensive communication communicates a presumption of its own optimal relevance." According to this principle, the hearer will automatically pay attention to the speaker's utterance and process it under the assumption that it is optimally relevant. The comprehension process follows a path of least effort: The most salient hypothesis is considered first and the process automatically stops when the hearer's expectations of relevance are satisfied.

In addition to reducing the maxims to a single principle governing human communication and cognition, relevance theory has also extended the focus of pragmatics to the explicit level of communication, whereas for Grice, pragmatics was mainly concerned with the interpretation of implicit meaning. In his definition of explicit communication ('what is said'), Grice only included the fleshing out of linguistic meaning by the disambiguation of ambiguous elements and the attribution of reference to referring expressions such as pronouns and proper names. By contrast, in relevance theory, several pragmatic phenomena such as metaphors and the pragmatic enrichment of scalar words, assimilated by Grice to cases of implicatures, have been reanalyzed as cases of explicit enrichment. We will discuss them in Chapters 6 and 7.

To summarize, since the work of Grice, pragmatics has undergone a radical paradigm shift. From the study of conventional conditions determining the production of speech acts, pragmatics has now also become part of the cognitive sciences and aims at understanding how listeners bridge the gap between the underspecified linguistic meaning of utterances and the speaker's full-blown meaning. Even though the conventional anchoring of speech act theory has been largely abandoned, social components related to verbal communication continue to be an active area of research, as we now outline.

1.1.4. Sociocultural models of pragmatics

In parallel to the development of pragmatic theories based on the Gricean notions of intention, rationality, and cooperation, other approaches have extended the field by focusing on the dynamics of social interactions and the interpersonal relations between speaker and hearer (Haugh, 2008; Mey, 1993; Verschueren, 1999). In Horn and Kecskes' (2013: 353) words: "socio-cultural interactional pragmatics maintains that pragmatics should include research into social and cultural constraints on language use as well as [linguistic constraints]." Two decades earlier, Leech (1983: 10) already stated that pragmatic principles "operate variably in different cultures or language communities, in different social situations, among different social classes, etc." and affirmed that "the main purposes of socio-pragmatics, as I envisage it, is to find out how different societies operate maxims in different ways, for example by giving politeness a higher rating than cooperation in certain situations" (1983: 80). The sociocultural trend in pragmatics thus aims at studying the variations induced by social contexts in the processes of verbal communication.

Many of the social aspects of verbal communication are culture-specific, with the consequence that speakers in a situation of intercultural communication cannot rely on the same set of assumptions than speakers interacting within the same culture (Kecskes, 2012, 2013). Thus, while neo- and post-Gricean pragmatics tend to focus on universal cognitive mechanisms underlying verbal communication, sociocultural models explore the aspects of language use that are variable across speakers of the same language – due to egocentric biases related to prior experiences and to the fact that intentions evolve and meanings are co-constructed in the course of interactions – and by contrasting aspects of language use across several languages and cultures. We will discuss the cross-cultural variations of pragmatic norms in Chapter 4.

The separation between social and cognitive approaches to pragmatics does not imply, however, that the topics covered by both trends of research do not have any intersection, and many researchers have emphasized the necessity to integrate both a social and a cognitive component in the study of pragmatics. For example, Ariel (2010: 143–144) argued that: "There is a crucial sociocultural foundation that interlocutors must assume before they can set the pragmatic cognitive process in motion. We have quite solid expectations for how much and what type of information is adequate on particular occasions, and these expectations play a crucial role in deriving pragmatic interpretations." Sperber and Wilson (1997) also recognized the importance of social factors and their complementarity with relevance theory: "it is true that most relevance-theoretic work so far has largely ignored aspects of communication discussed in the sociological literature: role playing, turn taking, class, gender, race and power, for example. Instead, the focus has been on issues typically discussed in psychology: attention, memory, intention, inference. However, this is more a reflection of what seems to us a sound initial research strategy (which is likely to change as the field develops) than some silly anti-sociological bias." Levinson (1983: 28) also noted that: "pragmatic accounts of language understanding will at least need access to sociolinguistic information." Similar convergences are also found in the work of researchers emphasizing the role of social factors. For example, Kecskes (2012, 2013) advocates a socio-cognitive approach to pragmatics. According to Horn and Kecskes (2013: 362–363): "interlocutors are considered as social beings searching for meaning with individual minds embedded in a socio-cultural collectivity." In this book, we also stress the importance of integrating social and cognitive factors in the study of the acquisition of pragmatic phenomena.

1.2. The acquisition of pragmatics

Despite the cognitive turn initiated in theoretical pragmatics since the work of Grice, in developmental pragmatics the focus was placed until the years 2000 on topics related to the use of language in social contexts rather than on cognitive competencies. This focus on social competencies will be made visible when we review the early studies on pragmatic development in Section 1.2.1. In the second part of the section, we introduce the main cognitive and social competencies that children must acquire in order to become pragmatically competent (Sections 1.2.2 and 1.2.3, respectively) and briefly explain in each case how their acquisition will be discussed in later chapters of the book.

1.2.1. A short introduction to the field of developmental pragmatics

Early studies in developmental pragmatics were limited to its social dimension. Ninio and Snow (1996: 10) noted, for example, that: "researchers using the label *developmental pragmatics* or *pragmatic development* for their own work study a wide range of disparate subjects whose communality is that they have some connections with both language and social interaction." The strong social grounding of developmental pragmatics is also evident in other monographs and articles devoted to this question. For instance the volume edited by Thompson (1997) includes a collection of papers addressing pragmatic development from a social perspective. The grounding of pragmatics in social norms is explicitly stated in Thompson's introduction (1997: 4): "The ingredients of pragmatic competence are: a knowledge of the structure and forms of language; a range of vocabulary, register, and formulaic exchanges; and knowing how to behave in specific social contexts." She reaffirms: "It is not sufficient to be able to speak the language grammatically, lexically and phonologically. Being communicatively competent requires combining social competence with linguistic competence."

The social dimension of developmental pragmatics continues to be an active area of research. For example, in her chapter on developmental pragmatics, Becker Bryant (2009) starts with the following statement: "When children are learning language, they must learn more than just phonology, semantics and syntax. Being a skilled language user means knowing how to use one's language appropriately and strategically in social situations. Children need to learn pragmatic skills [...] how to make language work in interactions with their peers, families, teachers and others." Similarly, Clark (2003) put a strong emphasis on social skills in her chapter devoted to the acquisition of pragmatics: "As children become more skilled at using language, they use it in more ways for greater effect. They make use of a growing array of linguistic options to mark social roles for both speaker and addressee. [...] They also learn how to do things with language: how to be polite and how to be persuasive. They learn how to negotiate to resolve conflicts. They learn to distinguish actual events from play. They learn how to talk inside the classroom as well as outside. And they learn how to tell stories [...]."

The focus on the development of social skills related to language use implied that in language acquisition research, cognitive aspects of pragmatic competencies were until recently less frequently studied compared with the structural aspects of the language faculty. It is noticeable that a number of textbooks on first language acquisition skip pragmatics altogether (e.g. Ambridge & Lieven, 2011; Fletcher & Garman, 1986; Saxton, 2010) or give it a very limited place as part of the study of meaning. For example, O'Grady (2005) only addressed very succinctly the acquisition of pronouns.

These omissions also reflect the fact that pragmatics is often not considered to be part of the language faculty because it is related to usage or, in Chomsky's words, to performance. Saxton (2010: 4) included, for example, the following four levels for the study of language: phonology, vocabulary, morphology, and syntax. He concedes that: "it all depends on one's theoretical perspective. For example, we could add pragmatics to the list above if we believe that the way language is *used* is particularly important." Lust (2006: 268) also mentioned the development of pragmatics as related to social skills: "The persistent mystery of language acquisition becomes even more compelling when we realize that the acquisition of language, assuming all its formal computational properties, must be integrated with the acquisition of pragmatics, a topic we have not directly addressed here. Unless children can embed the knowledge of language in a social system of shared and exchanged knowledge and reference, they cannot be said to have 'acquired language'. This area, one that involves its own cross-linguistic variation, may be the most difficult aspect of language knowledge for children to master."

The lack of space dedicated to pragmatics in textbooks on language acquisition is, however, rapidly changing, and recently edited textbooks and syntheses on language acquisition include chapters on pragmatics (e.g. Becker-Bryant, 2009; Pouscoulous & Noveck, 2009; Siegal & Surian, 2009). The importance given to pragmatics in this recent body of literature reflects the fact that the field has been rapidly growing over the past decade. The topics covered in these chapters also reflect the difference between theories emphasizing the acquisition of social skills (e.g. Becker-Bryant, 2009) and those focusing on cognitive abilities (e.g. Pouscoulous & Noveck, 2009). We will review both aspects of pragmatic competencies in turn in the next sections.

1.2.2. Cognitive pragmatic competencies

From a cognitive perspective, pragmatics seeks to explain how hearers bridge the gap between the semantically encoded meaning of words and sentences and the full-blown speaker's meaning. Enriching the linguistically encoded meaning of utterances requires several cognitive abilities.

First and foremost, pragmatically enriching linguistic meaning requires the ability to draw inferences. Inferences can be defined as a form of reasoning using premises as input from which a series of conclusions are drawn. These conclusions can either be directly deduced from the premises or are sometimes simply justified by them. Pragmatic inferences are said to be 'non-deductive' or 'abductive', because the truth of the premises used as input does not guarantee the truth of the conclusions. We will analyze children's growing ability to enrich the meaning of words and utterances by inference in two separate chapters. In Chapter 6, we address the question of pragmatic enrichment in cases of non-literal language uses such as metaphor and irony. In Chapter 7, we discuss children's growing ability to derive pragmatic inferences triggered by the use of scalar words such as 'some' and 'or', as well as numbers and aspectuals such as 'start' and 'finish'.

The inferential processes at work to understand the speaker's meaning are guided by expectations of cooperativeness and the search of the speaker's informative and communicative intentions. Reasoning about other people's mental states such as beliefs and desires in order to make sense of their actions is known in cognitive psychology as having theory of mind abilities. In Chapter 5, we present the development of theory of mind abilities in normally developing children and discuss its relationship with children's growing pragmatic competencies during their first years of life.

In addition to drawing inferences and reasoning about mental states, pragmatics rests on the cognitive ability to integrate contextual information from various sources such as world knowledge, physical perception, and prior discourse, and to use this information as premises for inferential reasoning. In Chapter 8, we discuss children's ability to integrate contextual information in order to adapt the level of informativeness of their referring expressions, depending on the common ground. We also discuss their growing ability to indicate the coherence relations linking sentences together in discourse through the use of discourse connectives. The use of pronouns as referring expressions and discourse connectives share another important property from a pragmatic perspective: they encode procedural rather than conceptual meaning (e.g. Wilson & Sperber, 1993). We also discuss in Chapter 8 the acquisition of procedural meaning.

If cognitive abilities are required in order to be pragmatically competent, it is expected that subjects showing evidence of pragmatic impairments should have deficits that can be linked to one or several of these cognitive abilities. In Chapter 9, from the perspective of autism spectrum disorders, we argue that the core pragmatic deficits of this population are related to the ability to reason about mental states, but also result from deficits in the structural aspects of language that have been until recently overlooked.

1.2.3. Social pragmatic competencies

From a social perspective, acquiring pragmatic competencies requires the ability to modulate the uses of language depending on the nature of interpersonal relations between the speaker and his addressee. For example, the linguistic formulation chosen to convey speech acts such as requests and directives are heavily dependent on perceptions of power relations. With addressees of lower social status, direct formulations such as imperatives are used. By contrast, addressing someone with a higher social status calls for more indirect formulations and the use of mitigators to increase politeness. Acquiring the social competencies enabling the adequate use of language in context thus involves learning a set of socially appropriate communicative behaviors and politeness rules. We address the acquisition of power relations and their influences on language use in Chapter 4.

Social norms governing the use of language are to some extent variable across languages and cultures. For example, while in Western European countries like the United Kingdom, requests are most often conveyed by means of conventionalized indirect forms (see Chapter 3), in Eastern European countries like Poland, direct forms are favored and politeness is achieved by the use of mitigators. We present examples of cultural variations in pragmatic norms in Chapter 4 and discuss the implications of these cross-cultural differences for children's acquisition of social and cognitive pragmatic competencies.

The existence of cross-cultural variations of pragmatic norms implies that second language learners may encounter difficulties in using language adequately in a second language. We present the challenges faced by second language learners in Chapter 10. We argue that even though cognitive pragmatic competencies relies on the universal mechanisms described above, learners still have problems understanding many forms of indirect communication, due to the necessity to integrate culture-specific premises as input to inferential processes.

Social models of pragmatic development emphasize the role of caregivers and peers as a means to acquire socially adequate behaviors, in other words to 'pragmatic socialization'. Blum-Kulka and Snow (2002: 3) stated, for example, that: "Researchers within the more anthropological paradigm [of language acquisition] see language as a cultural practice and thus describe language acquisition as a socializing process – a process played out through language of acquiring the language use skills, rights and values that constitute membership in a group." We discuss the role of social interactions for the development of pragmatic competencies in Chapter 4. For usage-based models of language acquisition, the influence of social interactions is not limited to the development of pragmatic competencies, but plays a crucial role as well for the development of the structural components of language such as the lexicon and syntax (e.g. Tomasello, 2003). Because of the increasing importance of usage-based approaches in language acquisition research, the field of developmental pragmatics is sometimes automatically associated with these models. The role of pragmatic competencies influencing language acquisition and the acquisition of the array of social and cognitive abilities forming pragmatic competencies are, however, two distinct research questions. The acquisition of pragmatic competencies, especially those associated with cognitive abilities, can be explained while maintaining a nativist model of language acquisition. Carston (1999) listed, for example, a large number of shared assumptions between relevance theory and generative grammar. The question of how pragmatic factors interact with the acquisition of other components of the language faculty will be discussed in Chapter 2.

1.3. Synthesis

In this chapter, we presented the main theoretical trends forming the field of pragmatics and introduced its social and cognitive dimensions, which must both be addressed in order to reach a complete picture of children's growing ability to use language for communication. We argued that acquiring pragmatic competencies requires the cognitive abilities to reason about mental states, to draw inferences, and to integrate contextual information from various sources. In addition, it requires the learning of social rules in order to communicate adequately in a given social situation and cultural context.

References

Ambridge, B. & Lieven, E. (2011). *Child Language Acquisition. Contrasting Theoretical Approaches*. Cambridge: Cambridge University Press.

Ariel, M. (2010). *Defining Pragmatics*. Cambridge: Cambridge University Press.

Austin, J. (1962). *How to Do Things with Words*. Oxford: Clarendon Press.

Bach, K. & Harnich, R. (1979). *Linguistic Communication and Speech Acts*. Cambridge: Cambridge University Press.

Becker-Bryant, J. (2009). Pragmatic development. In E. Bavin (ed), *The Cambridge Handbook of Child Language* (pp. 339–354). Cambridge: Cambridge University Press.

Blum-Kulka, S. (1987). Indirectness and politeness in requests: same or different? *Journal of Pragmatics*, *11*(2), 131–146.

Blum-Kulka, S. & Snow, C. (2002). *Talking to Adults: The Contribution of Multiparty Discourse to Language Acquisition*. Mahwah, NJ: Laurence Erlbaum.

Brown, P. & Levinson, S. (1987). *Politeness: Some Universals in Language*. Cambridge: Cambridge University Press.

Carnap, R. (1938). Foundations of logics and mathematics. In O. Neurath, R. Carnap & C. Morris (eds), *International Encyclopedia of Unified Science* (pp. 139–214). Chicago, IL: University of Chicago Press.

Carston, R. (1999). The relationship between generative grammar and (relevance-theoretic) pragmatics. *UCL Working Papers in Linguistics*, *11*, 21–40.

Carston, R. (2002). *Thoughts and Utterances: The Pragmatics of Explicit Communication*. Oxford: Blackwell.

Clark, E. (2003). *First Language Acquisition*. Cambridge: Cambridge University Press.

Fletcher, P. & Garman, M. (eds). (1986). *Language Acquisition: Studies in First Language Development*. Cambridge: Cambridge University Press.

Gazdar, G. (1979). *Pragmatics: Implicature, Presupposition and Logical Form*. New York: Academic Press.

Goffman, E. (1959). *The Presentation of Self in Everyday Life*. Edinburgh: University of Edinburgh Social Sciences Research Centre.

Grice, H.P. (1967/1989). *Studies in the Way of Words*. Cambridge: Harvard University Press.

Haugh, M. (2008). Intention in pragmatics. *Intercultural Pragmatics*, *5*, 99–110.

Hoff, E. & Shatz, M. (eds). (2009). *Blackwell Handbook of Language Development*. Malden/Oxford: Wiley-Blackwell.

Horn, L. (1984). A new taxonomy for pragmatic inference: Q-based and R-based implicatures. In Schiffrin, D. (ed), *Meaning, Form, and Use in Context: Linguistic Applications* (pp. 11–42). Washington, DC: Georgetown University Press.

Horn, L. (2004). Implicature. In L. Horn, & G. Ward (eds), *Handbook of Pragmatics* (pp. 3–28). Oxford: Blackwell.

Horn, L. & Kecskes, I. (2013). Pragmatics, discourse and cognition. In S. Anderson, J. Moeschler, & F. Reboul (eds), *The Language-Cognition Interface. Proceedings of the 19th International Congress of Linguists* (pp. 353–373). Geneva: Droz.

Huang, Y. (2007). *Pragmatics*. Oxford: Oxford University Press.

Kádár, D. & Haugh, M. (2013). *Understanding Politeness*. Cambridge: Cambridge University Press.

Kecskes, I. (2012). Is there anyone out there who is really interested in the speaker? *Language & Dialogue*, *2*, 285–299.

Kecskes, I. (2013). *Intercultural Pragmatics*. Oxford: Oxford University Press.

Leech, G. (1983). *Principles of Pragmatics*. London/New York: Longman.

Levinson, S.C. (1983). *Pragmatics*. Cambridge: Cambridge University Press.

Levinson, S.C. (2000). *Presumptive Meanings: The Theory of Generalized Conversational Implicatures*. Cambridge, MA: MIT Press.

Lust, B. (2006). *Child Language. Acquisition and Growth*. Cambridge: Cambridge University Press.

Mey, J. (1993). *Pragmatics: An Introduction*. Oxford: Wiley-Blackwell.

Morgan, J. (1978). Two types of convention in indirect speech acts. In P. Cole (ed), *Syntax and Semantics 9: Pragmatics* (pp. 261–280). London: Academic Press.

Morris, C. (1938). Foundations of the theory of signs. In O. Neurath, R. Carnap, & C. Morris (eds), *International Encyclopedia of Unified Science* (pp. 77–138). Chicago, IL: University of Chicago Press.

Ninio, A. & Snow, C. (1996). *Pragmatic Development*. Boulder: Westview Press.

Noveck, I. (2001). When children are more logical than adults: experimental investigations of scalar implicature. *Cognition*, *78*(2), 165–188.

O'Grady, W. (2005). *How Children Learn Language*. Cambridge: Cambridge University Press.

Pouscoulous, N. & Noveck, I. (2009). Going beyond semantics: The development of pragmatic enrichment. In Foster-Cohen, S. (ed), *Language Acquisition* (pp. 196–215). Basingstoke: Palgrave Macmillan.

Recanati, F. (2004). Pragmatics and semantics. In L. Horn, & G. Ward (eds), *Handbook of Pragmatics* (pp. 442–462). Oxford: Blackwell.

Recanati, F. (2010). *Truth-Conditional Pragmatics*. Oxford: Oxford University Press.

Saxton, M. (2010). *Child Language: Acquisition and Development*. London: Sage Publications.

Searle, J. (1969). *Speech Acts: An Essay in the Philosophy of Language*. Cambridge: Cambridge University Press.

Searle, J. (1975). Indirect speech acts. In P. Cole, & J. L. Morgan (eds), *Syntax and Semantics 3: Speech Acts* (pp. 59–82). New York: Academic Press.

Searle, J. (1979). *Expression and Meaning: Studies in the Theory of Speech Acts*. Cambridge: Cambridge University Press.

Siegal, M. & Surian, L. (2009). Conversational understanding in young children. In E. Hoff, & M. Shatz (eds), *Blackwell Handbook of Child Development* (pp. 304–323). Malden: Wiley-Blackwell.

Sperber, D. & Noveck, I. (2004). Introduction. In I. Noveck, & D. Sperber (eds), *Experimental Pragmatics*. London: Palgrave Macmillan.

Sperber, D. & Wilson, D. (1986/1995). *Relevance. Communication and Cognition*. Oxford: Blackwell.

Sperber, D. & Wilson, D. (1997). Remarks on relevance theory and the social sciences. *Multilingua*, *16*, 145–151.

Sperber, D. & Wilson, D. (2012). *Meaning and Relevance*. Cambridge: Cambridge University Press.

Thompson, L. (1997). *Children Talking: The Acquisition of Pragmatics*. Clevedon: Multilingual Matters.

Tomasello, M. (2003). *Constructing a Language: A Usage-Based Theory of Language Acquisition*. Cambridge, MA/London: Harvard University Press.

Verschueren, J. (1999). *Understanding Pragmatics*. London: Hodder Arnold.

Wilson, D. & Sperber, D. (1993). Linguistic form and relevance. *Lingua*, *90*, 1–15.

2

ASPECTS OF LANGUAGE ACQUISITION AND ITS STUDY

This chapter aims at providing theoretical and methodological background on language acquisition in order to set the context for the acquisition of pragmatic competencies in the next chapters. We first present an overview of the main milestones of language acquisition in the domains of phonology, syntax, and the lexicon (Section 2.1). We go on to demonstrate that the development pragmatic competencies, especially those related to theory of mind abilities, are in many ways interrelated with the acquisition the structural components of the language faculty (Section 2.2). Finally, we discuss some key methodological concepts such as the distinction between competencies in comprehension and production and introduce the most common empirical methods used to study the acquisition of pragmatics, assessing their main advantages and limitations (Section 2.3).

2.1. Milestones in first language acquisition

For all normally developing children, the acquisition of language follows a similar path during the first years of life. The stages of language acquisition can be divided into three periods, roughly corresponding to: (1) the early acquisition of language until the first words are combined (from birth to 18 months), (2) the acquisition of core syntactic structures and the vocabulary spurt (18 months to three years), and (3) the late acquisition of complex syntactic structures and the development of the lexicon (from three years onwards). The periods are only succinctly described in this section, and interested readers are referred to Lust (2006: especially Appendixes 1–6) for a detailed overview of the acquisition of the structural components of language.

2.1.1. From birth to 18 months

Almost immediately after their birth, babies already possess a number of skills in the perception of language. They are able to recognize the speech of their mother and to discriminate between speech and non-speech. They also perceive many contrasts between sounds, even when they do not pertain to their mother tongue (Mehler et al., 1988). They can even discriminate a number of prosodic differences of stress and accent (Christophe, Dupoux, Bertonicini & Mehler, 1994). By the age of four months, they show a preference for listening to words rather than other sounds (Colombo & Bundy, 1983) and start playing with the production of sounds. When they reach the age of six months, children can recognize their mother tongue compared with some others that do not resemble it closely, while starting to lose the ability to discriminate sounds that are not part of their exposure language(s) (Polka & Werker, 1994). They also begin to be able to identify some familiar words such as 'mommy' or their own name used in sentences (Jusczyk & Aslin, 1995) and to identify clauses in fluent speech (Nazzi, Kemler Nelson, Jusczyk & Jusczyk, 2000).

Between the ages of 6 to 12 months, children start babbling with identifiable syllables that include properties of the exposure language. When they are about eight-month old, they are also able to recognize words heard in stories several weeks earlier (Jusczyk & Hohne, 1997) and can discriminate words from their language from those of closely related languages (Jusczyk, Luce & Luce, 1994). At nine months, children can distinguish correct from incorrect phrasal segmentation in their mother tongue (Jusczyk et al., 1992) and at 10 months, children are sensitive to violations of word order, even when they target functional categories (Shady, Gerken & Jusczyk, 1995). At around 12 months, children start producing their first words.

After their first birthday, children's lexicon slowly starts to grow. They produce on average 10 words at 14 months but understand on average 50 words (Benedict, 1979). The semantics of children's first words is similar in all languages (Clark, 2003) and most of them correspond to nouns for concrete objects as well as words serving socio-pragmatic functions such as 'thank you' and 'hello'. Children start to combine words at around 15 months (Bloom, 1973) while undergoing a rapidly expanding vocabulary growth in comprehension. By the age of 16 months, children distinguish grammatical from ungrammatical function morphemes (Shady, 1996). At around 18 months, children start to produce sentences showing evidence of a correct word order even though most of them still often omit subjects and other arguments and inflections (Lust, 2006).

2.1.2. From 18 months to three years

By the age of 18 months, children become more sensitive to the syntactic constraints of their language. Around the age of 16 to 18 months, children look longer at a scene matching the sentence that they hear rather than a scene where the subject and object of the sentence are reversed (Hirsh-Pasek & Golinkoff, 1993). During the same period, their lexicon starts to expand more rapidly. Children learn on average 0.8 words per day between 16 and 23 months and are able to produce on average 300 words at the age of two.

After the age of two, children's vocabulary growth keeps accelerating: from 23 to 30 months, children learn on average 1.6 new words per day and produce around 600 words at the age of 30 months. Interindividual differences are very important, however, with a productive vocabulary typically ranging from 200 to 650 words at 30 months (Bloom, 2000). Morphosyntactic elements such as inflections are still often missing. Between the age of two and three, when their mean length of utterance (MLU) reaches about 3.5, children start to produce most types of syntactically complex sentences involving recursion (Lust, 2006) such as coordinated clauses and forms of embedded sentences such as relative and complement clauses.

2.1.3. Language acquisition after the age of three

Even though children already produce complex sentences at the age of three, their development continues for a number of operations involving language-specific lexicon and syntactic computations. One of the most evident aspects of language development after the age of three is related to the lexicon. The number of words acquired per day continues to increase: between the age of 30 months and six years, children acquire 3.6 new words per day and Anglin (1993) estimated that children understand about 14,000 words at the age of six. Between six and eight years they acquire 6.6 new words per day and between the age of 8 and 10, they acquire 12.1 words per day. This important growth in the lexicon enables children to reach as adults a mental lexicon between 60,000 and 80,000 words (Aitchison, 2003). The important growth of the lexicon during the school years is related to the acquisition of literacy and to the fact that children develop morphological skills enabling them to derive new words from already known ones (Anglin, 1993; Clark, 1993).

Even though children already produce most words and structures correctly by the age of five, language acquisition still continues to develop in some important ways after that age even for basic categories. For example, Karmiloff-Smith (1986) argued that polyfunctional words such as nouns and determiners are initially used only with one single function. In French, one example of such words is the determiner 'les' that indicates both pluralization (as opposed to 'le' and 'la') and totalization (as opposed to the partitive 'des'). Under the age of five, children use 'les' only to mark plural forms. During a second phase, children express totalization by an additional morpheme (e.g. 'tous') and it is only after the age seven or eight that they correctly use 'les' to simultaneously express both functions. The same pattern is found for many other polyfunctional words.

2.2. Mutual influences between pragmatics and language acquisition

In this section, we first demonstrate how children's growing ability to use social cues influences the way they acquire the meaning of words (Section 2.2.1) and then discuss the reciprocal influence of language for the development of some aspects of pragmatic competencies (Section 2.2.2). The resulting picture is that of a mutual influence scenario, in which pragmatics and other domains of the language faculty mutually bootstrap each other (see also de Villiers, 2007; Zufferey, 2010).

2.2.1. Cognitive and social factors enabling lexical acquisition

Children are exceptionally good at learning the meaning of words. Between the ages of 13 to 18 months, children start to do fast-mappings between words and meanings, in other words they are able to learn the meaning of a word after only a few exposures to a new label for an unfamiliar object (Carey, 1978). By the age of 18 months, children can even learn these associations on the basis of one exposure only (Baldwin et al., 1996). One of the questions raised by this exceptional ability is what exactly guides children during the process of word learning. In this section, we argue that children's growing ability to use social cues such as the speaker's gaze is a key element explaining children's ability to learn the meaning of words in a fast and very efficient manner, and also discuss other factors intervening in this process. We go on to demonstrate that pragmatic competencies guiding word learning are not limited to social cues, as children's growing ability to use the Gricean maxims during the school years also plays a role.

Different theories of word learning have evoked either the existence of specific principles, such as the principle of contrast (Clark, 1987) and the principle of taxonomic assumption (Markman & Hutchinson, 1984), or simple association rules driven by statistical regularities in the environment (e.g. Plunkett, 1997). An important body of literature has also tested the hypothesis that children are helped in this task by their developing socio-pragmatic abilities, such as the ability to take into account the speaker's gaze direction. For instance, Baldwin (1991, 1993) presented children with unfamiliar names given to unfamiliar objects. The children heard adults pronouncing a non-word (e.g. 'peri' or 'toma') while either looking at the unfamiliar toy that the child was holding in his hands or while looking at a toy that was not the object of the child's focus. Children were then asked comprehension questions (e.g. 'Where is the peri?') revealing that by the age of 18 months, they were able to correctly attribute the unfamiliar word to the object that the experimenter was focusing on rather than the object that they were holding.

The importance of joint attention was further demonstrated by Baldwin et al. (1996), who compared children's ability to learn the label for an unfamiliar object either when the speaker uttering the new word was seated within the children's view and displaying concurrent attention to the novel object, or when the speaker was seated outside the children's view. Their results indicate that by the age of 18 months, children learn stable associations between the label and the object, but only when they see the speaker uttering the label while looking at the object. When children do not have access to the speaker's gaze direction, they do not form such associations. In sum, these experiments reveal that the ability to take into account the gaze direction of another speaker, resulting in joint attention, is a crucial ability enabling children to assign the correct labels to unknown objects. Joint attention is also an important step for the development of theory of mind abilities. Baron-Cohen (1995) argued that children develop a cognitive module called 'shared attention mechanism' at the age of 18 months, representing the main precursor of full-fledged theory of mind abilities.

Tomasello (2004) also argued that aspects of theory of mind abilities such as joint attention and intention reading are foundational processes for word learning. Tomasello and Todd (1983) investigated joint attentional interactions between mothers and their 12- to 18-month-old children and measured the size of children's vocabulary at the end of the study. They found that the two factors were strongly correlated: the more time the mother–child dyad spent in joint attentional interactions, the higher their children's vocabulary. Carpenter, Nagell, and Tomasello (1998) found a similar correlation already at the age of 12 months, suggesting that joint attention plays a role at the very early stages of lexical production. Another result from these experiments is that mothers' tendency to follow their children's attentional focus also predicted the size of children's vocabulary in the following months. These results indicate that children's cognitive ability of achieving joint attention is crucial for word learning but so is the amount and quality of the social interactions that they are taking part in. Nelson (1988: 241) also stressed the importance of input for word learning and argued that in most cases "it is the adult who guesses what the child is focused on and supplies the appropriate word." These findings suggest that social and cognitive aspects of pragmatic competencies are interrelated, as both the development of a cognitive ability (i.e. joint attention) and the social context of exposure seem to matter for word learning.

Tomasello and his colleagues demonstrated in addition that children were taking adults' communicative intentions into account when learning a new label for an unfamiliar object, even when the situation was more complex than in Baldwin's experiments summarized above. For example, Tomasello and Barton (1994) found that 24-month-old children learned words from intentional actions but not from accidental ones. They also demonstrated children's ability to attribute a label to a correct referent in the context of a search game, in which the experimenter announced that he was "searching the toma" and then rejected several objects before finding the one he wanted. The speaker indicated that he had found the intended object by a smile and by stopping the search. In this situation, children correctly attributed the label to the intended referent and not to one of the distractor items that came up earlier during the search. Tomasello, Strosberg, and Akhtar (1996) replicated these findings with 18-month-old children. All this indicates that recognizing speaker's intentions is a crucial element guiding children in their label-object mappings, even in non-ostensive situations such as the search game set up in these experiments.

Bloom (2000) argued that children's ability to learn the meaning of words is to a large extent related to their developing theory of mind abilities. In a well known experiment by Markman and Wachtel (1988), three-year-old children were asked to show the *fendle* while being presented with a banana and a whisk. Most of the children consistently chose the whisk over the banana. According to Bloom (2000: 68), children intuitively apply the following reasoning when confronted with a new name and two possible referents for it:

1. I know that a banana is called *banana.*
2. If the speaker meant to refer to the banana, she would have asked me to show her the banana.
3. But she didn't; she used a strange word, *fendle.*
4. So she must intend to refer to something other than the banana.
5. A plausible candidate is the whisk.
6. *Fendle* must refer to the whisk.

In Bloom's description, children's referential attribution depends on their ability to (implicitly) reason about the speaker's mental states. Markman and Wachtel attribute children's tendency to choose the unfamiliar object to the application of a principle of mutual exclusivity, corresponding to a strong version of Clark's (1987, 1993) principle of contrast. The principle of mutual exclusivity states that children assume that differences in form correspond to differences in meaning. Following this principle, an object that already has a name in children's vocabulary cannot have a second name. When confronted with a familiar object and an unfamiliar one, they associate new words with unfamiliar objects (e.g. a whisk) rather than familiar ones (e.g. a banana). Markman and Wachtel believe that this principle is specific to word learning and therefore applies only to pair labels with referents. Bloom argues that the principle of contrast is not limited to word learning and therefore not only applied to labels. According to him, it is a pragmatic principle related to children's mindreading abilities, applied in all communicative situations, and indeed Diesendruck and Markson (2001) found that children use it in other communicative situations as well.

Another line of evidence of the role of theory of mind abilities for word learning comes from studies involving children suffering from autism spectrum disorders, a neurological condition involving deficits in theory of mind abilities (see Chapter 9, Section 9.2). According to the theory of mind account of word learning, autistic children should have difficulties making correct pairings between words and objects due to their theory of mind deficits. Indeed, in the literature, a number of studies relate inappropriate pairings between words and objects made by autistic children. One of the most famous anecdotes comes from Kanner (1943) who in his original description of autism described the case of a child who repeatedly used the phrase 'Peter eater' to talk about saucepan. This association was reportedly created when the child's mother once dropped a saucepan while singing the nursery rhyme 'Peter, Peter, Pumpkin Eater'. In a controlled set of experiments, Baron-Cohen, Baldwin, and Crowson (1997) investigated whether autistic children were able to use the speaker's gaze direction as a cue to his referential intents, the way normally developing children do by the age of 18 months (see Baldwin's 1991, 1993 experiments described above). Results from these experiments indicated that autistic children made mapping errors by attributing labels to the referents that were their own focus of attention rather than the speaker's focus. These findings confirm that deficits in theory of mind abilities lead to problems in word learning.

The studies reviewed so far indicate that children can very efficiently learn the meaning of words even in non-ostensive contexts thanks to their theory of mind skills. However, they also raise the question of whether theory of mind abilities are all that is required for learning the meaning of words or whether other abilities are also needed. Bloom (2000: 86–87) argued that children's theory of mind abilities help them in pairing words with referents in the world but that this is not sufficient for them to really learn the meaning of words. In order for children to have learned the meaning of a word, they also need to map it with a concept. Theory of mind abilities will not guide them in that respect. In addition, having theory of mind abilities does not help children to know whether a new label refers to an individual referent (e.g. the proper name of a specific dog) or to the category of dogs. For this, using cues from the speaker communicative behavior such as the direction of his gaze is not helpful, as speakers' overt behavior is the same when they speak about proper names and common nouns.

The existence of a set of cues complementing theory of mind abilities during the word learning process has been acknowledged by many different authors. For example, Jaswal and Markman (2001) found that two- and three-year-old children could learn the meaning of common and proper names in the absence of ostensive cues such as eye gaze and pointing by relying on semantic and syntactic cues. More generally, the 'emergentist coalition model' of word learning (Golinkoff et al., 1999; Hollich et al., 2000) includes an array of social, cognitive, linguistic, and attentional factors in order to explain the way children acquire the meaning of words. In this model, children are said to weigh the different types of cues differently in the course of word learning. In addition, the principles guiding children are emergent, because they are said to evolve from an immature to a mature state. During the first phase of word learning, children favor attentional cues such as temporal contiguity and perceptual salience, as predicted by associationist models. During a second phase, children incorporate linguistic cues related to grammar and prosody and socio-pragmatic cues such as eye gaze and social context, as soon as their linguistic and social-pragmatic skills are operational. During this second phase, the most sophisticated factors take precedence over the most simple association mechanisms. In his usage-based account of language acquisition, Tomasello (2004) also mentioned the existence of 'prerequisite processes' to word learning such as segmenting speech and conceptualizing referents and of 'facilitating processes' such as lexical contrast and linguistic context, that come into play during word learning, in addition to the foundational socio-pragmatic processes like joint attention, intention reading, and cultural learning.

To summarize, all the studies described in this section illustrate the correlation between theory of mind abilities and word learning, while stressing that socio-pragmatic cues related to theory of mind abilities must be complemented by other factors. Pragmatic competencies influence word learning in yet another way, as children have also been found to rely on other speakers' adherence to the maxims of quality and relation during word learning (Vázquez, Delisle & Saylor, 2012). In an experiment, children were witnessing a conversation between two adults on a television screen, one of them either respecting or violating Grice's maxim of relation or manner (defined in Chapter 1, Section 1.1.2). For example, the violation of the maxim of manner involved one of the conversation partners giving erroneous information about objects that children could see on the screen (e.g. "I have sixty balloons" while holding only two balloons). In a second phase, children had to pair a new label, for example, 'dake' with one of two objects, both presented as 'dakes' by one of the conversation partners. The experimenter made clear to the children that both objects could not be 'dakes' and asked them to choose one object as the 'dake'. At the age of four, children were sensitive to violations of the maxim of quality, as they tended not to trust the labels provided by speakers who did not adhere to it and consequently chose the object presented by the other conversation partner. They were, however, not sensitive to violations of the maxim of relation, as it was observed that these did not affect their trust in the speakers who did not adhere to them. Six-year-old-children on the other hand used both maxims to assess speakers' reliability as sources of knowledge for learning the meaning of new words, as they systematically chose to trust speakers who did not violate any of the maxims. This experiment thus indicates that pragmatic competencies continue to affect word learning even for older children.

2.2.2. Complex syntax and pragmatic competencies

We showed in the previous section that children's ability to reason about other people's mental states and to evaluate their communicative behavior represent strong cues guiding them in the task of word learning and that lack of these pragmatic abilities led to deficits in lexical acquisition, as evidenced by children suffering from autism. In this section, we argue that reciprocally, the influence of language on the development of theory of mind abilities and other pragmatic competencies is also a well-documented fact in the literature.

Evidence for the role of language in theory of mind development comes from studies of deaf children. Peterson and Siegal (2000) summarized 11 studies indicating that deaf children born from hearing parents and who suffered from an early lack of linguistic exposure presented an important delay in the development of theory of mind abilities. They also noted an important difference among different categories of deaf children, depending on their exposure to language during their preschool years. In their studies, they divided deaf children into three different categories. First, children of signing deaf parents who had a native speaker of sign language in their immediate household. Second, orally trained deaf children who, with the help of hearing aids, had been taught to speak and comprehend spoken language. Third, children who acquired sign language in school after a period of conversational deprivation in a family with no fluent signing member. Children from the first category did not present a delay in theory of mind development, which excludes the possibility that a deficit in the other categories of deaf children is exclusively due to this impairment. The other two groups suffered from an important delay in the development of theory of mind abilities. These results provide a strong argument in favor of the role of language for the development of theory of mind abilities.

The question then is whether the language faculty as a whole is related to theory of mind abilities or whether some specific components of language are more particularly required for developing theory of mind abilities. De Villiers and Pyers (2002) submitted that the mastery of complement clauses is the main linguistic prerequisite for the development of theory of mind, because it is the only structure that enables the embedding of a proposition with a different truth conditional status with respect to the main clause. For example, sentence (1) can be true while the embedded clause (2) is false. Other embedded structures such as relative clauses or adjunct clauses do not offer this possibility.

(1) Jane believes that lizards are venomous.
(2) Lizards are venomous.

In English, while mental state verbs like *believe* or *think* require embedding as in (1), verbs of desire such as *want* take an infinitival structure as in (3) and children also start to produce verbs of desire before verbs of belief or communication, which require embedding.

(3) Lisa wants to go swimming.

The relation between complement clauses and theory of mind abilities has been evidenced in two studies by Hale and Tager-Flusberg (2003) and Lohmann and Tomasello (2003) in which normally developing children were trained to understand false complements with communication verbs, with the result of increasing their theory of mind abilities, as measured by their performance on the false belief task (see Chapter 5, Section 5.1). Studies involving deaf children point to the same conclusion. For example, de Villiers and de Villiers (2003) found that deaf children's (both orally trained and ASL-learning) performance on both verbal and non-verbal versions of the false belief task was most closely predicted by their mastery of complement clauses. Pyers (2001) also tested first generation Nicaraguan signers who had not been exposed to formal signed language, and whose language did not contain complex structures. These subjects systematically failed even non-verbal versions of the false-belief task. On the other hand, younger signers who had acquired more evolved versions of Nicaraguan sign language did pass them.

This body of literature offers strong indicators that complex syntax is necessary for the development of theory of mind abilities, even though the nature and extent of the specific role of complement clauses is still debated (e.g. Perner, Sprung, Zauner & Haider, 2003; Smith, Apperly & White, 2003). The question is whether syntax is only constraining the development of theory of mind abilities or if other aspects of pragmatics competencies follow a similar pattern. We argue that they do, at least for a number of phenomena. For example, Ervin-Tripp (1977: 172) stressed that the kind of directives that children produce are limited by the complexity of the grammatical forms used to convey them (see also Chapter 3, Section 3.2). In addition, Diessel (2004) showed that the ability to use connectives is influenced by the syntactic complexity of the coherence relation in which they are used (see Chapter 8, Section 8.2).

2.3. Methodological aspects of language acquisition research

To complete this chapter, we introduce in this section some key concepts and methodological issues for language acquisition research such as the difference between comprehension and production (Section 2.3.1) and the various methods that are used to study the acquisition of pragmatics (Section 2.3.2). These methods will be further exemplified and discussed in all the subsequent chapters of the book.

2.3.1. Comprehension versus production

The outline of language acquisition sketched in Section 2.1.1 indicated that what children know about language is most of the time not reflected in the language they produce during the same period. The fact that comprehension precedes production is certainly one of the best attested facts about language acquisition. The asynchrony between comprehension and production has been demonstrated for all components of the language faculty. In the domain of phonology, children perceive in their first months of life an impressive array of phonological features of their exposure language, ranging from individual sounds to suprasegmental patterns of rhythm and stress, long before their vocal tract is mature enough to enable them to start producing sequences of sounds. In the domain of syntax, children demonstrate sensitivity to many core aspects of syntactic construction such as constituent structure and word order even when their own utterances are still at the telegraphic stage and lack such complexity. Finally, at all stages of lexical development, children understand more words than the ones they produce. For example, Goldin-Meadow, Seligman, and Gelman (1976) tested whether two-year-old children could comprehend and produce common words and found that they understood about two to three times more words than they produced. A form of imbalance between comprehension and production remains visible in studies of the adult mental lexicon (e.g. Aitchison, 2003) because people understand many more words than the ones they regularly produce.

Even though comprehension in many ways precedes production, it is also the case that production can precede a full comprehension of some aspects of language. For example, Levy and Nelson (1994) found that at the early stages of acquisition, children produce temporal words such as 'tomorrow', 'morning', and 'now' only in formulaic sentences. In that sense, their production of these words precedes a full mastery, as they are not used in all the possible contexts for which they are used in adult speech. Clark (2003) reported a similar discrepancy for the acquisition of function words like articles. At the beginning of the acquisition process, English-speaking children always produce a form of schwa before nouns, making it impossible to discriminate between 'the' and 'a'. By the age of two-and-a-half years, most children do produce the correct 'the' and 'a' forms, but these productions do not always reflect an appropriate adult-like usage. Therefore, in the case of articles too, production can be said to precede a full mastery of these items. Similar discrepancies are also reported for other areas of language development (see Hendriks & Koster, 2010 for a review).

From a methodological perspective, assessing comprehension relies on a variety of indirect measures of children's behavior (see Section 2.3.2). Some of these behaviors reflect the ability to explicitly reason about a pragmatic phenomenon, for instance, by explaining why a speaker produces a given utterance, while others reflect children's implicit understanding, as measured for example by the direction of their gaze or their ability to act on the basis of an utterance. Explicit and implicit aspects of comprehension do not always develop synchronously either. One of the best known cases of discrepancy in the development of implicit and explicit knowledge concerns the development of theory of mind abilities. Children do not show evidence of possessing explicit knowledge of false-belief reasoning before the age of four but have demonstrated in several studies an implicit understanding of this phenomenon through the direction of their gaze as early as their first birthday (see Low & Perner, 2012 for a review). We will come back to the issue of theory of mind development in Chapter 5. In second language learning, Zufferey et al. (submitted) have also found that advanced second language learners' implicit knowledge of the correct uses of discourse connectives also precedes their ability to explicitly judge their acceptability (see Chapter 10, Section 10.2.1).

In a nutshell, when studying the acquisition of a given pragmatic phenomenon, the two dimensions of comprehension and production must be taken into account, bearing in mind that they are most of the time not acquired synchronously. In the next chapters, we will always review both aspects of pragmatic development separately. In addition, conclusions about children's comprehension of a given phenomenon based on experimental evidence must also take into account the fact that different experimental methods can reflect explicit or implicit comprehension and that these two aspects of linguistic competence can be acquired at different schedules. We will therefore systematically compare different methods when such results are available in the literature.

2.3.2. Methods for assessing the acquisition of pragmatics

A number of methodological approaches are regularly used to assess children's developing pragmatic competencies. In this section, we briefly review and exemplify the most commonly used methods, separating those focusing on production, and those focusing on explicit and implicit comprehension.

One of the main resources used for studying children's linguistic productions are speech samples in the form of corpora. One of the main advantages of using corpus data is that they are collected in natural situations and that the potential biases induced by unnatural experimental settings are avoided. Children's linguistic behavior, both at home and in the laboratory, have in addition been found to be enhanced when they are speaking with their mother compared with strangers (Bornstein, Haynes, Painter & Genevro, 2000). A major drawback from corpus data is that the context in which language is produced is not controlled for, with the consequence that interpreting children's linguistic behavior in these speech samples relies on the experimenter's comprehension of the context of production. In addition, corpora only contain a reduced set of modalities, depending on the way it was collected. In many cases, only transcripts are available, sometimes with audio files. More recently, some corpora have included audio-visual recordings with single or multiple cameras (e.g. Roy, 2009). In addition, using corpora raises the question of how much linguistic data should be sampled in order to faithfully reflect children's abilities. The answer to this question depends on the frequency of the linguistic phenomenon under investigation. As Tomasello and Stahl (2004) observed, in many corpora from the CHILDES database (MacWhinney & Snow, 1985), children are recorded for one hour every one to two weeks, which represents only about 1 to 1.5% of the language they produce and hear over the recording period. Great care should therefore be taken before concluding that children are not yet able to produce language on the basis of corpus observations only.

A methodological question raised by production data is how many occurrences of a given phenomenon are necessary for concluding that acquisition has taken place. For example, if corpus data is used to determine the age at which children acquire discourse connectives such as 'but' and 'so', how many occurrences of these connectives are required for concluding that children master them? Two different factors are used to assess acquisition on the basis of production data: quantity and quality. In an acquisition model based on the notion of quantity, all occurrences produced are counted, whether correct or incorrect. A constraint is, however, placed on the minimal number of occurrences that have to be produced. This type of criterion has been applied to the acquisition of discourse connectives by Braunwald (1985), who counted all occurrences of connectives in her data, regardless of their meaning, while placing a quantitative lower limit of five occurrences. The quantitative method has the advantage of eliminating cases of isolated productions. From a methodological point of view, it also provides a simple way to extract data automatically, since no evaluation of the production is required. However, the application of purely quantitative criteria results in arbitrary decisions. Why should five occurrences rather than four or six be necessary? Another limitation of the quantitative approach is that it provides a binary view of the acquisition process (acquired or not). It seems more reasonable to think of this process as a continuum, where children go through several stages until they reach adult-like competencies. An alternative view is to take a qualitative approach and look for correct occurrences only. However, as judgments rely on researchers' interpretation of the data, they can be misleading. For this reason, many authors advocate the simultaneous use of quantitative and qualitative criteria to determine when a linguistic item is acquired based on children's productions.

Another frequently used method to assess children's production is elicitation. Contrary to corpus data, elicited data are not totally natural, as the experiment sets a context designed to trigger the production of a given linguistic phenomenon. Using this technique, Astington (1988) set up dialogs between two dolls in which the experimenter took one role and children were asked to take the other role. The speech turns of the experimenter were formatted to elicit various types of speech acts. One of the dialogs was designed to elicit the production of commissive acts (e.g. promises) as in (4):

(4) Context: Let's pretend that the mum wants the boy to clean up his room. But he doesn't want to do it. He wants to go out and play. Maybe he'll clean it up later but not now. What do they say?
Experimenter: Your room is a mess. Please will you clean it up?
Child: ...
Experimenter: How do I know that you'll make it later (or whatever commitment the child makes)
Child: ...
Experimenter: What can you say to me now so that I know (that you'll ...)
Child: ...
Experimenter: Is there anything/nothing you can say so I'll really know (that you'll ...)

The main advantage of elicitation is that it enables researchers to collect more data on a particular aspect of language compared with natural interactions, given that speech samples only represent a small portion of children's linguistic productions. However, elicitation also has a number of caveats. One of them is that experimenters must be very careful not to model, by their linguistic behavior, the answers that are expected from the children. For example, in (4) the experimenter should by all means avoid using the word 'promise' in the prompts. In addition, the pragmatic situation of the task should be set in such a way as to avoid inappropriate productions. For example, in (4), the experimenter must ascertain that on the basis of the context provided, children understand that a promise rather than a reason for not cleaning the room is expected of them.

In addition to the measures of language production, various non-corpus–based methods are used to assess children's comprehension of language. Some of them directly appeal to children's ability to form metalinguistic judgments. For example, in order to assess children's comprehension of ironic statements, Dews et al. (1996) asked children to choose, between two possibilities, the one corresponding to the speaker's meaning, as in (5).

(5) When the turtle said: 'Helpful, isn't he?' did the turtle mean that the man was *helpful* and *nice* or *selfish* and not *cooperating*?

Metalinguistic judgments have the advantage of clearly reflecting the meaning that has been understood. But such judgments are also very difficult for children to produce, and this method cannot be reliably used at an early age. In addition, Bernicot, Laval, and Chaminaud (2007) demonstrated that the observed order of acquisition between several pragmatic competencies such as the ability to understand indirect requests, figurative language, and conversational implicatures is not the same if the task required either pragmatic or meta-pragmatic skills.

Another method for assessing comprehension consists in asking questions targeting linguistic (rather than metalinguistic) content, for example, after listening to short stories. Zufferey *et al.* (submitted) have, for instance, assessed children's comprehension of causal relations conveyed by various discourse connectives in texts by asking them 'why' questions after reading portions of a story as for instance in (6).

(6) The mouse fell asleep because it was very tired.
Why did the mouse fall asleep?

These questions have the advantage of being easier for children to understand than metalinguistic questions, but they cannot be applied to all pragmatic phenomena. In many cases, comprehension and metalinguistic questions can also be combined to get a fine-grained picture of comprehension. In both cases, care must be taken with the formulation of test questions and with the pragmatic context set by the task, as children have been found to adequately report their ignorance to unanswerable questions by 'I don't know' more often in a context when the experimenter was ignorant of the answer and when the question was phrased with *wh-* rather than yes/no questions (Waterman, Blades & Spencer, 2004).

Another form of judgment that is regularly used to assess comprehension is the truth value judgment task (TVJT). Contrary to other judgment tasks, the TVJT does not require metalinguistic knowledge. According to Gordon (1996), the TVJT: "assumes only that the child has some conception of the notion of truth in the sense of a correspondence between what is said and the situation referred to.

[...] The advantage is that the task does not require that child to bring any of these processes to consciousness in any explicit way." Because of its relation to truth, this task is particularly useful to assess phenomena that lie at the semantics-pragmatics interface such as scalar implicatures (see Chapter 7). Guasti et al. (2005) used a version of the truth value judgment task in which children were watching a video with a puppet. At the end, the puppet described what happened in the story and children were asked to evaluate whether she had given a good or a bad description. This task was meant to measure children's evaluation of sentences containing quantifiers like *some*. It cannot ascertain, however, that children reject pragmatically infelicitous uses of quantifiers for the right reason. Guasti et al. have therefore also asked children to explain their answers when they judged that the puppet's description was incorrect. This example illustrates again how various methods can be combined to assess comprehension.

A more implicit way to assess language comprehension that does not require a verbal response is the use of an act-out task. These tasks involve asking children to perform an action such as passing an object, placing a figure, or selecting a picture based on a controlled linguistic stimulus. Such tasks are often used to assess children's mappings between objects and words, as discussed in Section 2.2.1. In pragmatics, they have been used in the study of scalar implicatures by Pouscoulous et al. (2007) who asked children to move tokens in boxes on the basis of sentences such as: "I would like some boxes to contain a token." This task revealed an earlier ability to handle scalar implicatures than tasks involving a conscious linguistic judgment.

Finally, implicit comprehension can be assessed through the study of eye gaze, as measured using eye-tracking devices. This method can be used either to track children's reading of sentences or the direction and duration of their gaze fixations on scenes depicted visually. The use of eye-tracking during reading is a powerful way to assess language processing by young readers, but it is obviously not applicable to younger children. The second technique, called the 'visual world paradigm', can be used even with babies. For example, Van Veen (2011) placed two- and three-and-a-half-year old children in front of a computer screen displaying pictures that were causally related to a linguistic stimulus. This method evidenced that very young children already have some understating of subtle differences between different types of causal relations, even though they do not yet express them correctly by the use of connectives.

2.4. Synthesis

We presented in this chapter a concise timeline of children's acquisition of the structural components of language and argued that while many aspects of the language faculty are already operational at the age of three, the acquisition of complex aspects of syntax continues until late during childhood and lexical acquisition reaches its peak only during the school years. We also showed that the acquisition of theory of mind abilities, an essential cognitive faculty related to pragmatics, and of other aspects of the language faculty are in many ways interrelated. From a methodological perspective, we demonstrated the importance of comparing production and comprehension and reviewed the most commonly used methods to assess the acquisition of pragmatic competencies from both perspectives. We discussed the advantages and drawbacks of these methods and suggested that complementary techniques can often be used in parallel.

References

Aitchison, J. (2003). *Words in the Mind: An Introduction to the Mental Lexicon* (3rd Edition). Oxford: Blackwell.

Anglin, J. (1993). Vocabulary development. A morphological analysis. *Monographs of the Society for Research in Child Development, 52*(10), 1–166.

Astington, J. (1988). Children's production of commissive speech acts. *Journal of Child Language, 15*, 411–423.

Baldwin, D. (1991). Infant's contribution to the achievement of joint reference. *Child Development, 62*, 875–890.

Baldwin, D. (1993). Infant's ability to consult the speaker for clues to word reference. *Journal of Child Language, 20*, 395–418.

Baldwin, D., Markman, E., Bill, B., Desjardins, R., Irwin, J., & Tidball, G. (1996). Infants' reliance on a social criterion for establishing word-object relations. *Child Development, 67*(6), 3135–3153.

Baron-Cohen, S. (1995). *Mindblindness: An Essay on Autism and Theory of Mind*. Cambridge, MA: MIT Press.

Baron-Cohen, S., Baldwin, D., & Crowson, M. (1997). Do children with autism use the speaker's direction of gaze strategy to crack the code of language? *Child Development, 68*, 48–57.

Benedict, H. (1979). Early lexical development: comprehension and production. *Journal of Child Language, 6*(2), 183–200.

Bernicot, J., Laval, V., & Chaminaud, S. (2007). Nonliteral language forms in children: in what order are they acquired in pragmatics and metapragmatics? *Journal of Pragmatics, 39*, 2115–2132.

Bloom, L. (1973). *One Word at a Time: The Use of Single Word Utterances before Syntax*. The Hague: Mouton.

Bloom, P. (2000). *How Children Learn the Meanings of Words*. Cambridge, MA: The MIT Press.

Bornstein, M., Haynes, M., Painter, K., & Genevro, J. (2000). Child language with mother and with stranger at home and in the laboratory: a methodological study. *Journal of Child Language, 27*, 407–420.

Braunwald, S. (1985). The development of connectives. *Journal of Pragmatics, 9*, 513–525.

Carey, S. (1978). The child as word learner. In M. Halle, J. Bresnan, & G. Miller. (eds), *Linguistic Theory and Psychological Reality* (pp. 264–293). Cambridge, MA: MIT Press.

Carpenter, M., Nagell, K., & Tomasello, M. (1998). Sixteen-month-old infants differentially imitate intentional and accidental actions. *Infant Behavior and Development, 21*, 315–330.

Christophe, A. Dupoux, E., Bertonicini, J., & Mehler, J. (1994). Do infants perceive word boundaries? An empirical study of the bootstrapping of lexical acquisition. *Journal of the Acoustical Society of America, 95*(3), 1570–1580.

Clark, E. (1987). The principle of contrast: a constraint on language acquisition. In B. MacWhinney (ed), *Mechanisms of Language Acquisition: The Twentieth Annual Carnegie Symposium on Cognition* (pp. 1–33). Hillsdale, NJ: Erlbaum.

Clark, E. (1993). *The Lexicon in Acquisition*. Cambridge: Cambridge University Press.

Clark, E. (2003). *First Language Acquisition*. Cambridge: Cambridge University Press.

Colombo, J. & Bundy, R. (1983). Infant response to auditory familiarity and novelty. *Infant Behavior and Development, 6*(3), 305–311.

de Villiers, J. (2007). The interface of language and theory of mind. *Lingua, 117*, 1858–1878.

de Villiers, J. & de Villiers, P. (2003). Language for thought: coming to understand false beliefs. In D. Gentner, & S. Goldin-Meadow (eds), *Language in Mind: Advances in the Study of Language and Thought* (pp. 335–384). Cambridge: MIT Press.

de Villiers, J. & Pyers, J. (2002). Complements to cognition: A longitudinal study of the relationship between complex syntax and false-belief-understanding. *Cognitive Development, 17*, 1037–1060.

Dews, S., Winner, E., Kaplan, J., & Rosenblatt, E. et al. (1996). Children's understanding of the meaning and functions of verbal irony. *Child Development, 67*(6), 3071–3085.

Diesendruck, G. & Markson, L. (2001). Children's avoidance of lexical overlap: a pragmatic account. *Developmental Psychology, 37*(5), 630–641.

Diessel, H. (2004). *The Acquisition of Complex Sentences*. Cambridge: Cambridge University Press.

Ervin-Tripp, S. (1977). Wait for me roller skate! In S. Ervin-Tripp, & C. Mitchell-Kernan (eds), *Child Discourse* (pp. 165–188). New York: Academic Press.

Goldin-Meadow, S., Seligman, M., & Gelman, R. (1976). Language in the two-year-old: receptive and productive stages. *Cognition, 4*(2), 189–202.

Golinkoff, R., Hirsh-Pasek, K., & Hollich, G. (1999). Emergent cues for early word learning. In B. MacWhinney (ed), *The Emergence of Language* (pp. 305–330). Mahwah, NJ: Erlbaum.

Gordon, P. (1996). The truth value judgment task. In D. MacDaniel, C. McKee, & H. Smith Cairns (eds), *Methods for Assessing Children's Syntax* (pp. 211–232). Cambridge, MA: MIT Press.

Guasti, M., Chierchia, G., Crain, S., Foppolo, F., Gualmini, A., & Meroni, L. (2005). Why children and adults sometimes (but not always) compute implicatures. *Language and Cognitive Processes, 20*(5), 667–696.

Hale, C. & Tager-Flusberg, H. (2003). The influence of language on theory of mind: a training study. *Developmental Science, 6*, 346–359.

Hendriks, P. & Koster, C. (2010). Production/comprehension asymmetries in language acquisition. *Lingua, 120*(8), 1887–1897.

Hirsh-Pasek, K. & Golinkoff, R. (1993). Skeletal supports for grammatical learning: What the infant brings to the language learning task. In C. Rovee-Collier, & L. Lipsitt (eds), *Advances in Infancy Research* (pp. 299–338). Norwood, NJ: Ablex.

Hollich, G., Hirsh-Pasek, K., & Golinkoff, R. (2000). Breaking the language barrier: An emergentist coalition model for the origins of word learning. *Monographs of the Society for Research in Child Development*. Chicago, IL: Chicago University Press.

Jaswal, V. & Markman, E. (2001). Learning proper and common names in inferential versus ostensive contexts. *Child Development, 72*, 768–786.

Jusczyk, P., Hirsh-Pasek, K., Nelson, D., Kennedy, L., Woodward, A., & Piwoz, J. (1992). Perception of acoustic correlates of major phrasal units to young infants. *Cognitive Psychology, 24*, 252–293.

Jusczyk, P. & Aslin, R. (1995). Infants' detection of sound patterns of words in fluent speech. *Cognitive Psychology, 29*(1), 1–23.

Jusczyk. P. & Hohne, E. (1997). Infants' memory for spoken words. *Science, 277*(5334), 1984–1986.

Jusczyk, P., Luce, P., & Luce, C. (1994). Infants' sensitivity to phonotactic patterns in the native language. *Journal of Memory and Language, 33*(5), 630–645.

Kanner, L. (1943). Autistic disturbances of affective contact. *Nervous Child, 2*, 217–250.

Karmiloff-Smith, A. (1986). Some fundamental aspects of language development after age 5. In Fletcher, P. & Garman, M. (eds), *Language Acquisition: Studies in First Language Development*. Cambridge: Cambridge University Press.

Levy, E. & Nelson, C. (1994). Words in discourse: A dialectical approach to the acquisition of meaning and use. *Journal of Child Language, 21*, 367–389.

Lohmann, H. & Tomasello, M. (2003). The role of language in the development of false belief understanding: a training study. *Child Development, 74*, 1130–1144.

Low, J. & Perner, J. (2012). Implicit and explicit theory of mind: State of the art. *British Journal of Developmental Psychology, 30*(1), 1–13.

Lust, B. (2006). *Child Language. Acquisition and Growth*. Cambridge: Cambridge University Press.

MacWhinney, B. & Snow, C. (1985). The child language data exchange system. *Journal of Child Language, 12*(2), 271–296.

Markman, E. & Hutchinson, J. (1994). Children's sensitivity to constraints on word meaning: Taxonomic versus thematic relations. *Cognitive Psychology, 16*, 1–27.

Markman, E. & Wachtel, G. (1988). Children's use of mutual exclusivity to constrain the meanings of words. *Cognitive Psychology, 20*, 121–157.

Mehler, J., Jusczyk, P, Lambertz, G., Halsted, N., Bertoncini, J. & Amiel-Tison, C. (1988). A precursor of language acquisition in young infants. *Cognition, 29*(2), 143–178.

Nazzi, T., Kemler Nelson, D., Jusczyk, P., & Jusczyk, A. M. (2000). Six-months-olds detection of clauses embedded in continuous speech: Effects of prosodic well-formedness. *Infancy, 1*, 123–147.

Nelson, K. (1988). Constraints of word learning? *Cognitive Development, 3*, 221–246.

Perner, J., Sprung, M., Zauner, P., & Haider, H. (2003). Want that is understood well before say that, think that, and false belief: A test of de Villier's linguistic determinism on German-speaking children. *Child Development, 74*, 179–188.

Peterson, C. & Siegal, M. (2000). Insights into theory of mind from deafness and autism. *Mind and Language, 15*, 123–145.

Plunkett, K. (1997). Theories of early language acquisition. *Trends in Cognitive Sciences, 1*(4), 146–153.

Polka, L. & Werker, J. (1994). Developmental changes in perception of nonnative vowel contrasts. *Journal of Experimental Psychology, 20*(2), 421–435.

Pouscoulous, N., Noveck, I., Politzer, G., & Bastide, A. (2007). A developmental investigation of processing costs in implicature production. *Language Acquisition, 14*(4), 347–375.

Pyers, J. (2001). Three stages in the understanding of false belief in Nicaraguan signers: The interaction of social experience, language emergence, and conceptual development. *Invited Symposium Conducted at the 31st Annual Meeting of the Piaget Society*. Berkley, CA: United-States.

Roy, D. (2009). New horizons in the study of child language acquisition. *Proceedings of Interspeech 2009*. Brighton: England.

Shady, M., Gerken, L., & Jusczyk, P. (1995). Some evidence of sensitivity to prosody and word order in 10-month-olds. In D. MacLaughlin, & S. McEwan (eds), *Proceedings of the 19th Boston University Conference on Language Development* (pp. 553–562). Somerville: Cascadilla Press.

Shady, M. (1996). *Infant's Sensitivity to Function Morphemes.* Unpublished dissertation. State University of New York at buffalo.

Smith, M., Apperly, I., & White, V. (2003). False belief reasoning and the acquisition of relative clause sentences. *Child Development, 74*(6), 1709–1719.

Tomasello, M. (2004). *Constructing a Language: A Usage-Based Theory of Language Acquisition.* Cambridge, MA: Harvard University Press.

Tomasello, M. & Barton, M. (1994). Learning words in non-ostensive contexts. *Developmental Psychology, 30*, 639–650.

Tomasello, M. & Stahl, D. (2004). Sampling children's spontaneous speech: how much is enough? *Journal of Child Language, 31*(1), 101–121.

Tomasello, M., Strosberg R., & Akhtar, N. (1996). Eighteen-month-old children learn words in non-ostensive contexts. *Journal of Child Language, 23*, 157–176.

Tomasello, M. & Todd. (1983). Joint attention and lexical acquisition style. *First Language, 4*, 197–212.

Van Veen, R. (2011). *The Acquisition of Causal Connectives.* Unpublished PhD Thesis, University of Utrecht, The Netherlands.

Vázquez, M., Delisle, S., & Saylor, M. (2012). Four- and six-year-olds use pragmatic competence to guide word learning. *Journal of Child Language, 40*(2), 291–306.

Waterman, A., Blades, M., & Spencer, C. (2004). Indicating when you don't know the answer: The effect of question format and interviewer knowledge on children's 'don't know' answers. *British Journal of Developmental Psychology, 22*, 335–348.

Zufferey, S. (2010). *Lexical Pragmatics and Theory of Mind: The Acquisition of Connectives.* Amsterdam: John Benjamins.

Zufferey, S., Mak, W., & Sanders, T. (submitted). Does linguistic encoding influence the acquisition of casual relations? A cross-linguistic study in French and Dutch. *Applied Psycholinguistics.*

Zufferey, S. Mak, W., Degand, L., & Sanders, T. (submitted). The role of L1 transfer for advanced learners' sensitivity to misuses of connectives.

PART II

Acquiring social aspects of pragmatic competence

3

LEARNING HOW TO DO THINGS WITH WORDS

Speech acts

Speech act theory has laid the foundations of pragmatics. In this chapter, we first introduce two aspects of speech act theory that have cognitive implications for acquisition, namely the difference between direct and indirect speech acts and the notion of conventionalization (Section 3.1). We then demonstrate that the difference between direct and indirect speech acts is not validated by developmental data on the acquisition of requests. We propose instead that linguistic and inferential development sets the pace for the acquisition of the linguistic forms to convey indirect speech acts (Section 3.2). We go on to discuss several interpretations of the notion of conventionalization, based on frequency and felicity conditions, and argue that conventionalization does not appear to play a crucial role for explaining the development of speech acts. Finally, we contend that differences in the age of acquisition between specific speech acts reflect the more general distinction between universal and culture-specific aspects of verbal communication (Section 3.3).

3.1. Cognitive implications of speech act theory

We introduced in Chapter 1 the main tenets of speech act theory. In this section, we focus more specifically on aspects of the theory that have cognitive implications for the way speech acts are acquired by children and processed by adult speakers, namely the difference between direct and indirect speech acts (Section 3.1.1) and the conventionalization of some linguistic forms to convey indirect speech acts (Section 3.1.2).

3.1.1. Direct and indirect speech acts

One of Searle's main contributions to the development of speech act theory is the observation that, in many cases, speech acts are not transparently communicated in language (Searle, 1969, 1975). For example, while (1) directly conveys a speech act of request by the use of an imperative form, (2) does not convey a speech act of question but a request despite its interrogative surface form.

(1) Be quiet.
(2) Can you be quiet?

As Levinson (1983: 263) pointed out, the notion of indirect speech act is dependent on the literal force hypothesis, in other words on the assumption that illocutionary force is built into sentence form. According to this hypothesis, the force of explicit performatives is given by performative verbs. For all other sentences, the force is given by the sentence type: interrogatives convey an illocutionary force of question, imperatives a force of request, and declaratives a force of statement (see also Gazdar, 1981). All sentences that do not contain performative verbs and that do not convey the force associated with their sentence form are indirect speech acts.

The main challenge then is to explain how a hearer can understand that (2) is a request even though it has the linguistic form of a question. According to Searle (1975: 64), understanding an indirect speech act requires the following elements: "mutual background information, a theory of speech acts, and certain general principles of conversation." In Searle's (1975) description of the steps necessary to recover the meaning of an indirect speech act, the indirect meaning is envisaged only if the surface meaning does not lead to a plausible interpretation of the speaker's meaning. Thus, Searle recognizes that understanding indirect speech acts requires the ability to draw inferences based on the principles of conversation described by Grice (1967/1989; see Chapter 1). But contrary to Grice, he believes, in addition, that understanding utterances such as (2) requires a theory of speech acts. The theory of speech acts that he formulates states that all illocutionary acts have a number of conditions that must be fulfilled in order to be felicitously communicated. Searle (1975: 71) listed these conditions, reproduced in Table 3.1, for directive and commissive acts (H stands for *hearer*, A for *act,* and S for *speaker*).

TABLE 3.1 Searle's felicity conditions for speech acts

	Directive (request)	*Commissive (promise)*
Preparatory condition	H is able to perform A.	S is able to perform A. H wants S to perform A.
Sincerity condition	S wants H to do A.	S intends to do A.
Propositional content condition	S predicates a future act A of H.	S predicates a future act A of S.
Essential condition	Counts as an attempt by S to get H to do A.	Counts as the undertaking by S of an obligation to do A.

These conditions provide a way to classify the different forms of indirect speech acts, depending on which condition they are related to. For example, (3) questions the hearer's ability to perform the act as stated in the preparatory condition, (4) states the sincerity condition, and (5) questions the propositional content condition. Other forms of indirect speech acts embed one of these conditions as in (6).

(3) Can you answer the phone?
(4) I want you to answer the phone.
(5) Won't you answer the phone?
(6) Would you mind terribly if I asked you to answer the phone?

These observations led Searle to make the following generalization: a speaker can perform an indirect speech act by questioning or stating one of its felicity conditions, depending on the speech act. This generalization explains why all linguistic forms cannot be used to conventionally perform an indirect speech act. For example, a request to answer the phone cannot be communicated by (7), as it does not refer to any of the conditions.

(7) Mobile phones use radio links.

Searle also points out, however, that these generalizations are not rules, as any of the linguistic forms mentioned in (3) to (6) can also be used to perform direct speech acts in some contexts. For example, it is the surface meaning of statement of (4) that is conveyed in (8), rather than an indirect request.

(8) I want you to answer the phone, but I am not asking you to because I know you are very upset.

Because Searle believes that even formulations that are frequently used to convey indirect speech acts can be used to communicate their literal meaning in some contexts, he rejects the idea that these sentences have an imperative force as a part of their meaning. As a consequence, he states that even when an utterance like (3) is used to convey an indirect speech act of request, it retains its literal meaning of question or statement and is uttered with this meaning as well. More specifically, when a speaker utters (3) he literally means that he wants to know whether the speaker has the ability to answer the phone. In (3), the sentence meaning is a question and the speaker's meaning is a request. Searle mentions as evidence that indirect speech acts retain their literal meaning the fact that responses appropriate to their literal meaning are also appropriate for the indirect speech act, as in (9). In this example, B starts by answering the literal question and then either provides the requested information or a reason for not complying with the request.

(9) A: Can you tell me what time it is?
B: No I can't, I don't have a watch.
B: Yes I can, it's three thirty.

The literal force hypothesis and the idea that indirect speech acts convey both their literal and non-literal meanings have some clear implications for the way adult speakers should process direct and indirect speech acts. It follows from Searle's description of the steps necessary to recover the meaning of an indirect speech act that literal meaning should always be accessed first and indirect speech acts are derived only if this first interpretation does not make sense in context. These predictions are, however, not verified in processing experiments. First, given the appropriate context, indirect speech acts are processed as quickly as direct ones (Gibbs, 1983). Second, literal meaning is not always straightforwardly recovered and requires an appropriate context to be accessed (Gibbs, 1984). In sum, the precedence of literal over non-literal speech acts is not verified empirically. In addition, subjects cannot ignore the indirect meaning of sentences containing frequently used formulations to perform indirect speech acts (see Section 3.1.2) even when they are presented in a literal context (Gibbs, 1983; Shapiro & Murphy, 1993). This result further confirms that the meaning of indirect speech acts is not secondary compared with the surface speech act and that indirect meaning is always accessed even when the literal meaning is plausible.

From a developmental perspective, the difference between direct and indirect speech acts leads to some predictions about their acquisition. Papafragou (2000) noted that according to speech act theory, indirect speech acts should be more difficult for children to acquire than direct speech acts as they require, in addition to understanding the literal surface meaning, deriving an indirect meaning by inference. We will discuss the early acquisition of direct and indirect speech acts in Section 3.2.

3.1.2. Indirect speech acts and conventionalization

Searle (1975) observed that some linguistic forms are more routinely used than others to convey indirect speech acts. For example, (10) is a very commonly used way to indirectly ask for salt during a meal, by questioning the speaker's ability stated in the preparatory condition. In contrast, Bill's reply in (11) is not a prototypical utterance used to refuse an invitation to lunch and it is not related to a felicity condition, even though the speaker's meaning can be recovered by inference.

(10) Can you pass the salt?
(11) Ann: Would you like to have lunch with me now?
Bill: I have a class starting in 10 minutes.

According to Searle, commonly used forms to communicate indirect speech acts such as (10) are to some extent conventionalized, because they are related to a felicity condition. He argues, however, that they are not conventionalized in the language the way idioms are, as their surface meaning is always communicated along with their indirect meaning. In addition, they can in some contexts be used as direct speech acts. Morgan (1978) elaborated on this idea and argued that indirect speech acts do not correspond to conventions of language such as idioms but to conventions of use. Morgan also argued that conventional indirect speech acts produce short-circuited implicatures. In other words, even though the route to their indirect meaning can be calculated by inference, it does not need to be calculated because the hearer's background knowledge gives him immediate access to the intended non-literal meaning. However, a hearer not possessing this background knowledge would still reach the correct interpretation by a regular inferential route.

Bach and Harnish (1979: 193) endorsed a weaker version of this idea by stating that some indirect speech acts become standardized. According to Bach (1998: 713): "a form of words is standardized for a certain use if this use, though regularized, goes beyond literal meaning and yet can be explained without special conventions. In each case, there is a certain core of linguistic meaning attributable on compositional grounds but a common use that cannot be explained in terms of linguistic meaning alone." Bach assimilated cases of standardized indirect speech acts to the phenomenon of generalized conversational implicatures (see Chapter 7). Morgan's notion of convention of use and Bach and Harnish's concept of standardization share the idea that the understanding of conventionalized or standardized indirect speech acts follows a distinct derivation procedure compared with other forms of indirect speech acts. Bach (1995: 678) stated that: "where there is standardization, the hearer's inference is compressed by precedent; one does not have to go through all the steps that would be required absent standardization." This corresponds to Morgan's idea of short-circuited implicatures.

The idea that standardization amounts to short-circuited implicatures has clear and testable consequences for processing. As indirect meaning does not need to be calculated, conventional indirect speech acts should be easier to process than unconventional ones. In a set of experiments, Gibbs (1981) found that subjects do indeed react faster to conventional indirect speech acts than to unconventional ones. He also found, however, that conventionality is a context-dependent notion. In other words, what is conventionally used to convey an indirect request varies from one context to another. For example, a conventional way for a speaker to indirectly ask for the time is (12), but the same indirect formulation addressed to request stamps from an employee at the post office is rather inappropriate (13):

(12) Can you tell me what time it is?
(13) Can you sell me some stamps?

Gibbs (1986) confirmed that context plays a crucial role in people's perception of the conventionality of indirect requests. According to him, the indirect formulation is chosen to anticipate the main obstacle that may prevent the addressee to perform the requested action. In the case of (12), the main obstacle to giving the time is not having a watch. Therefore a question bearing on the addressee's ability is appropriate. In (13), the ability of the employee to sell stamps is obvious and the same type of question therefore appears inadequate. Thus the choice of conventionalized forms appears to require the integration of contextual information and does not simply rely on a set of predetermined rules.

From a developmental perspective, the notions of conventionalization or standardization raise the question of how and when children acquire these specific form-function pairings. We will discuss in Section 3.3.1 how frequency may be related to children's acquisition of linguistic forms that are used to convey indirect speech acts. In Searle's theory, conventionalization rests on the list of felicity conditions explaining the transition between direct and indirect speech acts. The acquisition of the felicity conditions of speech acts will be discussed in Section 3.3.2.

3.2. The acquisition of direct and indirect speech acts

Requesting is a common communicative act that children start to produce in the form of imperative pointing even before they can use language. In addition, requests are frequently conveyed by means of indirect speech acts in adult communication. Requests represent therefore a good test bed to assess the early emergence of direct and indirect speech acts in children's speech and to provide insights on children's early understanding of non-literal language. We start this section by summarizing studies that have investigated children's production and comprehension of requests (Section 3.2.1). Based on this set of results, we argue that order of acquisition between various linguistic forms to convey speech acts does not corroborate the distinction between direct and indirect speech acts but rather reflects the maturation of children's linguistic and inferential skills (Section 3.2.2).

3.2.1. Studies on the acquisition of requests

Children's early productions of direct and indirect speech acts of requesting have been the object of a number of studies. For example, Garvey (1975) investigated 36 children aged 3;6 to 5;7 while they were interacting in dyads in a play room during 15 minutes. For data analysis, Garvey separated children in two age groups: the younger group ranged from 3;6 to 4;4 (12 children) and the older age group ranged from 4;7 to 5;7 (24 children). The speech produced by children was transcribed and occurrences of requests were identified by two judges. Results indicate that the two groups of children produce a comparable number of direct requests. Interestingly, when requests were performed through a direct speech act, Garvey notes that the adjunct clause following them often contained a felicity condition for requesting, such as the mention of a reason to perform the request as in (14). These productions provide some confirmation that children implicitly understand the felicity conditions of requests even when they choose to convey them with a direct speech act.

(14) Hey come here. I want to show you something.

Indirect requests were identified by looking for cases where the hearers' reaction indicated that they had interpreted the utterance as a request. Overall, 67 indirect requests were identified, among which 15 were produced by children from the younger age group. Even though the younger age group contained only half the number of children included in the older group, the number of requests produced is still somewhat lower than expected if the two groups had equal productions (22 requests). Still, the study indicates that children can use both direct and indirect speech acts by the age of 3;6 even though there is an increase in the indirect forms as children get older. Young children's ability to use both direct and indirect requests is corroborated by other studies. For example, Read and Cherry (1978) elicited the production of requests in 15 children divided into three age groups: 2;6, 3;6, and 4;6 and found no difference in the quantity of requests produced across the groups. They report, in addition, that at the age of 2;6, children already possess a variety of indirect means to express requests. Dore (1977) also studied the natural production of seven children from the age of three to four years and reports that requests are conveyed by different direct and indirect linguistic means.

At first sight, it seems therefore that children acquire the ability to perform direct and indirect speech acts in a synchronous manner. It could be argued, however, that the distinction between direct and indirect speech acts is too coarse to reveal a sequence of acquisition and that a more fine-grained classification would reveal a progression from direct to indirect ways to convey speech acts. Ervin-Tripp (1977) devised such a classification and argued that adults use at least five different types of indirect requests that she orders on a scale from the most explicit (2) to the most implicit (6).

1. Direct imperative: Pass the salt.
2. Embedded imperative: Can you pass the salt?
3. Permission directive: May I have the salt?
4. Personal need or desire statement: I want (need) the salt.
5. Question directive: Is there some salt?
6. Hint: The soup is tasteless.

If the scale between direct and indirect forms corresponds to a cognitive reality, it is expected that children should start by using the more direct forms first and should acquire the more implicit forms as they grow older. Ervin-Tripp (1977) used this scale to classify children's production of requests, from the data described in a series of different studies (by Bates, 1976; Carter, 1974; Dore, 1973; Halliday, 1975). From these datasets, Ervin-Tripp reports that the first telegraphic directives are found before the age of two, as in (15) to (17).

(15) I want dolly.
(16) Gimme. Apple me.
(17) Carol Hungry.

Early during children's third year, indirect requests in the form of (18) appear, and in the course of their third year, requests start to be conveyed by many indirect means as in (19) and (20), enabling children to develop a vast repertoire for conveying indirect speech acts.

(18) Is there truck?
(19) Would you like to play golf?
(20) Can you give me one car please?

By the age of four, children start to use various indirect forms such as (21) to (23). At this stage, the requested object is still always mentioned.

(21) He made sand go in my eyes.
(22) We haven't had any candy for a long time.
(23) If you are good, we won't use the wolf.

By the age of six, children make indirect requests without mentioning the desired objects. Ervin-Tripp (1982) added that by the age of seven or eight, children resort to the same forms of indirectness as adults.

It is noticeable that children's earliest productions already encompass both direct speech acts as in (16) and indirect ones as in (15) and (17). In addition, (17) can be assimilated to a form of hint and (18) to a question directive, which correspond to the most indirect forms in Ervin-Tripp's classification. Newcombe and Zaslow (1981) also reported that two-and-a-half-year-olds use both hints and question directives in their speech directed to adults. Is seems therefore that children's production of speech acts is not determined by their level of implicitness, even from a more fine-grained scalar view of implicitness.

Studies focusing on the comprehension of requests also lead to the conclusion that children understand indirect requests from an early age. In one such experiment, Reeder (1981) studied young children's ability to discriminate between the various possible illocutionary forces for an ambiguous sentence such as (24) that could in different contexts be interpreted in three different ways: as a direct speech act of question, as an indirect request, or as an indirect offer.

(24) Would you like to play on the slide?

In a first experiment, Reeder tested six children aged 3;6 on their ability to correctly identify the illocutionary force of (24) as either a question or a request depending on context. Children were presented with toys representing a playground with several puppets representing children and one representing a teacher. The teacher puppet either uttered (25) to induce a question interpretation or (26) to induce a request interpretation. When the context was set, the same stimulus sentence (24) was also uttered by the teacher puppet.

(25) Peter, off you go outside and play … you choose what you want to play with.
(26) Simon, leave the swing, Susan's on it …

Comprehension was assessed through a passive recall technique, in which children were asked to choose between, for example, (27) and (28), the one corresponding to what the speaker had said.

(27) Do you want to play on the slide?
(28) I want you to play on the slide.

Children chose significantly more often the question reformulation (27) when the context triggered a question interpretation (25) and the request reformulation (28) when the context triggered this interpretation (26). In a second experiment, Reeder compared 2;6 and 3;0 year-old children on their ability to discriminate requests from offers using the same stimuli. For the offer condition, the paraphrase was (29).

(29) I'll let you play on the slide.

Again, results confirm that children from both groups are able to choose the correct paraphrase in a given context. This study, therefore, indicates that children can pair different illocutionary forces with a single sentence from the age of 2;6. In addition, they do not have more difficulties doing so when the illocutionary force corresponds to an indirect speech act of request or offer than when it is a direct speech act of question.

Other comprehension studies have focused more specifically on children's comprehension of highly implicit speech acts according to Ervin-Tripp's classification, such as hints and question directives, with mixed findings. While some of them conclude that children do not understand these indirect speech acts before the age of five or six (Ackerman, 1978; Elrod, 1987; Leonard, Wilcox, Fulmer & Davis, 1978), in others, children appear to possess an early ability to handle them by the age of 2;6 to 3;0 (Schulze, Grassmann & Tomasello, 2013; Shatz & McCloskey, 1984; Spekman & Roth, 1985). This discrepancy can be partly explained by differences of methodology between the studies. Studies reporting a late acquisition of these indirect speech acts rely on complex meta-pragmatic skills such as appropriateness judgments (Leonard et al., 1978) or the choice of a sentence to continue a story (Ackerman, 1978). Similar tasks were also used in more recent experiments investigating children's ability to draw relevance inferences to understand indirect replies to questions, and such procedures consistently lead to the conclusion that children do not draw such inferences until the age of six (Bucciarelli, Colle & Bara, 2003; de Villiers, de Villiers, Coles-White & Carpenter, 2009; Verbuk & Schulz, 2010). In contrast, Shatz and McCloskey (1984) asked children to reply with a yes/no answer followed by an appropriate action and Schulze et al. (2013) asked children to perform an act-out task. We argued in Chapter 2 that tasks requiring meta-linguistic judgments delay the age of success compared with more implicit methods. Studies that made use of an implicit method to test comprehension confirm that children understand indirect speech acts from a very early age.

3.2.2. A cognitive explanation for the developmental pattern of speech acts

The literature review presented above lead us to conclude that children have an early ability to produce and understand both direct and indirect speech acts and that this distinction does not have an influence on the developmental pattern of speech acts. The question is, therefore, what other factors explain the developmental sequence reported by Ervin-Tripp (1977). We argue that one factor is children's acquisition of the syntactic structures encoding the formulations required to convey speech acts. Read and Cherry (1978) noted, for example, a developmental trend from more gesture-based requests to more verbal requests. Such development is also evident from the sequence reported by Ervin-Tripp (1977). The early requests produced around the age of two rely on telegraphic speech, but this linguistic limitation does not prevent children from performing various indirect speech acts. Between the age of three and four, when vocabulary and syntax rapidly develop (see Chapter 2, Section 2.1.2), children possess a larger repertoire of linguistic means to convey various forms of direct and indirect requests.

Further confirmation for the role of syntactic complexity comes from Carrell (1981) who studied the ability of four- to seven-year-old children to understand a wide variety of indirect requests, and reports that requests formulated as questions are more difficult to understand than statements and that negative requests are more difficult than positive requests. Ledbetter and Dent (1988) also report that syntactic complexity influences three- and five-year-old children's ability to understand requests. Reeder and Wakefield (1987) investigated whether linguistic and contextual factors were equally important for children's comprehension of speech acts by examining the consequences of reducing the amount of linguistic information by either truncating the stimulus utterance or acoustically distorting it. They found that degraded linguistic information is more detrimental to four-year-olds than to three-year-olds and conclude that children move from a context-based interpretation to reliance on linguistic form as they become more linguistically proficient. Young children's reliance on context to understand non-literal language has also been demonstrated in other domains of pragmatic development, for example, in the case of metaphors (see Chapter 6, Section 6.2). Reeder, Wakefield, and Shapiro (1988) confirmed that degraded linguistic input is particularly detrimental for children with high literacy levels.

In addition to the development of a linguistic code to convey speech acts, children must also possess the ability to derive the required inferences in order to enrich the encoded surface meaning and understand the speaker's meaning. We argue that children have the cognitive ability to derive inferences already when they start acquiring language, as demonstrated, for example, by their correct interpretation of speakers' intentions in communicative acts (see Chapters 2 and 5). However, inferences vary considerably in complexity, depending on the type of world knowledge that must be used as premises and to the number of inferential steps required to reach the speaker's meaning. Simply put, some inferences are harder for children to derive than others, and this factor might well explain why young children appear to understand some forms of indirect speech acts better than others. It is noticeable that studies concluding that children have a late ability to draw inferences in order to understand hints used situations involving rather complex inferences. For example, Spekman and Roth (1985) tested children's ability to understand (30) as a hint to bring something to dry the table.

(30) Some water spilled on the table.

In order to understand (30) as a request, the hearer must first ask himself why the speaker makes a statement about water being spilled on the table. Using his world knowledge about tables and what they are used for as well as the consequences of having water on objects, the hearer will conclude that the speaker wants him to dry the table. In contrast, Schulze *et al.* (2013) asked children to select an object when a speaker indirectly expressed which one he wanted by a different type of hint, as in (31).

(31) I find elephants good.

The difference of complexity between the inferences involved in (30) and (31) is clear. Schulze et al.'s example relies on children's understanding that a person who finds an object good probably wants this object. Many different studies in cognitive psychology have demonstrated that by the age of three, children are able to reason about other people's desires (see Chapter 5, Section 5.1). Spekman and Roth's example relies on more complex premises: what tables are used for as well as the consequences of having water on objects. It is not surprising therefore that drawing this inference was beyond the reach of five-year-olds.

To summarize, we argued in this section that the distinction between direct and indirect speech acts is not corroborated by acquisition data, as children are able to use and understand both direct and indirect speech acts from a very early age. We argued instead that children's gradual mastery of various indirect means to convey requests is dependent on the complexity of the syntactic structure used to convey them and on the complexity of the inferential process involved. The acquisition of indirect speech acts can, therefore, be accounted for by an inferential model of communication à la Grice, without the need to add a theory of speech acts.

3.3. The role of conventionalization

According to Bach and Harnish (1979), the standardization of some linguistic forms frequently used to convey indirect speech acts occurs because of usage. When a form is frequently used to convey an indirect speech act, the inference does not need to be calculated because it is compressed by precedent. In this section, we first discuss the role of frequency for children's acquisition of indirect speech acts (Section 3.3.1). In Searle's theory of speech acts (1969, 1975), the transition between direct and indirect acts is explained by a set of felicity conditions that speakers can question or state in order to conventionally trigger the derivation of an indirect speech act. We discuss the acquisition of the felicity conditions associated with the speech act of promising in Section 3.3.2 and conclude that differences in the acquisition of various felicity conditions is not straightforwardly explained by speech act theory. Finally, we argue in Section 3.3.3 that the difference evidenced throughout the chapter between the age of acquisition of requests and promises reflects a more general distinction between universal cognitive features and culture-specific aspects of verbal communication.

3.3.1. The role of frequency

The standardization of some forms to convey indirect speech acts in adult speech is said to enhance the efficiency of verbal communication, as it enables hearers to understand non-literal meanings without having to calculate the implicature upon each use. Papafragou (2000) pointed out, however, that the notion of standardization defined in terms of frequency raises a problem for acquisition, as children must first determine what the most frequent pairings between context and indirect speech acts are before standardization can take place, and this requires the ability to draw inferences. It could be argued, however, that children do not compute these inferences, but simply learn the most frequent forms as appropriate responses. If such were the case, then children should display only a limited ability to understand and produce indirect speech acts, by using and understanding only the most frequent forms, and without modulating them in context the way adult speakers do (Gibbs, 1986). Examples of children's early productions of speech acts indicate, however, that from the beginning of production, they are not limited to the most frequent and conventionalized forms to convey indirect speech acts (see Section 3.2.1).

A weaker hypothesis concerning the influence of frequency is that children's repertoire of forms to convey indirect speech acts is not limited to the most frequent ones, but that frequency in the input is nevertheless reflected in children's speech, with the most frequent forms acquired first and used more often by children than less frequent forms. In order to test this hypothesis, a study comparing the frequency of forms used to convey indirect speech acts in the input and the order in which they emerge in children's speech must be performed. To the best of our knowledge, such a study has not been conducted and firm conclusions can therefore not be reached on this point. It is likely, however, that frequency in the input plays a role in the acquisition of the forms used to convey indirect speech act, because such an influence, alongside children's conceptual and syntactic development, has been demonstrated for other pragmatic phenomena such as the order of acquisition between several discourse connectives (see Chapter 8, Section 8.2). It is also likely that that role of frequency for the acquisition of indirect forms to convey speech acts is complemented by children's inferential and linguistic development, as discussed in Section 3.2.2. Again, only a study pitching the role of each factor against the others can provide a definite answer on this point.

3.3.2. Children's understanding of felicity conditions

In Searle's theory of speech acts, the transition between direct and indirect acts rests on a set of felicity conditions. In order to assess the role of these conditions for the acquisition of speech acts, the four types of conditions listed by Searle must be systematically compared using coherent data and methodology. Such a comparison has, however, not been made in the literature, as empirical studies testing the role of felicity conditions, all focusing on the speech act of promising, only include a subset of them, thus providing a partial view of their order of acquisition.

In one such a study, Astington (1998a) assessed children's understanding of the propositional content and the essential conditions for promises. Recall that in Searle's formulations, these conditions are as follows: the utterance predicates a future act from the speaker (propositional content condition) and the utterance counts as an undertaking from the speaker of the obligation to perform that act (essential condition). In her experiment, 116 children aged 4 to 13 were presented with short stories, in which a character always said 'I promise' but sometimes violated one of Searle's conditions by either promising something outside of his control and thus producing a prediction rather than a promise (essential condition) or by promising something about an event occurring in the past, and therefore producing an assertion rather than a promise (propositional content condition). After each story, comprehension was assessed by asking children whether the character had made a promise or not. They were also asked to justify their answer ('Why do you say that?'). Results indicate that between the age of four and nine, children are insensitive to both felicity conditions, as they consider that promises can be made about all events occurring either in the past or in the future as long as they can be or have been accomplished. At this age, the outcome thus seems to determine whether a promise was made or not. By the age of nine, children become sensitive to the essential condition, as they take into account the fact that the speaker has control or not over the future action. Children become sensitive to the propositional content condition stating that the action is placed in the future between the age of 11 and 13. Thus both the essential and the propositional content condition appear to be acquired late, and this finding was confirmed in subsequent experiments (Maas & Abbedutto, 1998, 2001). Maas and Abbedutto (2001) reported in addition that nine year-olds still deny that a promise was made if the unfulfilled outcome of a promise cannot be explained by an obstacle and the speaker appears to have deliberately broken his promise. This result indirectly sheds some light on children's understanding of the sincerity condition. In Searle's description, the act of promising is still performed if the speaker is insincere and intentionally breaks his promise, but there is what Austin (1962) calls an abuse. Children seem to judge if the sincerity condition is not met, the promise is not valid and therefore did not take place at all.

An important aspect of Astington's (1988a) study is that a control group of adults were also included in the experiments, with the result that a quarter of them judged that a promise was still made when the felicity conditions were violated, in other words when an event was not under the speaker's control or when the event occurred in the past. Gibbs and Delaney (1987) also tested adults' intuitions about the felicity conditions of promises and found that while the essential and the preparatory conditions are clearly recognized as forming part of promises, adults accept that a speaker could promise to do something that they would have done anyway. Taken together, these results suggest that Searle's felicity conditions are too rigid to match even adults' concept of promising. It is not surprising, therefore, that children fail to recognize them until late in development.

Children's understanding of the preparatory condition, stating that the hearer must want the promised action to take place, has also been specifically assessed. Bernicot and Laval (2004) tested three-, six- and ten-year-olds in an experiment in which the sincerity condition was always met as indicated by the fact that the speaker always fulfilled his promise but in some cases, the hearer wanted the action to take place while in others the hearer made it clear that he didn't. At the end of the story, children were asked to choose between two pictures if the character representing the addressee of the promise would be happy or not about what had happened. Results show that satisfaction of the preparatory condition leads to a higher number of correct answers in all age groups. In addition, when the preparatory condition is met, children's answers are not influenced by the fact that an explicit performative is used or not.

As mentioned at the beginning of the section, the observed difference between the early acquisition of the preparatory condition and the late acquisition of the essential and propositional content conditions needs to be confirmed in an experiment consistently comparing the role of conditions using a unified population and methodology. Indeed, part of the observed difference can be attributed to methodological differences between the conscious metalinguistic task used by Astington and the more implicit pointing task used by Bernicot and Laval. In any case, if the age difference between felicity conditions emerging from the literature were confirmed in future experiments, this discrepancy could be explained by findings on children's growing theory of mind abilities (see Chapter 5). From the age of three, children are able to reason about desires, and this enables them to master the preparatory condition, whereas the essential condition requires children to understand complex aspects of the interpersonal relations involved in promises, which are acquired late in development. Mant and Perner (1988) reported, for example, that below the age of nine, children fail to understand that a speaker who informs someone of his intention to perform an action in the future is not committed to perform it unless the hearer relies on him. Maas (2008) also reported that the ability to reason about promises from the listener's perspective is related to performance at second-order theory of mind abilities tasks. In a nutshell, these results tend to indicate that a framework explaining the acquisition of promises through the lens of children's growing social cognition skills is better equipped to account for developmental data than a theory of speech acts listing conventional rules that are not recognized even by a sizable portion of adults.

3.3.3. The sequence of acquisition between speech acts

An important question for the acquisition of the felicity conditions associated with speech acts is whether the order of emergence between them is constant across speech acts. This question cannot be answered based on the literature, as the studies reported in the last section focused solely on the speech act of promising and no study has systematically compared the acquisition of felicity conditions across speech acts. There is, however, indirect evidence that differences exist between speech acts in the age at which children master their felicity conditions. In Section 3.2.1, we reported that three-year-olds' productions of requests used a variety of indirect means relying on several felicity conditions. In addition, we reported that when children produced direct speech acts, they often mentioned a felicity condition for requesting in an adjunct clause following the act of request. Even though the order of emergence between conditions cannot be inferred from this data, these findings indicate that children do master the felicity conditions of requesting from an early age, contrary to promises. It appears therefore that the content of each condition, which is variable across speech acts, determines the age of acquisition of a felicity condition.

There is additional evidence in the literature that requests and promises are acquired in sequence. First, contrary to requests, promises are not listed among children's early repertoire of speech acts (Dore, 1977). In addition, Astington (1988b) elicited the production of requests and promises by 96 children aged 4 to 11 in a constrained elicitation task. The experiment involved a role play in which children were asked to take the role of a child interacting with his mother or with a peer. Results indicate that children had more difficulties providing appropriate answers in the promise condition than in the request condition, as a number of them failed to produce any statement in this condition, while answering appropriately in the request condition.

The difference in the age of acquisition between requests and promises is not straightforwardly accounted for by Searle's classification of speech acts. It is, however, fully compatible with the relevance-theoretic account of speech acts, stating that there are only three basic and universal types of speech acts: saying, asking, and telling (to). These acts are encoded in the grammar by distinct form: declaratives, interrogatives, and imperatives. In this account (Sperber & Wilson, 1995: 245), all other speech acts such as promises "are institutional acts, that can be performed only in a society with the requisite institutions, and which must be recognized as such in order to be successfully performed." The complexity of such acts therefore comes from the fact that children must learn to set off social rules associated with their productions, and these can be variable across cultures. In the case of promises, important cross-cultural variations have been evidenced between the Western and the African's conceptions (Egner, 2006). We will discuss the role of social and cultural factors for children's development of pragmatic competencies in Chapter 4.

3.4. Synthesis

Speech act theory anchors pragmatics into the study of a set of conventionally determined rules and conditions governing the use of speech acts. These rules have cognitive implications for the way speech acts are acquired. In this chapter, we have argued that there is little evidence in the literature confirming their validity. First, the distinction between direct and indirect speech acts is not corroborated by acquisition data, as children produce and understand both direct and indirect speech acts from an early age. In addition, children's early comprehension and production of indirect speech acts is not limited to a set of conventionalized forms. We argued instead that the developmental pattern of indirect forms used to convey speech acts is related to their linguistic and inferential complexity. We also argued that children's late acquisition of the speech act of promising is not accounted for by speech act theory, but is compatible with a relevance-theoretic account separating basic and universal speech acts such as requests from socio-cultural acts like promising.

References

Ackerman, B. (1978). Children's understanding of speech acts in an unconventional directive frame. *Child Development, 49*(2), 311–318.

Astington, J. (1988a). Children's understanding of the speech act of promising. *Journal of Child Language, 15*, 157–173.

Astington, J. (1988b). Children's production of commissive speech acts. *Journal of Child Language, 15*, 411–423.

Austin, J. (1962). *How to Do Things with Words*. Oxford: Clarendon Press.

Bach, K. (1995). Standardization vs. conventionalization. *Linguistics and Philosophy, 18*(6), 677–686.

Bach, K. (1998). Standardization revisited. In A. Kasher (ed), *Pragmatics: Critical Concepts* (pp. 712–722). London: Routledge.

Bach, K. & Harnish, R. (1979). *Linguistic Communication and Speech Acts*. Cambridge: Cambridge University Press.

Bates, E. (1976). *Language and Context: The Acquisition of Pragmatics*. New York: Academic Press.

Bernicot, J. & Laval, V. (2004). Speech acts in children: the example of promises. In I. Noveck, & D. Sperber (eds), *Experimental Pragmatics* (pp. 207–227). London: Palgrave Macmillan.

Bucciarelli, M., Colle, L., & Bara, B. G. (2003). How children comprehend speech acts and communicative gestures. *Journal of Pragmatics, 35*, 207–241.

Carter, A. (1974). *Communication in the Sensorimotor Period*. Unpublished dissertation. Berkeley, CA: University of California.

Carrell, P. (1981). Children's understanding of indirect requests: comparing child and adult comprehension. *Journal of Child Language, 8*, 320–345.

de Villiers, P., de Villiers, J., Coles-White, D., & Carpenter, L. (2009). Acquisition of relevance implicatures in typically-developing children and children with autism. In J. Chandlee, M. Franchini, S. Lord, & G. M. Rheiner (eds), *Proceedings of the 33th Annual Boston University Conference on Language Development* (pp. 121–132). Somerville, MA: Cascadilla Press.

Dore, J. (1973). *The Development of Speech Acts*. Unpublished dissertation. New York: City University of New York.

Dore, J. (1977). Children's illocutionary acts. In R. Freedle (ed), *Discourse Comprehension and Production* (227–244). Hillsdale, NJ: Erlbaum.

Egner, I. (2006). Intercultural aspects of the speech act of promising: Western and African practices. *Intercultural Pragmatics, 3*(4), 443–464.

Elrod, M. (1987). Children's understanding of indirect requests. *Journal of Genetic Psychology, 148*, 63–70.

Ervin-Tripp, S. (1977). Wait for me, roller skate! In S. Ervin-Tripp, & C. Mitchell-Kernan (eds), *Child Discourse* (pp. 165–188). New York: Academic Press.

Ervin-Tripp, S. (1982). Ask and it shall be given you: children's requests. In H. Byrnes (ed), *Georgetown Roundtable on Languages and Linguistics*. Washington, DC: Georgetown University.

Garvey, C. (1975). Requests and responses in children's speech. *Journal of Child Language, 2*, 41–63.

Gazdar, G. (1981). *Pragmatics*. New York: Academic Press.

Gibbs, R. (1981). Your wish is my command: convention and context in interpreting indirect requests. *Journal of Verbal Learning and Verbal Behaviour, 20*, 431–444.

Gibbs, R. (1983). Do people always process the literal meanings of indirect requests? *Journal of Experimental Psychology: Learning, Memory, and Cognition, 9*, 524–533.

Gibbs, R. (1984). Literal meaning and psychological theory. *Cognitive Science, 8*, 275–304.

Gibbs, R. (1986). What makes some indirect speech acts conventional? *Journal of Memory and Language, 25*, 181–196.

Gibbs, R. & Delaney, S. (1987). Pragmatic factors in making and understanding promises. *Discourse Processes, 10*, 107–126.

Grice, H.P. (1967/1989). *Studies in the Way of Words*. Cambridge: Harvard University Press.

Halliday, M. (1975). *Learning How to Mean*. London: Arnold.

Ledbetter, P. & Dent, C. (1988). Young children's sensitivity to direct and indirect request structure. *First Language, 8*, 227–245.

Leonard, L., Wilcox, M., Fulmer, K., & Davis, G. (1978). Understanding indirect requests: An investigation of children's comprehension of pragmatic meanings. *Journal of Speech and Language Research, 21*(3), 528–537.

Levinson, S.C. (1983). *Pragmatics*. Cambridge: Cambridge University Press.

Maas, F. (2008). Children's understanding of promising, lying, and false belief. *The Journal of General Psychology, 135*(3), 301–321.

Maas, F. & Abbeduto, L. (1998). Young children's understanding of promising: Methodological considerations. *Journal of Child Language, 25*, 203–214.

Maas, F. & Abbeduto, L. (2001). Children's judgment about intentionally and unintentionally broken promises. *Journal of Child Language, 28*, 517–529.

Mant, C. & Perner, J. (1988). The child's understanding of commitment. *Developmental Psychology, 24*(3), 343–351.

Morgan, J. (1978). Two types of convention in indirect speech acts. In P. Cole (ed), *Syntax and Semantics 9: Pragmatics* (pp. 261–280). London: Academic Press.

Newcombe, N. & Zaslow, M. (1981). Do 2½ year-olds hint? A study of directive forms in the speech of 2½ year-olds to adults. *Discourse Processes, 4*(3), 239–252.

Papafragou, A. (2000). Early communication: Beyond speech-act theory. *Proceedings of the 24th Annual Boston University Conference on Child Development*. Somerville, MA: Cascadilla Press.

Read, B. & Cherry, L. (1978). Preschool children's production of directive forms. *Discourse Processes, 1*, 233–245.

Reeder, K. (1981). How young children learn to do things with words. In P. Dale, & D. Ingram (eds), *Child Language: An International Perspective* (pp. 135–150). Baltimore: University Park Press.

Reeder, K. & Wakefield, J. (1987). The development of young children's speech act comprehension: How much language is necessary? *Applied Psycholinguistics, 8*, 1–18.

Reeder, K., Wakefield, J., & Shapiro, J. (1988). Children's speech act comprehension strategies and early literacy experiences. *First Language, 8*, 29–48.

Searle, J. (1969). *Speech Acts: An Essay in the Philosophy of Language*. Cambridge: Cambridge University Press.

Searle, J. (1975). Indirect speech acts. In P. Cole, & J. L. Morgan (eds), *Syntax and Semantics 3: Speech Acts* (pp. 59–82). New York: Academic Press.

Schulze, C., Grassmann, S., & Tomasello, M. (2013). Three-year-old children make relevance inferences in indirect verbal communication. *Child Development, 84*(6), 2079–2093.

Shapiro, A. & Murphy, G. (1993). Can you answer a question for me? Processing indirect speech acts. *Journal of Memory and Language, 32*, 211–229.

Shatz, M. & McCloskey, L. (1984). Answering appropriately: a developmental perspective on conversational knowledge. In S. Kuczaj (ed), *Discourse Development* (pp. 19–36). New York: Springer.

Spekman N. & Roth, F. (1985). Preschool children's comprehension and production of directive forms. *Journal of Psycholinguistic Research, 14*(3), 331–349.

Sperber, D. & Wilson, D. (1986/1995). *Relevance. Communication and Cognition*. Oxford: Blackwell.

Verbuk, A. & Shultz, T. (2010). Acquisition of relevance implicatures: A case against a rationality-based account of conversational implicatures. *Journal of Pragmatics, 42*, 2297–2313.

4

SOCIAL AND CULTURAL ASPECTS OF PRAGMATIC DEVELOPMENT

In this chapter, we address the development of pragmatic competencies from a social and cross-cultural perspective. First, we review studies demonstrating that preschool children are able to modulate their communicative behavior depending on the social status of their addressee and discuss the role of the socialization received from parents and peers in the process of acquiring social pragmatic skills (Section 4.1). We then present some examples of cultural variations in pragmatic norms and discuss the implications of these cross-cultural differences for children's acquisition of social and cognitive pragmatic competencies (Section 4.2). We conclude that social and cultural variations affecting the acquisition of pragmatic competencies are limited by universal features of social cognition.

4.1. Pragmatic skills and interpersonal relations

In order to use language appropriately in context, children must learn to take into account the social role of their addressee. In adult speech, relations of power determine many linguistic choices made during communication, for example, in the production of face-threatening speech acts such as requests. Ervin-Tripp (1976) noted that the production of requests made by adults is directly related to the relations of power between interlocutors. For example, doctors are more likely to use direct speech acts to speak to nurses while nurses use more indirect forms to address doctors. In this section, we focus on the way children modulate their use of face-threating speech acts such as directives and requests, as well as their choice of politeness and discourse markers, depending on social relationships (Section 4.1.1). We then discuss the role of interactions with caregivers and peers for children's acquisition of social pragmatic skills (Section 4.1.2).

4.1.1. Using language to mark interpersonal relations

Children are able to use language to mark relations of power and negotiate with their addressee already during their preschool years. In a situation of role-play, children aged four to seven have been shown to associate the use of direct forms of requests with a higher status role, for example, doctor or teacher, and the use of more polite forms with lower statuses such as nurses or students (Andersen, 1990). During spontaneous interactions within their family, children already use different forms to convey requests to parents versus experimenters from the age of two-and-a-half years, thus adapting the level of politeness depending on their addressee. At this age, children use polite forms to convey requests in about 60% of the occurrences when they address experimenters, but only in 10% of the occurrences when speaking to their parents (Ervin-Tripp, O'Connor & Rosenberg, 1984). Another visible difference at this age concerns the politeness of requests addressed to mothers and fathers. While mothers elicit more direct imperatives, fathers elicit more polite requests and more uses of mitigating explanations. Between the age of two and three, 90% of the requests children make to their mothers do not include any use of polite markers (Ervin-Tripp & Gordon, 1986). Ervin-Tripp, Guo, and Lambert (1990) confirmed that children occasionally use the word 'please' to address an experimenter, a father, and older siblings, indicating their perceived higher social roles. Ryckebusch and Marcos (2004) also reported that French-speaking children aged 1;5 and 2;3 produce requests differently when they are speaking to their mother or father. With their mother, they use more assertive forms while they produce more action requests to their fathers.

Up to the age of three, children mark social relations mainly by their tone of voice. More specifically, they use more aggravated voices with their mothers and even more markedly with younger children, compared with their fathers and with experimenters. By the age of four, children make more subtle differences between family members and outsiders by using more modals and permission forms with experimenters compared with parents. At this age, children also learn to use their voice to act as a mitigator, and use a soft voice to produce directives to their fathers much more often compared with their mothers, indicating again a difference in their perceived social status. Ervin-Tripp, Guo, and Lambert (1990) noted that in traditional American families, mothers are considered as natural caregivers and children therefore do not feel the need to add politeness makers when requesting things from them but this assumption may vary depending on the role associated with mothers in other cultures (see Section 4.2). The choice of forms of address is also influenced by children's perception of the cost of their request for the addressee, in other words how intrusive it is. For example, between the age of two and three, children who request a toy belonging to a younger sibling use polite forms much more often than in other cases (Ervin-Tripp & Gordon, 1986).

In addition to family interactions, where roles and power are clearly established, children have also been demonstrated to maintain a hierarchy of high and low status members when they are interacting in groups of peers. For example, Goodwin (1993) reported that within groups of girls, older and more powerful members allocate themselves more powerful roles in pretend play and use imperatives to signal a change of frame of play. These hierarchies fluctuate, however, depending on aspects of the social situation, such as a child's expertise on a particular topic (Goodwin, 2001; Kyratzis, Marx & Wade, 2001). In addition, even when preschool children interact in peer group conversations encouraging the use of egalitarian language, they can modulate this register depending on context. Kyratzis and Tarım (2010) reported that Turkish preschool girls use egalitarian forms of directives such as tag questions and joint imperatives when they talk among themselves, but shift to more direct imperatives when they enact the role of mothers or talk to boys. These results thus indicate that already at the ages of three and four, children modulate their use of language to index power shifts and use more direct speech acts with lower group members, more deferential indirect acts with higher status members and egalitarian forms within social groups valorizing solidarity more than power distinctions. In addition, children also adapt their non-verbal behavior such as body orientation to reflect relations of power (Griswold, 2007).

Differences of gender represent a dimension of social variation often studied in relation to the use of language, and a question for children's social development is whether girls and boys have different styles to express social hierarchies. Kyratzis, et al. (2001) noted that the observed differences of social status within peer groups and the way these differences are expressed in language are not intrinsically correlated with gender, as girls use as many direct assertive acts as boys in their observation of an American mixed preschool classroom. Ladegaard (2004) also reported that Danish girls and boys equally use assertive and unmitigated forms during play. Differences in the forms used have, however, been found depending on the gender of the addressee. Goodwin (1990) reported that girls shift their choice of speech acts to more direct imperative forms when they speak to boys compared with when they speak to other girls. In addition, Kyratzis and Guo (2001) observed that in a mixed-sex friendship group of nursery school children, the power relations varied depending on the context of play. Boys were using more assertive forms in the context of a doctor play while girls used more such forms during borderwork play, in other words when a group of girls plays with a group of boys (Thorne, 1993). Cook-Gumperz and Syzmanski (2001) also reported that Latina girls dominate boys in family scenarios, reflecting their perception of social organizations within the family.

A number of studies have evaluated children's metapragmatic ability to judge the appropriateness of requests. Bates (1976) assessed whether children aged four to five could assess the 'niceness' of pairs of requests differing in syntactic directness, the use of semantic softeners such as 'please', and the tone of voice. She reported that children aged four to five are already sensitive to all three factors in their evaluation of the niceness of requests. Other studies have assessed the influence of power relations for children's judgments of the tone of a request. Becker (1986) replicated Bates' (1976) experiment with similar requests performed by peers, and asked children to assess their level of bossiness. Direct requests without semantic softeners pronounced in an aggravated tone of voice were judged to be bossy even by four- and five-year-olds. This result is consistent with children's awareness of social status: peers are not intrinsically superior socially (even though relations of power are established in some contexts) and such direct requests are not acceptable from them. Children thus show an awareness of the role of power in their judgment of requests from the age of four, but their sensitivity to social cues continues to develop over many years. For example, Baroni and Axia (1989) reported that five- and seven-year-olds' ability to judge polite and impolite requests depending on the degree of familiarity between the addresses still progresses between the two age groups.

In addition to the production of face-threatening speech acts, the presentation of arguments in conversations, especially during conflicts, is also correlated with relations of power between speakers. Children have been found to modulate their argumentative behavior depending on their addressee in situations of conflict. Dunn (1997) reported that when children aged 33 to 47 months address friends in natural interactions they are more likely to use conciliatory arguments than when they address their siblings or their mothers. Dunn noted that this difference reflects power relations, as children are in a more equal position with their friends than with their siblings and mothers. It may also reflect children's understanding that relationships with friends can discontinue when conflicts arise, contrary to family relations that consequently do not require similar efforts and conciliation.

Another way to look at children's marking of differences of social status in language is through their use of discourse markers, as one of the functions of these lexical items is the marking of social relationships between interlocutors (Schiffrin, 1987). For example, some markers like 'well' and 'now' are used in sentence-initial position to add authority in communicative contexts where there is an unequal power status between the participants, such as conversations between a teacher and a student (Coulthard, 1977). Andersen, Brizuela, DuPuy, and Gonnerman (1999) studied the production of such discourse markers by children aged four to seven during role play involving an unequal situation in terms of power, such as dialogs between doctors and patients or parents and children. Results indicate that children use the discourse marker 'well' much more frequently when they play the role of a parent than a child and when they address a child than when they address another parent. They are also able to modulate this use depending on the communicative context. In a medical context, where doctors and nurses have a higher status than both children and their parents, children playing doctors and nurses use discourse markers more than children playing parents. Similar differences were found in classroom settings. Children playing teachers used discourse markers indicating power much more than children playing students. In this situation, they even combined the use of several markers such as "OK, well, now." When a power relation was introduced between students, for example, between a native-speaker and a foreigner, children playing native-speakers used discourse markers in the speech addressed to their non-native speaker peers, reflecting again the perception of power associated with their role. This pattern became more apparent as children grew older, and Andersen et al. conclude that at least by the age of six, children have a sophisticated understanding of how to use discourse markers to mark status asymmetry with their hearer. Kyratzis (2007) also reported that in role-play involving a friendship group of three girls in nursery school aged four and five years, power relations were sometimes marked by the use of discourse markers like 'well' and 'now' in some of the contexts set for the role play.

In conclusion, already between the ages of two and three, children are able to modulate their speech depending on their addressee, and from their preschool years, children show great sensitivity to interpersonal relations in their use of language. They are able to shift register depending on the social status of their addressee and can also adapt and shift their register with the same addressee depending on the context of talk, and the relative social rank of their addressee in this particular context. From a methodological perspective, this difference implies that experimental research on pragmatic development that involves interactions with children must take into account the fact that children do not produce the same speech acts with all their addressees and also do not react in the same way to an identical communicative act depending on the social role of its producer. This should be acknowledged when designing experiments and discussing the generalization of results. As Dunn (1997: 202) pointed out: "rather than regarding social understanding as 'within child' characteristic or trait we should acknowledge that how children use their social understanding depends on the nature of the particular relationship."

4.1.2. Pragmatic socialization

An important question for studies emphasizing the role of social relations for children's pragmatic development is whether children are taught to use pragmatic skills through their interpersonal relationships, in other words, what is the impact of the input that children receive for the development of their pragmatic skills. The ethnographic approach to language acquisition includes a well-established research trend on language socialization (e.g. Duranti, Ochs & Schieffelin, 2011), a term including "both socialization through language and to use language" (Ochs & Schieffelin, 1986: 2). In this definition, the difference between the acquisition of language in general and the development of pragmatic competencies appears to be only a distinction of scope and perspective, as language socialization is seen as an attempt to get children to use language appropriately and meaningfully (Li, 2008). Blum-Kulka (1997: 3) defined the more specific term of 'pragmatic socialization' as "the ways in which children are socialized to use language in context in socially and culturally appropriate ways." This definition includes cultural factors in addition to social factors, and research in the domain of pragmatic socialization has focused on cultural specificities of parental input, and their attempt to encourage their children's use of culturally important communicative acts. Some well-known examples include the acquisition of the speech act of clarification by Samoan children (Ochs, 1988) and the acquisition of teasing and shaming by Kaluli children in Papua New Guinea (Schieffelin, 1985). We will come back to the impact of pragmatic socialization for the development of culture-specific aspects of pragmatic competencies in Section 4.2.1.

A number of studies have analyzed parents' techniques for teaching pragmatic skills to their children as well as their effectiveness, focusing mostly on aspects of language use related to politeness and appropriateness in conversation, an area that is perceived as particularly important by parents as a reflection of good parenting (Becker & Hall, 1989). Several researchers have noted that other areas of language acquisition do not trigger similar teaching by parents (e.g. Becker, 1990; Goodwin, 1985). Blum-Kulka (1990) categorized parent's indirect comments to improve their children's pragmatic skills during dinner time conversations into four categories: (1) discourse management, including comments about turn taking and smooth flow; (2) maxim violation, for example, comments about relevance and quantity; (3) behavior, encompassing reprimands and sanctions due to bad behavior such as fighting and not eating; (4) metapragmatic comments consisting of talk about language. Becker (1990) also noted that American parents use a variety of techniques to teach politeness to their children. For example, they model the expected behavior by enacting it in adult interactions, as in (1) from Becker (1990: 12):

(1) Father: Go get my milk.
Mother: What do you say?
Father: Please.
Mother: All right.

Parents also tend to reinforce their children's appropriate uses of language by positive comments and by prompting the appropriate behavior. For example, parents take the hand of their young child and make them say hello to someone. With preschoolers, parents also produce a series of indirect comments to remind their children of politeness rules, such as (2) and (3).

(2) Daddy is speaking to you.
(3) What is the magic word?

Snow, Perlmann, Gleason, and Hooshyar (1990) noted that children receive a lot of indirect feedback about politeness rules. It may seem surprising that parents do not choose to issue direct commands to change their children's behavior. The reasons of this indirectness noted in the literature is that parents may want to model the proper way to request by using a polite formulation and to save their own face by not mentioning explicitly the rule violation, as parents consider that impolite behavior from children reflects poor parenting skills (Becker & Hall, 1989). It has also been suggested that parents may want to punish children for their behavior by using deliberate vagueness and sarcasm (Becker, 1988). Another question arising from this research is to what extent parents' comments succeed in changing their children's behavior. Becker (1988) assessed the effectiveness of parent's indirect comments and found that they are followed by an appropriate reaction from the children in 59% of the cases. However, this study does not elucidate the more general question of whether such pragmatic socialization affects children's use of language in the long run or only triggers routinized sequences.

Early studies of pragmatic socialization focused on the context of family interactions, and more specifically on relations between parents and their children. However, the study of different communicative contexts has revealed differences, both in the type of pragmatic socialization that children receive and also in their reaction to them. For example, Yifat and Zadunaisky-Ehrlich (2008) studied the violations of maxims and discourse management between school teachers and children in preschool and kindergarten and found that teachers pay more attention to violations of the quantity than the quality maxims, contrary to home conversations (Blum-Kulka, 1997; de Geer, Tulvisite, Mizera & Tryggvason, 2002). Recent studies have also demonstrated that children become socialized in great part through multiparty dialogs rather than dyadic contexts, and that this context provides them with the opportunity to learn from a richer and more complex environment (Blum-Kulka & Snow, 2002).

Another shift in anthropological studies has been the move from family interactions to the study of peer groups, a context in which children become agents of their own socialization (Cook-Gumperz & Kyratzis, 2001; Goodwin & Kyratzis, 2007, 2011). The influence of parents and peers is not constant through a child's development. In traditional European and American families, many young children spend a lot of time with their mothers and then move on to interacting with peers and siblings as they grow older. Dunn, Brown, Slomkowki, Tesla, and Youngblade (1991) studied 50 second-born children interacting at 33, 40, and 47 months with their mothers and older siblings and with a close friend at 47 months. They noted that between the ages of 33 to 47 months, the time children spend with their mothers drops. As a consequence their conversation time drops as well and is replaced by an increase of conversation time with siblings. This transition implies a new communicative context: while relations between children and mothers are usually marked with affection and care, relations with siblings are often more ambivalent and hostile (Buhrmester, 1992).

Dunn (1997) studied children's argumentative style during conflicts using the same corpus of recorded conversations as above. She observed that children's arguing style was influenced by the argumentative style of their mothers, as a significant correlation emerged in the use of conciliatory arguments between mothers and their children (in other words, arguments in which the speaker takes the other's needs and desires into account in an attempt to negotiate). Another important finding is that children did not reproduce the same argumentative behavior with all their communicative partners: "some children who took their siblings' viewpoints into consideration in their sibling conflicts simply repeated their protests and unreasoned accusations when in conflict with their mothers; others who negotiated and compromised within conflicts with their mothers simply yelled and protested without arguments within their disputes with their siblings" (Dunn, 1997: 198). Children's argumentative style does, therefore, not appear to be exclusively conditioned by the model provided by their mother, as their behavior and discourse style in situations of conflicts is not constant across addressees.

Dunn et al. (1991) measured whether the family style of handling conflicts was correlated with the development of children's ability to understand other people's emotions and minds, in other words, with their theory of mind abilities. They administered children at the age of 40 months tests measuring their understanding of others' emotions and minds. Results indicate over-time correlations between sibling–child interactions at the age of 33 months and children's understanding of others' minds and emotions at 40 months. Children who showed greater abilities to negotiate during conflicts at the age of 33 months reached a higher performance on the emotion understanding and theory of mind tasks seven months later (Slomkowski & Dunn, 1992). Importantly, however, no over-time correlations were found when children's discourse was measured during interactions with their mothers. This indicates that peer interactions do indeed seem to make a unique contribution for children's pragmatic socialization, and such interactions should therefore be an important object of investigation. In contrast, there are no correlations between mothers' own argumentative styles and their children's performance on emotion understanding and theory of mind tasks. Thus, children's argumentative style is not a reproduction of a style modeled by their mothers. It appears as well that children's discursive skills are not simply a social construct but are related to their cognitive abilities to understand others' minds and emotions. We will discuss the development of children's developing theory of mind abilities and its relations with the acquisition of pragmatics in Chapter 5.

4.2. Cross-cultural differences in the acquisition of pragmatics

We presented in the last section some examples of cultural variations in the use of social pragmatic skills and the socialization that children receive from parents and peers. In this section, we review studies assessing the extent of these variations and discuss their consequences for children's development of social (Section 4.2.1) and cognitive (Section 4.2.2) pragmatic skills.

4.2.1. Cultural differences in the management of interpersonal relations

Many aspects of interpersonal relationships are variable across cultures. For example, speakers' representations about what constitutes polite behavior as well as the linguistic encoding of politeness and routines vary widely across cultures. As a result, the system that children have to learn is quite different across languages and cultures. For example, Samoan children are taught to produce speech acts reserved to the lower-status members of the family, such as the reporting of news to the older members of the family (Ochs & Schieffelin, 1995), Japanese children are taught to bow and to use a complex system of honorifics (Burdelski, 2011; Nakamura, 2006), and American Koreans are taught to use honorific requests and greetings with their grandparents (Park, 2006). These culture-specific aspects of politeness and communication routines cannot be directly compared cross-linguistically. However, some aspects of communication seem to be more universal and therefore more comparable across cultures. In this section, we mainly focus on directive speech acts such as requests and also discuss the use of discourse markers and the linguistic strategies used to deal with conflicts.

Sperber and Wilson (1986) argued that directives are part of the three universal speech acts encoded in the grammar (see Chapter 3). It is, therefore, expected that in all languages and cultures, some forms of directives exist. Cultural differences exist, however, in what is perceived as a polite directive in adult communication. Ogiermann (2009) compared the requests produced by English, German, Polish, and Russian speakers and reported a continuum of directness going from West to East. While English and German speakers use direct imperatives in only 4% and 5% of the cases, respectively, Polish speakers used them in 20% of the cases and Russian speakers in 35% of the cases. In English and German, the majority of requests are conveyed by conventional indirect means such as questions bearing on the hearer's ability to perform the request. In contrast, in Russian, using an indirect means to convey a speech act of request has a negative connotation, as the hearer perceives it as an attempt to waste his time and assimilates it to a manipulative game. Wierzbicka (1991) also noted that in Polish, politeness is not achieved by the use of indirect question forms, and those would in most cases not be understood as requests at all. In this language as well, the use of direct imperatives is expected, and politeness is achieved by the addition of mitigators such as 'please'.

Cultural specificities have also been found to influence the mode of production of requests. For example, in Navajo culture, the production of directives follows some specific rules related to power relations, as the production of requests indicates intimate relationships between the speaker and the addressee (Field, 2001). In this culture, strangers and people in certain relations within the family such as adult siblings of the opposite sex, or men related through marriage, do not make direct requests to each other. Instead, they appeal to a third party such as mothers and sisters to convey the request. Parents and teachers use a similar routine to address a request to children, by including another child as intermediary. When using this routine, they simultaneously accomplish two communicative goals: they request something of one child and remind an (often older) child used as intermediary of his responsibility toward his sibling or peer.

Cross-cultural differences have been reported in the type of requests that parents address to their children. For instance, in order to convey a polite request to their children during a family meal, Israeli parents favor the use of direct acts accompanied by mitigators such as terms of endearments, modals, and politeness markers. In the same context, American parents prefer to convey politeness through indirectness. This difference has been interpreted as reflecting the more general cultural trend in American culture to favor the child's independence, while Israeli parents prefer to rely on emotional involvement (Blum-Kulka, 1990). Other differences are also found in the quantity of metapragmatic comments that parents address to their children, as American parents produce many more metapragmatic comments directed to their children than Israeli parents. Differences in the type of pragmatic socialization practices used by parents are also evidenced in studies comparing other cultures. For example, during dinner time conversations, Estonian and Finnish parents produce more metapragmatic comments to their children than Swedish parents (de Geer, Tulviste, Mizera & Tryggvason, 2002). The type of comments made also differ, with Swedish parents focusing more on ethical behavior and Estonian and Finnish parents emphasizing table manners. Swedish children were also found to negotiate and respond to their parents' comments more than the other children. More generally, the kind of socialization that children receive from their parents also differs depending on which aspects of interpersonal relations are emphasized in a given culture (see Gaskins, 2006 for a review).

In spite of these differences in socialization practices across cultures, some common features have also been reported in the literature. For example, in both American and Israeli cultures, parents use many more direct requests with their children compared with adult speech outside the family. In addition, parents' metapragmatic comments about the linguistic behavior of their children mostly target their adherence to Gricean maxims in both cultures (Blum-Kulka, 1990). Some universals have also been found in the way mothers address their young children in cross-cultural studies. For instance, in Argentina, France, Japan, and the United States, mothers all show great similarities in the type and frequency of the functional classes of speech used. More specifically, all mothers favor affect-oriented speech, containing expressions, onomatopoeias, and endearments with their five-month-old babies. In contrast, they use more information-oriented speech, such as questions, direct statements, and reports, with their 13-months-olds (Bornstein et al., 1992). Still, several cultural specificities were identified, such as the tendency of Japanese mothers to use more affect-oriented speech than in the other cultures, of Argentinian mothers to resort more to direct statements, French mothers to include more reports, and American mothers to question their babies more.

In the case of requests as well, universals exist. Studies on the acquisition of requests have been conducted in many different languages such as French, Swedish, and Greek, and all of them report that young children produce directives from an early age. In all cultures as well, children show some sensitivity to relations of power in school and in the family by adapting their directive speech acts depending on their addressee (Aronsson & Thorell, 1999; Georgalidou, 2008; Ryckebusch & Marcos, 2004). These results lead to the conclusion that requests are among the first speech acts acquired by children across cultures and that sensitivity to the social status of the addressee is a universal trait as well. Küntay, Nakamura, and Şen (2014) also conclude that "despite the fact that children may be learning very different directive forms depending on their language, crosslinguistic studies show that development of directives happens relatively early, and that children are sensitive to contextual factors such as activity type and age of interactant and vary the level of politeness accordingly."

Another area where cross-linguistic comparisons are possible is the use of discourse markers like the English 'well' and 'now' to mark relations of power, as we reported in Section 9.1.1. Andersen et al. (1999) compared the use of these markers across English-speaking, French-speaking, and Spanish-speaking children aged four to seven and reported striking cross-linguistic similarities in the way these markers are used by children. In all languages, markers like 'well' and 'now' are used, sometimes even in sequence, by speakers with higher social status. Conversely, disfluency markers such as 'uh' and 'hmm' are used by children enacting lower social status speakers in role-play. In addition, in all languages, children rarely used discourse markers at the age of four but systematically used them to mark power relations by the age of six or seven. The main cross-linguistic difference reported by Andersen et al. is that French-speaking children used more discourse markers than the other two populations, regardless of the social role they portrayed, and they also used more markers in sequence (up to four markers against only three for the English speakers). The authors note that this may reflect cross-linguistic differences in adult discourse, with discourse markers being more used in French compared with English or Spanish. This study indicates, therefore, that while cross-linguistic differences exist in the way children learn to use discourse markers to reflect adult-like usage in their exposure language, the age of acquisition for these markers and the way children use them to mark social relations is remarkably similar across languages.

Lastly, cross-cultural comparisons have been conducted to compare the way people handle arguments in conflicts. Peng and Nisbett (1999) argued that the Western world is influenced by the ancient Greek civilization, emphasizing the role of individual persons and leading people to act on the basis of their own personal decisions. In contrast, in Eastern civilizations like China and Japan, social obligations are emphasized and individuals are expected to act in such a way as to preserve the cohesion of society. Peng and Nisbett provided some empirical evidence that these differences affect the way people deal with contradiction in communication. In their experiments, they presented Chinese and American students with a situation of conflict between a mother and a daughter and were asked to provide solutions. While Chinese students favored solutions of compromise, American students preferred solutions favoring one side over the other. There is, however, evidence that these differences do not affect the way both cultures deal with contradictions in their everyday lives. Van der Henst, Mercier, Yama, Kawasaki, and Adachi (2006) reported from a set of experiments that both Chinese and French students tend to favor their own opinion over that of another when contradictions arise, reflecting a universal cognitive trait that evolved in order to prevent the acquisition of false beliefs during interactions. Some universal characteristics of conflict talk also exist in children's speech, as Chinese and American children equally use direct conflict strategies, such as criticizing and scolding (Kyratzis & Guo, 1996). Differences of gender were found, however, between the two cultures: while in America boys tended to use more direct strategies than girls, in China the reversed pattern was found.

In sum, despite cross-linguistic and cross-cultural differences in the use of requests and discourse markers for communication, children seem to learn how to use them at a comparable schedule and also consistently show some sensitivity to the social contexts associated with the use of specific forms. The handling of conflicting opinions shows some universal traits across cultures as well, such as a preference for one's opinion and the resort to direct strategies with opponents.

4.2.2. Variations in cognitive aspects of pragmatic competencies

So far, we have focused on aspects of pragmatic competencies related to social practices such as the use of politeness to convey face-threatening acts. Other studies have focused on the way some cross-linguistic and cross-cultural variations may potentially affect children's acquisition of cognitive aspects of their pragmatic competencies, such as joint attention, theory of mind abilities, and the production of referring expressions. Some of these variations are due to cultural differences in the way interactions between children and caregivers take place while others are related to differences in the way languages encode information. We review them in turn in this section.

We reported in the last section many cross-cultural differences in the way parents interact with their children and also in the type of pragmatic socialization that they provide them. The existence of such cross-cultural differences in communication opens the possibility that parents' different communicative styles across cultures may shape the way children develop basic cognitive competencies related to verbal communication. For example, pointing behaviors as well as their functions in communication have been found to be quite variable across cultures (Wilkins, 2003). Yet, in spite of these differences, children from different cultures display similar pointing behaviors in controlled experiments. Liszkowski, Brown, Callaghan, Takada, and De Vos (2012) studied the pointing behaviors of children aged 9 to 15 months from seven very different cultures including Japan, Papua New Guinea, and Peru, while they were interacting with their main caregivers. Interactions took place in a decorated room, containing pictures of animals and plants as well as objects. The authors found evidence of pointing with a similar frequency in children from all the cultures studied between the ages of 10 to 14 months. In addition, children all pointed in order to look together with their caregiver at an object in the room.

Brown (2011: 49) drew a similar conclusion from her cross-cultural review of studies on joint attention: "children are socialized through and into different interactional styles across different cultural settings, yet the evidence so far supports the view that there is a universal propensity for children to engage in episodes of joint attention over objects and events by around the age of 12 months." In their comparison of children from three cultures (Canada, Peru, and India), Callaghan et al. (2011) also concluded that pointing and shared attention were not culture-specific behaviors, as some children tended to point often while others did not in all three cultures. An important environmental factor explaining differences between children's pointing gestures is the socialization provided by their parents (Rowe & Goldin-Meadow, 2009). More specifically, parents from high socio-economic status use gestures to communicate a broader range of meanings compared with parents from a lower background. This parental behavior leads to making children also gesture to convey a broader range of meanings and subsequently developing a higher vocabulary. Thus it seems that social rather than cultural factors have a stronger influence than cultural ones on children's development of pointing behaviors.

Joint attention is an important precursor to children's developing theory of mind abilities (see Chapter 5) and cross-cultural studies also reveal that children succeed at false-belief tasks at a comparable age across cultures (Callaghan et al., 2005). Differences in the socio-economic status of the families have, however, been shown to affect theory of mind development (Shatz, Diesendruck, Martinez-Beck & Akar, 2003). Taken together, these results tend to indicate that basic cognitive skills related to pragmatic competencies are likely to be universal aspects of human communication, even though social factors influence their pace of acquisition and cultural factors affect later development leading children to develop culture-specific functional uses in adult speech.

In addition to cultural differences, children growing in different parts of the world have also been said to develop pragmatic skills at different paces depending on the way some distinctions are encoded or not in their exposure languages. For example, in the domain of theory of mind development, Vinden (1996) analyzed theory of mind development in Peruvian children speaking Junín Quechua. The peculiarity of this dialect of Quechua is that it does not include a specific linguistic form to communicate about mental states. Experiments conducted with children from the age of four to eight years show that the rate of success at the false-belief task is significantly lower than the occidental average, independently of the age of the children. These results therefore seem to indicate that children's mother tongue plays a fundamental role in the development of their theory of mind. A more general study by Shatz et al. (2003), using tasks adapted to cultural differences between children, indicates, however, that there is no difference between children acquiring a language with different words to refer to true and false beliefs (such as Turkish and Puerto Rican Spanish) and those that do not make this distinction (such as English). By contrast, interactions in the family, and more specifically parent–child conversations, plays a role in the pace at which children develop theory of mind abilities (Sabbagh & Callanan, 1998; de Rosnay & Hughes, 2006).

Another example of differences of linguistic encoding between the languages discussed in the literature concerns the use of referring expressions conveying a certain degree of accessibility for the hearer. In some languages like French and English, the use of an article marking accessibility is compulsory in the grammar. Some studies indicate that children acquire the function of these markers earlier in these languages compared with languages like Chinese or Japanese and that lack such systems of articles and express such differences by other linguistic means such as word order and case marking. In this case as well, some universals are found.

Demir, So, Özyürek, and Goldin-Meadow (2012) reported that both Turkish and English children preferentially use full nouns in the absence of perceptual context. In the presence of perceptual cues, English-speaking children shifted to pronouns and Turkish-speaking children to omitted arguments, thus following the rules of their languages. In addition, even though Turkish-speaking children used more underspecified referents even when the referent was present in the perceptual context, they also used more gestures than English-speaking children, in order to specify the referents. This result indicates that children from both cultures are equally sensitive to the communicative needs of their addressee even though they express reference differently depending on specificities of their mother tongue. We will provide further evidence for children's early ability to modulate their choice of referring expressions in Chapter 8 (Section 8.1).

We conclude from this section that children develop cognitive pragmatic skills at a similar pace across cultures, despite differences of linguistic encoding in their exposure languages. We will provide in Chapters 4 to 8 more examples of cognitive pragmatic skills acquired by children learning different languages. In addition, environmental factors related to the quality of the input that children are exposed to such as mothers' preferences for mental state explanation or pointing behavior seem to be more important factors than cross-cultural differences for explaining inter-individual differences in the pace of acquisition for these skills. As Küntay et al. (2014) rightly observe, in many studies these two factors are intertwined, as the background of parents is often unequal across cultures. This factor must be controlled for before cultural differences can be called for to explain differences between cohorts of children.

4.3. Synthesis

In this chapter, we showed evidence that children are able to adapt their communicative behavior depending on the social status of their addressee from an early age. This ability reflects children's more general sensitivity to the need to integrate contextual information for producing adequate communicative acts. We also discussed the extent of cross-cultural variations in pragmatic norms as well as the effect of variable socialization strategies for children's developing pragmatic skills. We argued that while culture affects the end state that children have to learn in order to become proficient communicative partners, such variations are limited by the development of universal aspects of social cognition skills such as theory of mind abilities.

References

Andersen, E. (1990). *Speaking With Style: The Sociolinguistic Skills of Children*. London: Routledge.

Andersen, E., Brizuela, M., DuPuy, B., & Gonnerman, L. (1999). Cross-linguistic evidence for the early acquisition of discourse markers as register variables. *Journal of Pragmatics*, *31*, 1339–1351.

Aronsson, K. & Thorell, M. (1999). Family politics in children's play directives. *Journal of Pragmatics, 31*(1), 25–47.

Baroni, R. & Axia, G. (1989). Children's meta-pragmatic abilities and the identification of polite and impolite requests. *First Language, 9*, 285–297.

Bates, E. (1976). *Language and Context: The Acquisition of Pragmatics*. New York/San Francisco: Academic Press.

Becker, J. (1986). Bossy and nice requests: children's production and interpretation. *Merrill-Palmer Quarterly, 32*, 393–413.

Becker, J. (1988). The success of parents' indirect techniques for teaching their preschoolers pragmatic skills. *First Language, 8*, 173–182.

Becker, J. (1990). Processes in the acquisition of pragmatic competence. In G. Conti-Ramsden, & C. Snow (eds), *Children's Language, Volume* 7 (pp. 7–24). Hillsdale: Lawrence Erlbaum Associates.

Becker, J. & Hall, M. (1989). Adult beliefs about pragmatic development. *Journal of Applied Developmental Psychology, 10*, 1–17.

Blum-Kulka, S. (1990). You don't touch lettuce with your fingers. Parental politeness in family discourse. *Journal of Pragmatics, 14*, 259–288.

Blum-Kulka, S. (1997). *Dinner Talk. Cultural Patterns of Sociability and Socialization in Family Discourse.* Hillsdale: Lawrence Erlbaum Associates.

Blum-Kulka, S. & Snow, C. (2002). *Talking to Adults. The Contribution of Multiparty Discourse to Language Acquisition.* Hillsdale: Lawrence Erlbaum Associates.

Bornstein, M., Tal, J. Rahn, C. Galperín, C., Lamour, M., Ogino, M., Pêcheux, M., Toda, S., Azuma, H., & Tamis-LeMonda, C. (1992). Functional analysis of the contents of maternal speech to infants of 5 and 13 months in four cultures: Argentina, France, Japan, and the United States. *Developmental Psychology, 28*(4), 593–603.

Brown, P. (2011). Language socialization and the cultural organization of attention. In A. Duranti, E. Ochs, & Schieffelin, B.B. (eds), *Handbook of Language Socialization* (pp. 29–55). Malden/Oxford: Wiley-Blackwell.

Buhrmester, D. (1992). The developmental course of sibling and peer relationships. In F. Boer, & J. Dunn (eds), *Children's Sibling Relationships: Developmental and Clinical Issues* (pp. 19–40). Hillsdale: Lawrence Erlbaum Associates.

Burdelski, M. (2011). Language socialization and politeness routines. In A. Duranti, E. Ochs, & B. Schieffelin, B. (eds), *Handbook of Language Socialization* (pp. 275–295). Malden/Oxford: Wiley-Blackwell.

Callaghan, T., Moll, H., Rakoczy, H., Warneken, F., Liszkowski, U., Behne, T., & Tomasello, M. (2011). *Early Social Cognition in Three Cultural Contexts*. Boston: Wiley-Blackwell.

Callaghan, T., Rochat, P., Lillard, A., Claux, M., Odden, H., Itakura, S., Tapanya, S., & Singh, S. (2005). Synchrony in the onset of mental-state reasoning: evidence from five cultures. *Psychological Science, 16*, 378–384.

Cook-Gumperz, J. & Kyratzis, A. (2001). Child discourse. In D. Schiffrin, D. Tannen, & H. Hamilton (eds), *The Handbook of Discourse Analysis* (pp. 590–611). Oxford: Blackwell.

Cook-Gumperz, J. & Szymanski, M. (2001). Classroom "families": cooperating or competing – girls' and boys' interactional styles in a bilingual classroom. *Research on Language and Social Interaction, 34*(1), 107–129.

Coulthard, M. (1977). *An Introduction to Discourse Analysis*. London: Longman.

De Geer, B., Tulvisite, T., Mizera, L., & Tryggvason, M. T. (2002). Socialization in communication: pragmatic socialization during dinnertime in Estonian, Finnish and Swedish families. *Journal of Pragmatics, 34*, 1757–1786.

De Rosnay, M. & Hughes, C. (2006). Conversation and theory of mind: Do children talk their way to socio-cognitive understanding? *British Journal of Developmental Psychology, 24*, 7–37.

Demir, O., So, W-C., Özyürek, A., & Goldin-Meadow, S. (2012). Turkish- and English-speaking children display sensitivity to perceptual context in the referring expressions they produce in speech and gesture. *Language and Cognitive Processes, 27*(6), 844–867.

Dunn, J. (1997). Arguing with siblings, friends and mothers: developments in relationships and understanding. In D. Slobin, J. Gerhardt, A. Kyratzis, & J. Guo (eds), *Social Interaction, Social Context and Language: Essays in Honor of Susan Ervin-Tripp* (pp. 191–204). Mahwah, NJ: Laurence Erlbaum Associates.

Dunn, J., Brown, J., Slomkowki, C., Tesla, C., & Youngblade, L. (1991). Young children's understanding of other people's feelings and beliefs: Individual differences and their antecedents. *Child Development, 62*, 1351–1366.

Duranti, A., Ochs, E., & Schieffelin, B. (2011). *Handbook of Language Socialization*. Malden/ Oxford: Wiley-Blackwell.

Ervin-Tripp, S. (1976). Is Sybil there? The structure of some American English directives. *Language in Society, 5*, 25–66.

Ervin-Tripp, S. & Gordon, D. (1986). The development of children's requests. In R. Schiefelbusch, (ed), *Communicative Competence: Assessment and Intervention* (pp. 61–96). San Diego: College Hill Press.

Ervin-Tripp, S., Guo, J., & Lampert, M. (1990). Politeness and persuasion in children's control acts. *Journal of Pragmatics, 14*, 195–219.

Ervin-Tripp, S. O'Connor, M., & Rosenberg, J. (1984). Language and power in the family. In Schulz, M. and Kramerae, C. (ed), *Language and Power* (pp. 116–135). Belmont: Sage Press.

Field, M. (2001). Triadic directives in Navajo language socialization. *Language in Society, 30*(2), 249–263.

Gaskins, S. (2006). Cultural perspectives on infant–caregiver interaction. In N. J. Enfield, & S. C. Levinson (eds), *Roots of Human Sociality* (pp. 279–298). Oxford, UK: Berg.

Georgalidou, M. (2008). The contextual parameters of linguistic choice: Greek children's preferences for the formation of directive speech acts. *Journal of Pragmatics, 40*(1), 72–94.

Goodwin, M. (1985). The serious side of jump rope: Conversational practices and social organization in the frame of play." *Journal of American Folklore 98*, 315–330.

Goodwin, M. (1990). *He-Said-She-Said: Talk as Social Organization Among Black Children*. Bloomington: Indiana University Press.

Goodwin, M. (1993). Accomplishing social organization in girls' play: Patterns of competition and cooperation in an African-American working-class girls' group. In S. T. Hollis, L. Pershing, & M. J. Young (eds), *Feminist Theory and the Study of Folklore* (pp. 149–165). Urbana: University of Illinois Press.

Goodwin, M. (2001). Organizing participation in cross-sex jump-rope: Situating gender differences within longitudinal studies of activities. *Research on Language and Social Interactions, 34*, 75–105.

Goodwin, M. & Kyratzis, A. (2007). Children socializing children: Practices for negotiating the social order among peers. *Research on Language and Social Interactions, 40*(4), 279–289.

Goodwin, M. & Kyratzis, A. (2011). Peer language socialization. In A. Duranti, E. Ochs, & B. Schieffelin, B. (eds), *Handbook of Language Socialization* (pp. 365–390). Malden/ Oxford: Wiley-Blackwell.

Griswold, O. (2007). Achieving authority: Discursive practices in Russian girls pretend play. *Research on Language and Social Interaction, 40*(4), 291–319.

Küntay, A., Nakamura, K., & Şen, B. (2014). Crosslinguistic and crosscultural approaches to pragmatic development. In D. Matthews (ed), *Pragmatic Development in First Language Acquisition* (pp. 317–342). Amsterdam: John Benjamins.

Kyratzis, A. (2007). Using the social organizational affordances of pretend play in American preschool girls' interactions. *Research on Language and Social Interaction, 40*(4), 321–352.

Kyratzis, A. & Guo, J. (1996). "Separate worlds" for girls and boys? Views from U.S. and Chinese mixed-sex friendship groups. In D. I. Slobin, J. Gerhardt, A. Kyratzis, & J. Guo (eds), *Social Interaction, Social Context, and Language: Essays in Honor of Susan Ervin Tripp* (pp. 555–578). Mahwah, NJ: Lawrence Erlbaum Associates, Inc.

Kyratzis, A. & Guo, J. (2001). Preschool girls' and boys' verbal conflict strategies in the United States and China. *Research on Language and Social Interaction, 34*, 45–74.

Kyratzis, A., Marx, T., & Wade, E. (2001). Preschoolers' communicative competence: Register shift in the marking of power in different contexts of friendship group talk. *First Language, 21*, 387–431.

Kyratzis, A. & Tarım, S. (2010). Using directives to construct egalitarian or hierarchical social organization: Turkish middle-class preschool girls' socialization about gender, affect, and context in peer group conversations. *First Language, 30*, 473–492.

Ladegaard, H. (2004). Politeness in young children's speech: Context, peer group influence and pragmatic competence. *Journal of Pragmatics, 36*, 2003–2022.

Li, D. (2008). Pragmatic socialization. In C. Chapelle (ed), *The Encyclopedia of Applied Linguistics* (pp. 71–83). Wiley Online Library. Available at: http://onlinelibrary.wiley.com/book/10.1002/9781405198431.

Liszkowski, U., Brown, P., Callaghan, T., Takada, A., & De Vos, C. (2012). A prelinguistic gestural universal of human communication. *Cognitive Science, 36*(4), 698–713.

Nakamura, K. (2006). The acquisition of linguistic politeness in Japanese. In M. Nakayama, R. Mazuka, & Y. Shirai (eds), *Handbook of Japanese Psycholinguistics* (pp. 110–115). Cambridge: Cambridge University Press.

Ochs, E. (1988). *Culture and Language Development: Language Acquisition and Socialization in a Samoan Village*. Cambridge: Cambridge University Press.

Ochs, E. & Schieffelin, B. (1986). *Language Socialization across Cultures*. New York: Cambridge University Press.

Ochs, E. & Schieffelin, B. (1995). Language acquisition and socialization: Three developmental stories and their implications. In B. Blount (ed), *Language, Culture and Society: A Book of Readings* (pp. 470–512). Second Edition. Prospect Heights: Waveland Press, Inc.

Ogiermann, E. (2009). Politeness and in-directness across cultures: A comparison of English, German, Polish and Swedish requests. *Journal of Politeness Research, 5*, 189–216.

Park, E. (2006). Grandparents, grandchildren, and heritage language use in Korean. In K. Kondo-Brown (ed), *Heritage Language Development: Focus on East Asian Immigrants* (pp. 57–86). Amsterdam: John Benjamins.

Peng, K. & Nisbett, R. (1999). Culture, dialecticism, and reasoning about contradiction. *American Psychologist, 54*, 741–754.

Rowe, M. & Goldin-Meadow, S. (2009). Differences in early gesture explain SES disparities in child vocabulary size at school entry. *Science, 323*(5916), 951–953.

Ryckebusch, C. & Marcos, H. (2004). Speech acts, social context and parent-toddler play between the ages of 1;5 and 2;3. *Journal of Pragmatics, 36*(5), 883–897.

Sabbagh, M. & Callanan, M. (1998). Metarepresentation in action: 3-, 4-, and 5-year-olds developing theories of mind in parent-child conversations. *Developmental Psychology, 34*(3), 491–502.

Schieffelin, B. (1985). The acquisition of Kaluli. In D. Slobin (ed), *The Cross-linguistic Study of Language Acquisition* (pp. 525–593). Hillsdale: Laurence Erlbaum.

Schiffrin, D. (1987). *Discourse Markers*. Cambridge: Cambridge University Press.

Shatz, M., Diesendruck, G., Martinez-Beck, I., & Akar, D. (2003). The influence of language and socioeconomic status on children's understanding of false belief. *Developmental Psychology, 39*, 717–729.

Slomkowski, C. & Dunn, J. (1992). Arguments and relationships within the family: Differences in young children's disputes with mother and sibling. *Developmental Psychology, 28*, 919–924.

Snow, C., Perlmann, R., Gleason, J. B., & Hooshyar, N. (1990). Developmental perspectives on politeness: sources of children's knowledge. *Journal of Pragmatics, 14*, 289–305.

Sperber, D. & Wilson, D. (1986). *Relevance: Communication and Cognition*. Oxford: Blackwell.

Thorne, B. (1993). *Gender Play: Boys and Girls in School*. New Brunswick: Rutgers University Press.

Van der Henst, J.-B., Mercier, H., Yama, H., Kawasaki, Y., & Adachi, K. (2006). Dealing with contradiction in a communicative context: a cross-cultural study. *Intercultural Pragmatics*, 3–4, 487–502.

Vinden, P. (1996). Junín Quechua children's understanding of mind. *Child Development, 67*, 1707–1716.

Yifat, R. & Zadunaisky-Ehrlich, S. (2008). Metapragmatic comments indexing conversational practices of preschool children in institutional discourse. *First Language, 28*, 329–347.

Wierzbicka, A. (1991). *Cross-Cultural Pragmatics: The semantics of Human Interactions*. Berlin/ New York: Mouton de Gruyter.

Wilkins, D. (2003). Why pointing with the index finger is not a universal. In S. Kita (ed), *Pointing: Where Language, Culture, and Cognition Meet* (pp. 171–215). Mahwah, NJ: Lawrence Erlbaum Associates.

PART III

Acquiring cognitive aspects of pragmatic competence

5

UNDERSTANDING SPEAKERS' INTENTIONS

Theory of mind

In Gricean pragmatics, understanding speakers' meanings is a matter of recognizing their intentions. The study of humans' ability to understand intentions in verbal communication has brought pragmatics and cognitive psychology together through the notion of theory of mind abilities, a cognitive faculty allowing people to reason about other peoples' mental states such as beliefs and desires in order to understand and predict their behavior. In order to relate the acquisition of pragmatics with the development of theory of mind abilities, we first address the question of how and when children develop theory of mind abilities. We conclude in the light of recent experimental findings that children already possess theory of mind abilities around their first birthday (Section 5.1). We go on to demonstrate how these early mind-reading skills contribute to children's development of pragmatic competencies as soon as other linguistic, conceptual, and metarepresentational knowledge become available. Finally we discuss the hypothesis, put forward by Sperber and Wilson, that verbal communication rests on a sub-module of theory of mind specifically dedicated to it (Section 5.2).

5.1. Defining theory of mind abilities

The concept of theory of mind has been the object of an important body of literature during the past 30 years in cognitive psychology. In this section, we first introduce the origins of this concept and describe the false-belief task, a commonly used tool to assess children's developing theory of mind abilities (Section 5.1.1). We explain how developmental studies have recently taken a radical turn, when a new set of findings has put into question the developmental milestones established based on results at the classical versions of the false-belief task (Section 5.1.2).

5.1.1. The classical debate

During the past decades, theory of mind abilities has come to be considered as one of the main skills characterizing human cognition and separating humans from other non-human primates. Indeed, despite the quite sophisticated social behavior of some species of primates, none of them have been proved to possess theory of mind abilities comparable to humans (e.g. Kaminski, Call & Tomasello, 2008). In addition, recent neuroimaging studies have revealed that specific brain regions are associated with theory of mind reasoning in human adults (Gallagher et al., 2000; Saxe & Baron-Cohen, 2006). One of these regions is the right temporo-parietal junction that is specifically activated when people think about mental states but not when they think about other aspects of people such as their personality traits or their appearance (Saxe & Kanwisher, 2003; Perner, Aichhorn, Kronbichler, Staffen & Ladurner, 2006). Such findings led to the conclusion that the possession of theory of mind abilities is a key component of human social cognition.

From a developmental perspective, the questions are when and how do children develop the ability to reason about other peoples' mental states. In order to determine at what age children possess adult-like theory of mind abilities, most studies have focused on one aspect of this development: the ability to attribute false beliefs to others. The importance of testing the attribution of false rather than true beliefs was already emphasized by Dennett (1978) who remarked that it is not enough to observe that an individual can predict the actions of another to conclude that he has theory of mind abilities, because he may do so without attributing mental states to him but only by using his own world knowledge. For example, if Mary sees John going toward the fridge with an empty glass in his hand, she may conclude that he is looking for orange juice, not because she attributes to him the belief that there is orange juice in the fridge but because she knows that it is there. With false beliefs on the other hand, the subject must be able to dissociate his own true belief from the false belief of another person in order to make sense of his actions. For example, in order for Mary to understand why John is looking inside the fridge with a glass in his hand although she knows that there is no orange juice left, she must attribute to him the false belief that there is orange juice in the fridge in order to make sense of his behavior. This observation has led to the design of a false-belief task to assess children's possession of theory of mind abilities.

In the first version of the false-belief task (Wimmer & Perner, 1983), a child called Maxi puts chocolate into a blue cupboard and leaves the kitchen. During his absence, his mother takes the chocolate, uses some for a cake, and puts the rest back into a green cupboard. When she leaves the kitchen, Maxi comes back to eat some chocolate. Children who take the test are then asked where Maxi will look for his chocolate. Many variants of this task have been designed, such as the well-known Sally-Ann task (Baron-Cohen, Leslie & Frith, 1985) and used with children across the world (Avis & Harris, 1991; Callaghan et al., 2005; Liu, Wellman, Tardif & Sabbagh, 2008). The results reported by most studies are invariably the same: children fail to provide the correct answer to the false-belief question until the age of four (Wellman, Cross & Watson, 2001). Another indicator that has also been used to assess the possession of theory of mind abilities is the understanding that things can be different from what they appear to be, an ability tested in the appearance-reality task (Flavell, Flavell & Green, 1983). In this task, children are presented with an object looking like another object, for example, a stone that resembles an egg and asked questions regarding the appearance of the tested object and the object's true nature. Children also succeed at this task at around the age of four, thus consistently confirming results from the false-belief task.

While the ability to pass the false-belief task is usually considered to be the main milestone indicating the possession of theory of mind abilities, children have been found to develop a number of important precursors to theory of mind abilities during their first years of life. One such milestone is shared attention, a competence that children achieve around 18 months and which enables them to share representations with another speaker (see Chapter 2, Section 2.2.1). Around the same age, children start to understand that some preferences, for example, in food, are subjective (Repacholi & Gopnik, 1997). Shortly after 18 months, children start to engage in pretend play, which has been considered by some authors as the crucial faculty enabling them to later attribute false beliefs to others by simulation (e.g. Leslie, 1994). Around the age of three, children become aware of other peoples' desires and their consequences. They understand, for example, that a person will be happier if she achieves what she wants than when she does not.

In sum, this body of literature indicates that children's understanding of false beliefs at the age of four builds upon a series of previous acquisitions of concepts such as goals, intentions, and desires. But the development of children's theory of mind abilities does not stop when they succeed at the false-belief task either, as a number of important mentalizing abilities continue to develop until late childhood. For example, children are able to pass advanced versions of the false-belief task, requiring a double embedding of mental states, between the age of five to eight depending on the difficulty of the task used (Sullivan, Zaitchik & Tager-Flusberg, 1994). In the first version of this task (Perner & Wimmer, 1985), John wrongly believes that Mary believes that the ice-cream van is located in a specific place. In order to succeed at the task, children must be able to reason about the beliefs that John entertains about the beliefs of Mary. Because of this double recursion, this task is also often called second-order theory of mind task. Another important dimension of theory of mind abilities is the understanding that beliefs can be formed based on several types of evidence such as visual perception, hearsay, or inference. By the age of three, children understand that seeing leads to believing (Pratt & Bryant, 1990) but it is not before the age of six that they understand that beliefs can rely on inferences as well as on direct perception (Sodian & Wimmer, 1987).

Despite the long development of theory of mind abilities described above, the transition between failure and success at the false-belief task during the preschool years is traditionally considered as the major milestone indicating the possession of theory of mind abilities. This transition has been accounted for in different ways in the literature. According to the 'theory account' (e.g. Gopnik & Astington, 1988; Perner, 1991; Wellman, 1990;), the transition between failure and success at the task reflects a radical change occurring in children's cognition around the age of four. Before that age, children fail at the false-belief task because they do not have a concept of belief yet. The acquisition of the concept of belief around the age of four is due to general processes of learning and interaction with the child's environment. The 'modular account' states that theory of mind abilities represent an innate mental module, present from birth (Baron-Cohen, 1995; Leslie, 1994). In this view, the transition between failure and success at the false-belief task reflects a change in performance rather than competence. The main assumption behind this view is that the development of theory of mind is a continuous process of maturation taking place at the contact of the environment, but that does not undergo a radical transition during the preschool years. Thus, for different reasons (the maturation of a mental module vs. the learning of a concept), both accounts emphasize the importance of the input for the development of theory of mind abilities during the first years of life. Indeed, numerous evidence suggests that the development of theory of mind abilities is influenced by environmental factors, such as the presence of an older sibling (Ruffman, Perner, Naito, Parkin & Clements, 1998), the socio-economic status of the child's family (Shatz, Diesendruck, Martinez-Beck & Akar, 2003), the mental state explanations given by mothers (Peterson & Slaughter, 2003; Ruffman, Slade & Crowe, 2002), and more generally the parent–child conversations (de Rosnay & Hughes, 2006; Sabbagh & Callanan, 1998).

Yet another account suggests that having a theory of mind only implies simulation skills (Gordon, 1986). According to the simulation account, it is possible to infer other people's intentions and therefore their actions by using one's own mind as a model of theirs. For example, it is possible to anticipate the solution that somebody else will find to a problem by solving this problem ourselves, while taking into account the differences in abilities that differentiate us from the other person. This position does not imply the necessity of possessing a complex device for mental state attribution, but only the ability for pretense and taking another person's perspective.

All these models of theory of mind have their own merits and have been corroborated by some kind of empirical validation. For instance, the simulation model correctly predicts the early acquisition of pretend play in young children. Moreover, from a neuroscience perspective, the discovery of mirror neurons in the monkey's premotor cortex (see Rizzolatti & Sinigaglia, 2008) has also given it strong support, especially since some experimental evidence seems to suggest that a similar matching system also exists in humans (Gallese & Goldman, 1998). From a cognitive point of view, the simulation model is the only one which does not imply that theory of mind abilities require the more general ability to form higher-order representations or 'metarepresentations', since it only rests on the ability to translate a representation and apply it to another person. For this reason, the simulation account is not as well equipped as the other two accounts to explain how theory of mind abilities are related to pragmatic enrichment, as simulation is used to predict another person's behavior whereas pragmatics enrichment is performed in order to understand the speaker's already performed communicative act. In addition, Southgate (2013) convincingly argued that children's ability to understand an action performed by someone else as goal-oriented is not determined by their motor ability to perform this action, as predicted by the mirror neuron theory of action understanding, thus casting some doubts on the role of mirror neurons and simulation theory to account for children's growing ability to understand other's mental states and behaviors.

To summarize, for several decades, research on theory of mind development has focused on explaining the transition occurring during the preschool years and enabling children to succeed at the false-belief task, based on the development of theoretical knowledge, a mental module, or simulation skills. This research landscape has radically changed since 2005, when a series of new experimental results questioned the fact that children do not possess the ability to attribute false beliefs before the age of four.

5.1.2. New results and puzzles

One of the main limitations of the false-belief task described above is that it requires verbal skills in order to understand the story and the false-belief question, and cannot be used with very young children. In order to overcome this problem, Onishi and Baillargeon (2005) used gaze fixations as an indicator of 15-months-old infants' reaction to false beliefs. They showed infants scenes in which the experimenter hides a toy in one of two boxes displayed in front of them. Then a change occurs, for instance, the object is moved from one box to another. The experimenter sometimes sees the change occur and sometimes not, thus producing a situation of false belief. In some cases, the experimenter acts according to his false belief and looks for the object in the wrong location but in others he looks in the correct box despite not witnessing the change. If infants have some understanding of false belief, Onishi and Baillargeon reasoned that they should be surprised and therefore look longer when the experimenter acts in an unexpected way. This is exactly what the results obtained in this experiment have shown.

So unexpected were these results given the long-established transition during the preschool years reported by hundreds of studies that a number of researchers looked for alternative, simpler explanations of children's behavior, not involving the ability to reason about false beliefs (e.g. Perner & Ruffman, 2005). These alternative explanations have, however, become less and less likely as other studies have replicated the new findings in different situations (Scott & Baillargeon, 2009; Song, Onishi, Baillargeon & Fisher, 2008; Surian, Caldi & Sperber, 2007) and using different dependent variables than the surprise-looking paradigm used by Onishi and Baillargeon. In some cases, the variable was expectancy looking (Southgate, Senju & Csibra, 2007) or even active helping in a referential task (Southgate, Chevallier & Csibra, 2010). The exact age at which infants demonstrate an understanding of false belief based on their gaze fixations has, however, not yet been firmly established in this body of literature. While some studies have found that children display an understanding of false belief as early as 13 months or even 7 months (Kovács, Téglás & Endress, 2010), others have not found it in 18-month-old children (Southgate et al., 2007). Despite this variability, all these studies confirm that very young children have at least some understanding of false beliefs long before the age of success at the classical version of the false-belief task.

A possible explanation for these new findings is that the classical false-belief task provided an inaccurate picture of children's theory of mind abilities. Indeed, it has often been observed in the literature that passing the classical false-belief task requires more than the ability to reason about mental states (e.g. Bloom & German, 2000; Surian & Leslie, 1999). One of the potential problems is that children have to be able to follow and understand a story, which may be too demanding for young children's short-term memory. In order to overcome this problem, an alternative task called the unexpected content or Smarties task was developed (Gopnik & Astington, 1988; Perner, Leekam & Wimmer, 1987), that simply requires children to tell what they thought was in a Smarties box before the experimenter opened it and revealed its true content. However, this modified task has not led to improvements in children's performance, as most of them also pass it at the age of four. Another possibility is that the formulation of the test question may be too complex and pragmatically ambiguous. Some researchers have indeed found that a simple modification of the test question into "*Where will Maxi look first for his chocolate*?" was enough to improve the rate of success amongst three-year-old children (Lewis & Osborne, 1990; Siegal & Beattie, 1991). In addition, some studies have found that three-year-olds (but not two-and-a-half-year-olds), while giving the wrong answer to the false belief question in classical false belief tasks, were looking at the correct location where the character should look for his object based on his false belief (Clements & Perner, 1994; Ruffman, Garnham, Import & Connolly, 2001).

In sum, the changes made to the classical verbal false-belief task only led to small changes in the age of success, as children younger than three still mostly fail. This means that the discrepancy observed between the age of success at the classical task and infants' ability evidenced in the eye gaze studies cannot be explained away by problems with the classical version of the task nor by dismissing the new set of findings. The main challenge in the current literature on theory of mind is to provide a way to reconcile both sets of findings. Different accounts are currently competing in the literature.

According to the 'negative release account' (Low & Perner, 2012), infants already possess operational theory of mind abilities but they cannot express these abilities in classical versions of the false-belief task because of external limitations in memory or because of their inability to inhibit interfering processes due to immature executive control. According to this account, the transition between infants and preschoolers occurs when these disturbing external factors can be controlled for. Carruthers (2013) elaborated a negative release account stating that classical verbal false-belief tasks require three capacities: (1) mental states processing in order to understand and keep in mind the mental states of an agent and derive expectations of behaviors, (2) pragmatic processing in order to understand the speech of the experimenter and attribute to him an informative intention, and (3) formulation of an action representing the mental states of an agent. All three elements require theory of mind abilities, and this might cause an overload for young children. Following this account, success at the classical theory of mind tasks comes when the processing resources allocated to the theory of mind module increase and when the relations between this module and executive control become more operational.

The competing account states that the transition reflects a 'positive gain' corresponding to the discovery of new principles or the maturation of existing capacities. According to this second account, infants' early mental state attribution is limited in scope and flexibility and it is only by the time they pass classical versions of the false-belief task that they reach adult-like, flexible theory of mind abilities. The positive gain of abilities between infants and preschoolers has been conceptualized in several different ways (Low & Perner, 2012). One of the most popular distinctions lies between implicit and explicit abilities, a distinction already used to explain many different areas of children's development such as playing the piano, drawing (e.g., Karmiloff-Smith, 1992), and the development of children's understanding of numbers (Apperly & Butterfill, 2009). However, the notion of implicitness has received different interpretations. For example, Ruffman et al. (2001) related explicitness to consciousness. In a set of experiments, they tested the possibility that three-year-old children who fail at classical versions of the false-belief task but look at the correct location are still unaware of their behavior. They therefore asked children to bet counters on where the character would go to retrieve his object. If children have some awareness of the answer suggested by their eye gaze, they should bet modestly on the validity of their explicit answer. The results indicate, however, that three-year-olds bet very confidently on their explicit answers, indicating that they are still totally unaware of the alternative answer suggested by their eye gaze. Clements and Perner (1994) related the notion of explicitness to meta-cognition and argued that implicit theory of mind abilities allow children to represent beliefs but not to judge them. Yet another way to characterize the implicit-explicit distinction is to relate it to spontaneous versus elicited behavior, as eye gaze corresponds to spontaneous behavior while the classical theory of mind task involves a prompted response eliciting a controlled action. San Juan and Astington (2012) argued in addition that the development of some functional aspects of language, and more specifically of epistemic verbs and their related syntax, is a key factor accounting for the transition between implicit and explicit theory of mind abilities. The most serious counterargument for all versions of the positive gain theory is that the limitations in infants' abilities to deal with mental states at the implicit stage have not yet been evidenced.

Saxe (2013) suggested that one of the possible ways to solve the puzzle of theory of mind development will come from studies of brain imagery. These studies have already led to the identification of areas dedicated to thinking about thoughts in adults. Saxe pointed out that similar studies with children could shed some additional light on the development of theory of mind abilities. However, the few existing studies tend to indicate that the brain regions dedicated to theory of mind reasoning in adults become specialized only by the age of nine, while in younger children they are activated when thinking about anything concerning another person (Gweon, Dodell-Feder, Bedny & Saxe, 2012; Saxe, Whitfield-Gabrieli, Scholz & Pelphrey, 2009). As a result, these studies deepen even further the puzzle of infants' abilities and suggest that mindreading skills in young children, enabling them to pass both implicit and explicit versions of the false-belief task, may rely on a different neural system than adults. This system remains, however, to be identified.

To summarize, the current literature on theory of mind abilities has demonstrated that shortly after their first birthday, infants have an implicit understanding of false beliefs that turns into the ability to answer an explicit question about a character's false belief at the age of four. Children's development of theory of mind abilities is not completed at the age of four; however, as their ability to attribute second-order beliefs (beliefs about beliefs) develops only a couple of years later, as does their ability to reason about the sources of beliefs.

5.2. Theory of mind and pragmatic development

In the literature, many studies have reported a correlation between the age of success at the classical false-belief task and the acquisition of various aspects of pragmatic competencies around the age of four. The challenge raised by the new eye-gaze studies with infants is to explain why the acquisition of many pragmatic competencies has been found to correlate with classical versions of the false-belief task, if pragmatics requires theory of mind abilities that are operational by the age of one. We address this question in Section 5.2.1. We go on to discuss the possibility that verbal communication requires a specific sub-module of theory of mind abilities in Section 5.2.2.

5.2.1. Theory of mind development and the acquisition of pragmatic competencies

The relationship between the development of theory of mind abilities and pragmatic competencies has been explored from many different angles over the past decades. One of the first studies that have explicitly related theory of mind and pragmatics was conducted by Happé (1993) who compared children with autism spectrum disorder in their ability to pass first- and second-order theory of mind tasks and to understand similes, metaphors, and irony. Results from these experiments revealed a correlation between the ability to pass first-order theory of mind tasks and to understand metaphor and between the ability to pass second-order theory of mind tasks and to understand irony. These results were interpreted as an indication that understanding metaphors involve the ability to go beyond the literal meaning of the sentence in order to recognize the speaker's intention and that this requires first-order theory of mind abilities. In this interpretation, similar capacities are not required for similes, because the comparison is linguistically explicit ('X is like a Y'). Irony requires second-order theory of mind abilities because it involves the ability to understand a thought about a thought, in other words the fact that the speaker presents his own negative attitude toward a thought or utterance attributed to someone else.

Similar correlations with first-order theory of mind abilities were also found with other aspects of pragmatic competencies such as the use of Gricean maxims in communication. For example, Surian, Baron-Cohen, and van der Lely (1996) observed that children suffering from autism, who fail false-belief tests, also have great difficulties in recognizing when a Gricean maxim has been flouted, but those of these children who pass these tests do not have the same difficulties. Another example of correlation for normally developing children comes from pragmatic tasks involving reference disambiguation. For example, Bezuidenhout and Sroda (1998) showed children a ball and asked them to "put the ball in *the* box." In the test situation, the children had two boxes in front of them. The most salient one for the children was not visible to the experimenter, whereas the less salient one was visible from both the children's and the experimenter's point of view. Up to the age of four, children mostly chose the most salient box from their perspective (but see Chapter 8, Section 8.1.2 for experimental results showing evidence of earlier abilities to select objects based on perceptual common ground). Again the transition between failure and success at this task coincides with the age of success at the false-belief task. Similar correlations were also found in other studies of referential communication (Maridaki-Kassotaki & Antonopoulou, 2011; Mitchell, Robinson & Thompson, 1999; Resches & Pérez-Pereira, 2007).

In spite of this body of evidence, there are good reasons to question the validity of a correlation between the development of theory of mind abilities as measured by classical versions of the false-belief tasks and the development of pragmatic competencies. Indeed, while the correlation between irony and theory of mind abilities has been replicated in numerous studies (see Chapter 6, Section 6.2), the relation between metaphors and first-order theory of mind abilities has become widely contested. In recent pragmatic accounts, metaphors are said to be part of normal communication and to rest on the same processes as any other utterance (see Chapter 6, Section 6.1). From this perspective, it becomes implausible that metaphors, but not all other utterances, should require theory of mind abilities that are not available before the age of four, as children can engage in verbal communication long before this age. Another indication that the correlation between the acquisition of pragmatic competencies and the ability to pass first-order theory of mind task is not genuine comes from the fact that correlations were also found between the ability to pass the false-belief task and the development of aspects of language that do not directly appeal to theory of mind abilities but to metalinguistic awareness, such as the comprehension of synonymy (Doherty & Perner, 1998) and homonymy (Doherty, 2000). These results imply that the developmental link is not limited to aspects of pragmatic competencies related to the attribution of mental states to the speaker.

An even more serious problem for the validity of the observed correlations is that most sentences, and not only metaphors, contain some kind of ambiguity that needs to be resolved in context, by going beyond the decoded meaning of sentences. This implies that children should be unable to engage in inferential communication before the age of four. They appear, however, to understand most utterances long before they pass false-belief tests. More generally, they are able to engage in verbal communication adequately from a very early age. For example, we reported in Chapter 2 that children use inferential cues in the process of word learning. In Chapter 3, we presented results indicating that children can draw relevance inferences enabling them to understand hints from the age of two-and-a-half years, when the task is simple. These results tend to indicate that inferential communication does not start when children pass explicit versions of the false-belief task. In this respect, the eye-gaze infant studies described above, indicating that children do possess theory of mind abilities shortly after their first birthday, resolve this paradox and explain children's early success at verbal communication.

The question then is what accounts for the observed correlations described above? In the case of metaphor, Wilson (forthcoming) argues that the correlation may be due to the development of a metalogical ability (Sperber, 2000), enabling humans to assess a proposition as being true or false and therefore to assess the benevolence of a speaker (e.g. Mascaro & Sperber, 2009). In this view, it is not theory of mind abilities that are needed to understand metaphor but another metarepresentational ability to assess the truth of an argument, which develops during the preschool years.

We argue in addition that the acquisition of pragmatic competencies such as the ability to understand non-literal language or to assign the correct referent to a pronoun cannot be reduced to the possession of theory of mind abilities. Enriching the linguistic form of sentences to understand the speaker's meaning also requires the ability to select and integrate contextual information as input for inferential processes and to possess conceptual and linguistic knowledge. Indeed, we present evidence in Chapter 6 (Section 6.1) that young children can understand and produce metaphors as soon as they have access to the relevant conceptual properties on which they are built. This account is corroborated by Norbury (2005), who studied the ability of children with communication impairments to understand metaphors and found that not only do theory of mind skills not ensure comprehension of metaphors but also that the strongest predictor of success is semantic ability. Similarly, we reported in Chapter 3 that children's ability to draw relevance inferences depended on the accessibility of contextual information that must be used as input to inferential processes. This ability is not dependent on theory of mind abilities (see also Chapter 9) and accounts for many of the limitations encountered by young children.

In a nutshell, children's acquisition of pragmatics during the preschool years does not appear to be limited by their lack of theory of mind abilities. It seems most likely that children already have the required theory of mind abilities from a very early age and that this enables them to develop pragmatic competencies as soon as other linguistic and conceptual knowledge are acquired, and when meta-representational processes enabling them to judge the truth or falsity of arguments become operational. We will discuss in more details the factors enabling children to develop specific pragmatic competencies in the next chapters.

5.2.2. Pragmatics as a sub-module of theory of mind

We argued above that theory of mind abilities could be conceived as a mental module and we reported evidence that, in human adults, dedicated brain regions are activated when people think about thoughts. A theoretical question for the study of inferential communication is whether the specificities of verbal communication justify the existence of a specific module dedicated to it. In his discussion of the role of theory of mind abilities for word learning, Bloom (2002) explicitly argued against the idea that children require different theory of mind abilities for lexical acquisition than for understanding non-verbal behaviors, on the grounds that the attribution of intentions that are necessary for word learning also apply in non-communicative contexts. For example, children are able to infer from a very young age that when a speaker uses an unknown label, he refers to the object that he is paying attention to (see Chapter 2, Section 2.2.1). Similar results have been reported for cases of non-communicative acts. Baldwin and Moses (1994) found, for example, that children understand that when an adult looks at an object on the ground and scrunches up his nose in disgust, this emotion is related to the object that the adult is looking at. In other words, children use the same reasoning for object labeling and emotion understanding. Bloom also argued that it is highly suggestive that the non-communicative aspects of theory of mind abilities emerge at a time when children start to learn words. He therefore suggested that while children progressively become more skilled with the attribution of intentions in the context of verbal communication compared with other domains, it is because of practice effects rather than the existence of a specialized sub-module dedicated to verbal communication.

In the context of relevance theory, Sperber (2000) and Sperber and Wilson (2002) took the opposite view and argued in favor of the existence of a specific sub-module of theory of mind dedicated to verbal communication, working according to the principle of relevance. They argued that the comprehension procedure for utterances described by relevance theory (Sperber & Wilson, 1995) meets the requirements of modularity because it is a frugal heuristic that leads the hearer to follow a path of least effort. Indeed, it is generally assumed that generic modules can only use the formal properties of the input to derive conclusions whereas dedicated modules can exploit the regularities in their specific domain. The existence of a sub-module is in addition justified by the fact that all utterances convey a presumption of their own optimal relevance (described in the communicative principle of relevance) and that the scope of such a module would be limited to ostensive-inferential communication.

Another major difference between verbal communication and other cases of mental state attribution mentioned by Sperber and Wilson (2002) is that in non-verbal situations, the subject must first identify the effect that the agent might have predicted and desired by performing his action, and then conclude that this was the intended effect. In verbal communication, however, hearers cannot proceed in a similar manner, as the speaker's intention is precisely to have the hearer recognize his informative intention. In other words, while it is possible to infer the intention behind an action by viewing its physical outcome, an ostensive act of communication such as pointing has no physical effect. It seems therefore plausible that two different mechanisms are involved in both cases.

Lastly, Sperber and Wilson (2002) noted that the number of non-communicative actions that someone can perform at a given time is rather limited and therefore the interpretation of these actions is quite simple. By comparison, the gap that hearers have to bridge between the sentence's meaning and speaker's meaning is wide, as several types of enrichment of explicit and implicit meaning are required. It seems therefore unlikely that a general heuristic may be sufficient to explain both non-communicative behaviors and ostensive–inferential communication. In addition, in Gricean pragmatics, inferential communication implies the recognition of a double level of intention: an informative intention and a communicative intention. This process, requiring a double embedding of mental states, is not problematic for young children who produce communicative acts from a very early age. Sperber and Wilson argued that the discrepancy between the early onset of ostensive–inferential communication in children and their late ability to succeed at false-belief tasks brings some confirmation for the existence of a dedicated sub-module.

Sperber and Wilson's as well as Bloom's views on the relation between pragmatics and theory of mind module were both published before the new eye-gaze studies involving infants were conducted. How do the new infant studies affect these two accounts? We argue that the new findings still leave both accounts open, as they do not provide empirical data contradicting either of them. The discovery that young children possess some form of theory of mind abilities much earlier than was previously thought and can use their abilities in communicative situations (e.g. Southgate et al., 2010) only invalidates Sperber and Wilson's argument about the discrepancy between the onset of verbal communication and the age of success at the false-belief task. Given the new findings, there is no longer a major discrepancy between the onset of verbal communication and theory of mind abilities to be explained. The other arguments in favor of the specificities of verbal communication remain valid and require further empirical testing to be evaluated.

5.3. Synthesis

We started this chapter by introducing the debate that took place during several decades in cognitive psychology about the development of theory of mind abilities during the preschool years. We explained that recent findings coming from infant eye-gaze studies raised many new questions for the definition of theory of mind abilities and their acquisition. Most of these questions are still open. Saxe (2013) even stated that explaining children's developing theory of mind abilities represents one of major puzzles ahead for cognitive sciences. In the second part of the chapter, we have assessed the correlations between children's developing theory of mind abilities and their acquisition of various pragmatic competencies such as the ability to understand non-literal language uses. We concluded that the correlations observed at the age of four did not reflect a genuine transition in children's pragmatic competencies due to their possession of theory of mind abilities. In view of the recent infant studies, we argued that children already possess theory of mind abilities by the time they start to communicate verbally and that this explains many of their early successes at verbal communication. The development of pragmatic competencies such as the ability to understand metaphors and indirect speech acts occurs when the required linguistic and metarepresentational skills become available.

References

Apperly, I. & Butterfill, S. (2009). Do humans have two systems to track beliefs and belief-like states? *Psychology Review, 116*, 953–970.

Avis, J. & Harris, P. (1991). Belief-desire reasoning among Baka children: evidence for a universal conception of mind. *Child Development, 62*, 460–467.

Baldwin, D. & Moses, L. (1994). Early understanding of referential intent and attentional focus: Evidence from language and emotion. In C. Lewis, & P. Mitchell (eds), *Children's Early Understanding of Mind: Origins and Development* (pp. 133–156). Hillsdale, NJ: Erlbaum.

Baron-Cohen, S. (1995). *Mindblindness: An Essay on Autism and Theory of Mind*. Cambridge: The MIT Press.

Baron-Cohen, S., Leslie, A., & Frith, U. (1985). Does the autistic child have a "theory of mind"? *Cognition, 21*, 37–46.

Bezuidenhout, A. & Sroda, M. (1998). Children's use of contextual cues to resolve referential ambiguity: An application of relevance theory. *Pragmatics and Cognition, 6*, 265–299.

Bloom, P. (2002). Mindreading, communication and the learning of names for things. *Mind & Language, 17*, 37–54.

Bloom, P. & German, T. (2000). Two reasons to abandon the false belief task as a test of theory of mind. *Cognition, 77*, B25–B31.

Callaghan, T., Rochat, P., Lillard, A., Claux, M., Odden, H., Itakura, S., Tapanya, S., & Singh, S. (2005). Synchrony in the onset of mental-state reasoning: Evidence from five cultures. *Psychological Science, 16*, 378–384.

Carruthers, P. (2013). Mindreading in infancy. *Mind & Language, 28*(2), 141–172.

Clements, W. & Perner, J. (1994). Implicit understanding of belief. *Cognitive Development, 9*, 377–395.

Dennett, D. (1978). Beliefs about beliefs. *Behavioral and Brain Sciences, 1*(4), 568–570.

De Rosnay, M. & Hughes, C. (2006). Conversation and theory of mind: Do children talk their way to socio-cognitive understanding? *British Journal of Developmental Psychology, 24*, 7–37.

Doherty, M. (2000). Children's understanding of homonymy: Metalinguistic awareness and false belief. *Journal of Child Language, 27*, 367–392.

Doherty, M. & Perner, J. (1998). Metalinguistic awareness and theory of mind: Just two words for the same thing? *Cognitive Development, 13*, 279–305.

Flavell, J., Flavell, E., & Green, F. (1983). Development of the appearance-reality distinction. *Cognitive Psychology, 15*, 95–120.

Gallagher, H., Happe, F., Brunswick, N., Fletcher, P. C., Frith, U., & Frith, C. (2000). Reading the mind in cartoons and stories: An fMRI study of "theory of mind" in verbal and nonverbal tasks. *Neuropsychologia, 38*, 11–21.

Gallese, V. & Goldman, A. (1998). Mirror neurons and the simulation theory of mind-reading. *Trends in Cognitive Sciences, 4*(7), 252–254.

Gopnik, A. & Astington, J. (1988). Children's understanding of representational changes and its relation to the understanding of false belief and the appearance-reality distinction. *Child Development, 59*, 26–37.

Gweon, H., Dodell-Feder, D., Bedny, M., & Saxe, R. (2012). Theory of mind performance in children correlates with functional specialization of a brain region for thinking about thoughts. *Child Development, 83*(6), 853–1868.

Happé, F. (1993). Communicative competence and theory of mind in autism: A test for relevance theory. *Cognition, 48*, 101–119.

Kaminski, J., Call, J., & Tomasello, M. (2008). Chimpanzees know what others know, but not what they believe. *Cognition, 109*, 224–234.

Karmiloff-Smith, A. (1992). *Beyond Modularity: A Developmental Perspective on Cognitive Science*. Cambridge, MA: MIT Press.

Kovács, A., Téglás, E., & Endress, A. (2010). The social sense: Susceptibility to others' beliefs in human infants and adults. *Science, 330*, 1830–1834.

Leslie, A. (1994). Pretending and believing: Issues in the theory of ToMM. *Cognition, 50*, 193–200.

Lewis, C. & Osborne, A. (1990). Three-year-olds' problems with false belief: Conceptual deficit or linguistic artifact? *Child Development, 61*, 1514–1519.

Liu, D., Wellman, H., Tardif, T., & Sabbagh, M. (2008). Theory of mind development in Chinese children: A meta-analysis of false-belief understanding across cultures and languages. *Developmental Psychology, 44*, 523–531.

Low, J. & Perner, J. (2012). Implicit and explicit theory of mind: State of the art. *British Journal of Developmental Psychology, 30*, 1–13.

Maridaki-Kassotaki, K. & Antonopoulou, K. (2011). Examination of the relationship between false-belief understanding and referential communication skills. *European Journal of Psychology of Education, 26*, 75–84.

Mascaro, O. & Sperber, D. (2009). The moral, epistemic and mindreading components of children's vigilance towards deception. *Cognition, 112*, 367–380.

Mitchell, P., Robinson, D., & Thompson, D. (1999). Children understanding that utterances emanate from minds: using speaker belief to aid interpretation. *Cognition, 72*, 45–66.

Norbury, C. (2005). The relationship between theory of mind and metaphor: Evidence from children with language impairment and autistic spectrum disorders. *British Journal of Developmental Psychology, 23*, 383–399.

Onishi, K. & Baillargeon, R. (2005). Do 15-month-old infants understand false beliefs? *Science, 308*(255), 255–258.

Perner, J. (1991). *Understanding the Representational Man.* Cambridge: The MIT Press.

Perner, J., Aichhorn, M., Kronbichler, M., Staffen, W., & Ladurner, G. (2006). Thinking of mental and other representations: the roles of left and right temporo-parietal junction. *Social Neuroscience, 1*(3–4), 245–258.

Perner, J., Leekham, S., & Wimmer, H. (1987). Three-year-olds' difficulty with false belief: The case for conceptual deficit. *British Journal of Developmental Psychology, 5*, 125–137.

Perner, J. & Ruffman, T. (2005). Infants' insight into the mind: how deep? *Science, 308*, 214–216.

Perner, J. & Wimmer, H. (1985). "John thinks that Mary thinks that ...": attribution of second-order beliefs by 5-to 10-year old children. *Journal of Experimental Child Psychology, 39*, 437–471.

Peterson, C. & Slaughter, V. (2003). Opening windows into the mind: mothers' preference for mental state explanations and children's theory of mind. *Cognitive Development, 18*, 399–429.

Pratt, C. & Bryant, P. (1990). Young children understand that looking leads to knowing (so long they are looking into a single barrel). *Child Development, 61*, 973–982.

Repacholi, B. & Gopnik, A. (1997). Early reasoning about desires: Evidence from 14- and 18-month-olds. *Developmental Psychology, 33*, 12–21.

Resches, M. & Pérez-Pereira, M. (2007). Referential communication abilities and theory of mind development in preschool children. *Journal of Child Language, 34*, 21–52.

Rizzolatti, G. & Sinigaglia, C. (2008). *Mirrors in the Brain: How Our Minds Share Actions and Emotions*. Oxford: Oxford University Press.

Ruffman, T., Garnham, W., Import, A., & Connolly, D. (2001). Does eye gaze indicate implicit knowledge of false belief? Charting transitions in knowledge. *Journal of Experimental Child Psychology, 80*, 201–224.

Ruffman, T., Perner, J., Naito, M., Parkin, L., & Clements, W. (1998). Older (but not younger) siblings facilitate false belief understanding. *Developmental Psychology, 34*, 161–174.

Ruffman, T., Slade, L., & Crowe, E. (2002). The relation between children's and mothers' mental state language and theory of mind understanding. *Child Development, 73*(3), 734–751.

Sabbagh, M. & Callanan, M. (1998). Metarepresentation in action: 3-, 4-, and 5-year-olds developing theories of mind in parent-child conversations. *Developmental Psychology, 34*(3), 491–502.

San Juan, V. & Astington, J. (2012). Bridging the gap between explicit and implicit understanding: How language development promotes the processing and representation of false belief. *British Journal of Developmental Psychology, 30*, 105–122.

Saxe, R. (2013). The new puzzle of theory of mind development. In M. Banaji, & S. Gelman (eds), *Navigating the Social World: What Infants, Children and Other Species can Teach us* (pp. 107–112). Oxford: Oxford University Press.

Saxe, R. & Baron-Cohen, S. (2006). Editorial: The neuroscience of theory of mind. *Social Neuroscience, 1*, i–ix.

Saxe, R. & Kanwisher, N. (2003). People thinking about thinking people: The role of the temporo-parietal junction in "theory of mind." *Neuroimage, 19*, 1835–1842.

Saxe, R., Whitfield-Gabrieli, S., Scholz, J., & Pelphrey, K. (2009). Brain regions for perceiving and reasoning about other people in school-aged children. *Child Development, 80*, 1197–1209.

Scott, R. & Baillargeon, R. (2009). Which penguin is this? Attributing false beliefs about object identity at 18 months. *Child Development, 80*, 1172–1196.

Shatz, M., Diesendruck, G., Martinez-Beck, I., & Akar, D. (2003). The influence of language and socioeconomic status on children's understanding of false belief. *Developmental Psychology, 39*, 717–729.

Siegal, M. & Beattie, K. (1991). Where to look first for children's understanding of false beliefs. *Cognition, 38*, 1–12.

Sodian, B. & Wimmer, H. (1987). Children's understanding of inference as a source of knowledge. *Child Development, 58*, 424–433.

Song, H. J., Onishi, K. H., Baillargeon, R., & Fisher, C. (2008). Can an agent's false belief be corrected by an appropriate communication? Psychological reasoning in 18-month-old infants. *Cognition, 109*, 295–315.

Southgate, V. (2013). Do infants provide evidence that the mirror system is involved in action understanding? *Consciousness and Cognition, 22*, 1114–1121.

Southgate, V., Chevallier, C., & Csibra, G. (2010). Seventeen-month-olds appeal to false beliefs to interpret others' referential communication. *Developmental Science, 13*, 907–912.

Southgate, V., Senju, A., & Csibra, G. 2007. Action anticipation through attribution of false belief by 2-year-olds. *Psychological Science, 18*, 587–592.

Sperber, D. (2000). Metarepresentations in an evolutionary perspective. In D. Sperber (ed), *Metarepresentations: A Multidisciplinary Perspective* (pp. 117–137). New York: Oxford University Press.

Sperber, D. & Wilson, D. (1995). *Relevance: Communication and Cognition*. Oxford: Blackwell.

Sperber, D. & Wilson, D. (2002). Pragmatics, modularity and mind-reading. *Mind and Language, 17*, 3–23.

Sullivan, K., Zaitchik, D., & Tager-Flusberg, H. (1994). Preschoolers can attribute second-order beliefs. *Developmental Psychology, 30*(3), 395–402.

Surian, L., Baron-Cohen, S., & van der Lely, H. (1996). Are autistic children deaf to Gricean maxims? *Cognitive Neuropsychiatry, 1*, 55–71.

Surian, L., Caldi, S., & Sperber, D. (2007). Attribution of beliefs by 13-month-old infants. *Psychological science, 18*, 580–586.

Surian, L. & Leslie, A. (1999). Competence and performance in false belief understanding: a comparison of autistic and normal 3-year-old children. *British Journal of Developmental Psychology, 17*, 141–155.

Wellman, H. (1990). *The Child's Theory of Mind*. Cambridge: The MIT Press.

Wellman, H., Cross, D., & Watson, J. (2001). Meta-analysis of theory-of-mind development: the truth about false belief. *Child Development, 72*(3), 655–684.

Wilson, D. (forthcoming). Pragmatic processes and metarepresentational abilities: the case of verbal irony. In T. Matsui (ed), *Pragmatics and Theory of Mind*. Amsterdam: John Benjamins.

Wimmer, H. & J. Perner (1983). Beliefs about beliefs: Representation and constraining function of wrong beliefs in young children's understanding of deception. *Cognition, 13*, 103–114.

6

UNDERSTANDING NON-LITERAL LANGUAGE

Metaphor and irony

An important dimension of pragmatic competencies from a cognitive perspective is the ability of listeners to understand a different meaning from the one conveyed literally by sentences, for instance in the case of metaphors and irony. In classical rhetoric, metaphor and irony both fall into the category of tropes and Grice also analyzed them together as cases of violations of the first maxim of quality. Recent pragmatic accounts of these phenomena have demonstrated, however, that metaphor and irony serve distinct functions and appeal to different cognitive processes. In this chapter, we address them in turn, starting with metaphor in Section 6.1 and following with irony in Section 6.2. In both cases, we discuss the way children start to understand and produce these figures of speech as well as the factors influencing comprehension. We conclude that acquisition data confirm the differences between metaphor and irony put forward by recent pragmatic accounts.

6.1. Metaphor

We start with a brief overview of the main contemporary accounts of metaphor provided by cognitive linguistics and relevance theory (Section 6.1.1). We go on to discuss the difficulty of studying children's spontaneous productions of metaphors (Section 6.1.2) and review studies of children's understanding of metaphors in controlled experiments (Section 6.1.3). We also discuss the factors influencing children's performance in these tasks (Section 6.1.4).

6.1.1. Theoretical accounts of metaphor

In his brief discussion of metaphor and irony, Grice (1967/1989) associated both figures of speech to instances of blatant violations of the first maxim of quality (i.e. "do not say what you believe to be false"), triggering conversational implicatures. Indeed, when a speaker uses either a metaphoric or an ironic statement, he purposefully asserts a proposition that is literally false in order to communicate something else. Inherent in the Gricean account is the idea that deriving a metaphorical or ironic interpretation requires first to access and then to reject literal meaning. Thus, in this view, endorsed also by Searle (1979), the non-literal meaning conveyed by metaphors and irony is always secondary compared with the literal meaning of sentences that are used to convey them, and is accessed only if the latter does not make sense in context. The prediction that non-literal meaning is only secondary compared with literal meaning is, however, not corroborated by empirical studies of the way speakers process metaphorical meaning. For example, Glucksberg (2001) asked subjects to judge the literal truth or falsity of three different types of statements: literally true statements (1), literally false statements (2), and metaphors (3).

(1) Some birds are robins.
(2) Some birds are apples.
(3) Some birds are singers.

Glucksberg reasoned that if people can ignore metaphorical meanings when they have to perform a judgment of the sentence's literal meaning, then statements (2) and (3) should lead to similar reaction times, as they are both literally false. If on the other hand people cannot ignore metaphorical meanings, type (3) statements should take longer to process than type (2) statements, because they are literally false but metaphorically true. Results indicate that subjects do indeed take longer to judge statements like (3) as literally false compared with statements like (2), an effect that Glucksberg attributes to the interference created by metaphorical meaning. Many other processing experiments confirm that not only does metaphorical meaning not take longer to process compared with literal meaning, but also that hearers cannot refrain from accessing a metaphorical interpretation even when the task they are asked to perform does not require them to do so, as in Glucksberg's experiment (e.g. Gibbs, 1994, 2002; Gibbs & Colston, 2012). In view of these empirical findings, the classical rhetoric and Gricean accounts of metaphors are no longer supported. Current linguistic and psychological models of metaphor processing share the assumption that metaphors are a natural component of human communication that is not secondary compared with the literal meaning of utterances.

One such account is cognitive linguistics (e.g. Fauconnier, 1985; Gibbs, 1994; Kövecses, 2002; Lakoff, 1987; Lakoff & Johnson, 1980; Talmy, 2000), a theoretical model stating that metaphors represent a fundamental aspect of human cognition and that people use metaphors in communication because they think and even feel metaphorically. In this view, the formal structures of language also reflect the way concepts are organized and categorized in the mind. In Tendahl and Gibbs's words (2008: 1825) "metaphor is not merely a figure of speech, but a specific mental mapping and a form of neural coactivation that influences a good deal of how people think, reason, and imagine in everyday life." The existing metaphors in language thus reflect conceptual mappings between abstract domains of knowledge, such as time or emotions and concrete knowledge such as motion in space. In addition, cognitive linguistics states that metaphors are not simply the mapping of a single element from a source to a target domain, but include relational structures and inferences as well. For example, many metaphorical expressions used to describe a love relationship as in (4) to (6) follow the structured metaphor LOVE IS A JOURNEY, a metaphor mapping the domain of emotions with the domain of motion in space.

(4) We have reached a dead end.
(5) We are at the crossroads.
(6) You and I go a long way.

From a developmental perspective, cognitive linguistics predicts that young children should possess at least a rudimentary ability to draw cross-domain mappings, as it is a fundamental component of human thought that is involved in many aspects of linguistic and cognitive development. In addition, Tendahl and Gibbs (2008: 1856) noted that "cognitive linguists assume that early metaphor development is primarily based on correlations in embodied experience." For example, through their sensory experiences, very young children experience a correlation between their feeling of affection and the warmth associated with the embrace of a parent or a caretaker. At first, these domains are undifferentiated but as children get older, they retain only some links between these domains, which form the sensory basis of their early metaphors. Another prediction made by cognitive linguistics is that children should learn the meanings of metaphorical expressions faster when they rely on well-known conceptual metaphors, for example, MORE IS UP or SEEING IS KNOWING, than when they are not related to these structured metaphors. We will see how these predictions can be assessed in the next section.

In the context of relevance theory, metaphor has also been an active area of research (e.g. Carston, 2002, 2010; Sperber & Wilson, 2008; Vega Moreno, 2007; Wilson, 2010; Wilson & Carston, 2007). According to relevance theory, metaphors represent a case of loose talk that arise in verbal communication from the mapping between complex thoughts and the existing linguistic means to convey them. Relevance theory does not consider metaphors as a unified and natural kind, but rather as a phenomenon that diverges only in scale from other cases of loose talk such as approximation and hyperbole. One of the reasons why metaphors are assimilated with other kinds of loose talk comes from the observation that the same sentence can convey an approximation, a hyperbole, or a metaphor depending on context. For example, in some contexts, (7) could convey an approximation if Peter is not literally starving but only very hungry. In other contexts, if Peter were only slightly hungry at the time of speaking, the same utterance would convey a hyperbole. In other cases still, if Peter were not at all hungry at the time but did simply not make a good living and found it difficult to make ends meet, (7) would convey a metaphor.

(7) Peter is starving.

This example illustrates the fact that the boundary between the various types of loose talk is difficult to draw and that approximation, hyperbole, and metaphor all rest on the application of a same principle of broadening of lexically encoded concepts to various degrees, leading to the creation of occasion-specific or 'ad hoc' concepts (see Barsalou, 1987; Sperber & Wilson, 1998).

According to Wilson (2010), "typically, a loose interpretation [is] based on a few highly accessible encyclopedic properties [that] will satisfy the hearer's expectation of relevance." For example, in (8), the ad hoc concept ROSE* (noted by convention with a star in order to differentiate it from the lexically encoded concept) includes only part of the conceptual properties of the lexically encoded concept ROSE: the beauty, the fragility, but not the fact of being a vegetal or of having petals.

(8) Mary is a rose.

Gernsbacher and Robertson (1999) provided empirical confirmation that metaphor interpretation requires both the selection of salient conceptual properties and the suppression of some irrelevant ones. Testing adult subjects' reaction times in a statement verification task, they find that subjects are faster to verify the statement 'sharks are tenacious' after reading the metaphor 'lawyers are sharks'. Conversely, subjects are slower in verifying the statement 'sharks are good swimmers' after reading the same metaphor. This result provides some indication that metaphors involve both the activation and the inhibition of some conceptual properties of lexically encoded concepts. Thus, similarly to all other utterances, metaphors are processed by looking for the most accessible interpretations satisfying the hearer's expectations of relevance, and do not rely on a distinct derivation procedure.

From a developmental perspective, the lexical pragmatics account proposed by relevance theory implies that understanding metaphors requires several linguistic and pragmatic skills: (1) the ability to draw inferences in order to construct the relevant ad hoc concept, (2) the ability to integrate contextual information as input for the derivation of inferences, and (3) knowledge of conceptual information related to the topic and vehicle of the metaphor. Each of these factors can prevent young children from understanding and producing metaphors. However, it seems likely that the ability to draw inferences does not represent an obstacle for children's understanding of metaphors (see Pouscoulous, 2011). Indeed, in many other domains of development, children have demonstrated their ability to draw inferences from a very early age. We discussed in Chapter 2 the way children use their inferential skills to make correct object-labels pairings from a very early age. In Chapter 3, we also argued that young children were able to use inferential skills to understand the meaning of some unconventional indirect speech act such as hints. Therefore, it seems likely that children's ability to understand and produce metaphors is not limited by their inferential skills but rather rests on the accessibility of the contextual and conceptual information on which the metaphor is built. We will discuss the role of these factors in the next section (Section 6.1.2).

To conclude, even though they operate from very different frameworks, cognitive linguistics and relevance theory share a number of important assumptions about metaphors, and such convergences have been discussed in the literature (Gibbs & Tendahl, 2006; Tendahl & Gibbs, 2008; Wilson, 2010). Scholars from both schools of thought emphasize that in both approaches, metaphors are not considered to be special cases of communication, contrary to the classical rhetoric view. Both approaches also recognize the central role of concepts for the construction of metaphors, but differ in how they conceive their origin. While cognitive linguists believe that metaphors originate in thought and reflect conceptual mappings in the mind, relevance theorists contend that their origins lie in verbal communication and in the creation of occasion-specific concepts that in some cases become conventionalized. Wilson (2010) noted that because of this diverging view, both approaches have focused on different types of metaphors: cognitive linguistics has mainly addressed metaphors reflecting conceptual mappings as in (4) to (6), while relevance theory has mainly discussed comparison metaphors as in (8). Both approaches represent therefore complementary views on metaphors that address related but partially distinct questions, and that are to a large extent compatible. We argue in Section 6.1.4 that acquisition data corroborate both theoretical views.

6.1.2. Do young children produce metaphors?

From a very early age, children's linguistic productions include non-literal uses of words that resemble metaphors. For example, Winner, McCarthy, Kleinman, and Gardner (1979) reported the case of an 18-month-old child who called a toy car a snake while twisting it up his mother's arm. Similarly, Winner (1988) reported the case of a child who used the expression 'fire engine in my tummy' in order to refer to his stomach ache. Another example given by Winner (1988) is a child saying 'I am an N' while running up and down the stairs. Such examples suggest that children may have the ability to use words in a non-literal manner from an early age. However, it has often been pointed out in the literature that these early usages do not necessarily represent genuine cases of metaphors. An alternative explanation is that these productions represent cases of overextensions rather than metaphors. Indeed, young children often tend to use words with a broader denotation than adults, for example, by calling all round objects a ball (e.g. Bloom, 2000; Clark, 1973, 2003). The difference between metaphors and overextensions is that children who overextend words do not know the real name for an object. For this reason, overextensions stop as soon as children learn the appropriate word.

Winner (1979) studied the speech productions of one child between the age of 2;3 and 4;10 using corpus data, applying systematic criteria to exclude anomalies and overextensions in order to identify genuine productions of metaphors. Non-literal uses of words were categorized as over-extensions according to the following criteria: (1) the word was used for a set of similar referents and (2) there was no evidence that the child knew the correct label or literal name for the object. Non-literal uses of words were labeled as metaphors under the following conditions: (1) either prior or after the non-literal use of a word, the child renamed the object with its literal name; and (2) the object was transformed through a pretend gesture and named according to this gesture, for example, if the child put a banana on his ear like a telephone and then uttered the word 'phone'.

During the 112 hours of recording from the corpus, the child studied by Winner produced 185 non-literal uses of words satisfying her criteria for metaphors. All of them corresponded to cases of renaming of familiar objects with other nouns. These metaphors were either part of the child's symbolic play or instances of sensory metaphors arising from perceived physical similarity, mostly related to the object shape. For example, the child named a pencil a 'big needle' and the letter J 'a cane'. Winner noted a developmental pattern going from more metaphors related to pretense at the age of two to a majority of sensory metaphors at the age of four. In order to test the generalization of these findings, Winner et al. (1979) studied longitudinal speech samples from two other children. Their results indicate that symbolic play metaphors declined with age in one of the children but not the other. The authors concluded that early metaphors are rooted either in pretend play or in the perception of sensory resemblances. Children's preference for one of these modes might reflect individual differences in style.

Vosniadou (1987) argued that Winner's criteria may not be adequate to assess children's production of metaphors. On the one hand, some cases of overextensions should be treated as genuine metaphors, as one of the functions of metaphors in adult speech is precisely to express something that cannot be easily conveyed by existing words and conventional metaphors are often created from the need to fill gaps in the lexicon. Thus, she argues that what is needed is a criterion to separate literal from non-literal overextensions. On the other hand, not all cases of renaming labeled by Winner as metaphors are necessarily genuine metaphors, as children may in some cases simply compare two objects as being literally similar. In that case, she argues that what is needed is the proof that the child is aware of the fact that the two objects compared belong to different conceptual domains. Vosniadou and Ortony (1983) designed an experiment to test preschoolers' ability to understand literal and non-literal comparisons. They found that by the age of four, children can distinguish between literal and non-literal resemblances. For instance, in a sentence completion task involving comparisons, children preferred the non-literal comparison (9) over the literal comparison (10). In another sentence completion task involving categorization as in (11) and (12), they preferred the literal (11) over the non-literal choice (12).

(9) Rain is like tears.
(10) Rain is like snow.
(11) Rain is the same kind of thing as snow.
(12) Rain is the same kind of thing as tears.

This experiment tends to confirm that by the age of four, children can distinguish between literal and metaphorical resemblance. In addition, Vosniadou (1987: 17) noted that "it is possible that younger children could do better in tasks in which the comparisons were embedded in a meaningful context, or in non-verbal tasks." We will come back to the influence of context and the nature of the task on children's understanding of metaphors in Section 6.1.3.

To summarize, assessing children's ability to use metaphors based on their spontaneous productions is a complex issue, as it is in most cases impossible to ascertain that children truly intend to convey a metaphorical meaning by the non-literal use of a word. However, most authors agree that young children do intend to use words in non-literal manners at least in some occasions. For example, Bloom (2000: 37) stated that "sometimes it is clear that children use words in a non-literal fashion, as when a two-year-old says that wheeling searchlights on top of a building are 'like a helicopter'." Therefore, despite the numerous limitations of children's early productions, a rudimentary ability to produce some metaphors is clearly within their reach, as predicted by both cognitive linguistics and relevance theory. These results must also be complemented by data from comprehension experiments in order to get a full picture of the processes underlying children's acquisition of metaphors.

6.1.3. When do children understand metaphors?

Early studies of metaphor comprehension concluded that children do not understand them until very late in their development. In one of them, Asch and Nerlove (1960) asked 3- to 12-year-old children questions about the meaning of dual-function adjectives such as 'cold' or 'sweet', which can either refer to a physical property or a psychological trait. They found that while preschoolers understand the physical properties of these adjectives, they fail to perceive their psychological meaning. Thus, three-year-old children deny that a person can be sweet or cold. By the age of five or six, children do apply the adjectives to people but only with their physical meaning. For these children, a cold person is a person who feels physically cold. It is only by the age of 11 or 12 that children understand both meanings and relate them.

However, more recent studies lead to the conclusion that children understand metaphor much earlier than these early studies indicate, and discuss several limitations with the procedures used in early experiments. One problem is that in many of them, metaphors were presented to children out of context, and this does not correspond to the way metaphors are interpreted in normal communication. In a set of experiments, Vosniadou, Ortony, Reynolds, and Wilson (1984) assessed four- to eight-year-old children's understanding of metaphors in the context of short stories. They found that young children understand metaphors better when their meaning represents the probable outcome of the story than when it contains a less predictable outcome. This provides some confirmation that children use contextual cues to infer the metaphorical meaning of sentences and that in an adequate context, even young children display an understanding of metaphors.

Another well-identified problem comes from the nature of the task used to assess children's comprehension (e.g. Gibbs, 1994; Pouscoulous, 2011; Vosniadou, 1987; Winner, 1988). In many of the early experiments, children were asked to perform metalinguistic judgments and to paraphrase metaphorical meaning. This is a very difficult task for young children (see Chapter 2) that prevents them from demonstrating some understanding of metaphors. Studies relying on a simpler task reveal that by the age of three, children do understand some metaphors. For example, Pearson (1990) used a repetition task to assess three- to five-year-old children's ability to understand literal, metaphorical, and semantically anomalous sentences matched for length, vocabulary, and sentence structure. Results indicate that even three-year-olds display a similar ability to repeat literal and metaphorical sentences. By contrast, across all age groups, children had poorer performances with semantically anomalous sentences. This experiment provides indirect evidence that young children can process metaphorical meaning. Vosiadou et al. (1984) used an act-out task, another procedure representing a simpler alternative to metalinguistic tasks. Their results confirm that even the youngest children in their study, who were only four-years old, can understand metaphors when the task is made optimally simple.

6.1.4. What are the factors influencing children's understanding of metaphors?

According to cognitive linguistics, children's early understanding of metaphors should be related to their bodily experience (Gibbs, 2006). This prediction finds some confirmation in the literature. Winner (1988) found, for example, that there is a difference between the ability to perceive sensory and relational metaphors. While in the former case children can rely on their bodily experience, in the latter case they must possess the required world knowledge to build the metaphor. She concluded that "verbal metaphors based on innately perceived sensory similarities are understood at as soon an age as can be tested, whereas nonsensory metaphors are only understood if children possess sufficient knowledge of domains in question" (1988: 88).

Another prediction made by cognitive linguistics is that as soon as children understand a conceptual metaphor, they should be able to apply it to different domains. A number of studies confirm that conceptual metaphors play an important role in children's understanding of metaphorical expressions. For example, Ozçalişcan (2005) tested three- to five-year-old Turkish-speaking children's ability to understand metaphors structured by the source domain MOTION IN SPACE across three target domains (time, sickness, and ideas) and depending on the degree of conventionality of the metaphorical expression, determined by the frequency of the verb used. The tasks involved story continuations and semi-structured interviews. Results indicate that three-year-olds fail to understand all the tested metaphors; four-year-olds understand them provided that the context is set to support the metaphorical interpretation, and five-year-olds are able to verbally reason about the metaphorical mappings. This study provides some confirmation for cognitive linguistics, as no effect of the target domain was found in any age group. This means that once children develop the understanding of a structured metaphor in a source domain, they can apply it to various target domains with equal ease, whether the metaphor is constructed with a high- or a low-frequency verb. This study also confirms that metaphors are acquired early and that context plays a crucial role for young children's understanding of them. In this experiment, children showed an understanding of metaphors by the age of four, but it is possible that the meta-linguistic nature of the tasks prevented three-year-olds from demonstrating some understanding of these metaphors as well.

Keil (1986) also studied the role of conceptual domains for children's acquisition of metaphors. He compared five-, eight- and nine-year-old children's ability to understand metaphors across different source and target domains. His results confirm that once a domain is acquired, all the metaphors related to it are understood in a synchronous manner. However, different conceptual domains are acquired at different ages. For example, preschoolers already master the animate versus inanimate distinction and this leads to their understanding of metaphors such as 'the car is tired'. By contrast, preschoolers do not understand metaphors when they lack the underlying conceptual distinctions, as for example between physical and abstract properties of objects. Finally, Gentner (1988) tested children's interpretation of comparative metaphors involving shared object attributes such as 'a cloud is like a marshmallow' and relational metaphors involving shared relational structures but few shared attributes as for example 'a cloud is like a sponge'. Results indicate a developmental shift from a more attribute-based interpretation of metaphors to a more relational-based interpretation, similar to that of adults.

Taken together, these studies confirm that once a domain is acquired, children understand all metaphors that pertain to it in a synchronous manner. They also confirm more generally the importance of conceptual knowledge for children's understanding of metaphors. These findings are therefore also compatible with the account of metaphor provided by relevance theory. In order to construct the appropriate ad hoc concept, children must have access to the relevant conceptual properties of the lexically encoded concept. Relevance theory also contends that metaphors are constructed on a subset of contextually salient properties of lexically encoded concepts. The importance of this factor has also been confirmed in developmental data. Evans and Gamble (1988) asked eight-, ten- and twelve-year-olds to generate a list of attribute saliency for a number of terms forming the topics and the vehicles of metaphors. Six weeks later, they asked the same children to verbally explain metaphors containing these terms. Their results indicate that for all age groups, children's incorrect understanding of metaphors was explained by the attributes that they listed for the concepts involved. This experiment confirms that children's understanding of metaphors is related to the properties that they saliently associate with concepts. However, according to relevance theory, salience is context-dependent, and this experiment has not tested children's ability to integrate contextual information in order to modulate the salience of the properties used to build a metaphorical interpretation.

In a nutshell, the comprehension experiments summarized in this section indicate that even young children aged three to four can demonstrate some understanding of metaphors when the task demands are kept minimal and they possess the required conceptual knowledge. These findings are compatible with both cognitive linguistics and relevance theory, but contradict the classical rhetoric view stating that metaphors are argumentative devices limited to specific communicative situations.

6.2. Irony

In classical rhetoric, irony is treated on a par with metaphor, as a figure of speech consisting in asserting something false in order to communicate something else. However, contrary to metaphor, the non-literal meaning conveyed by irony must not be understood as resembling the literal meaning in some way but as standing in opposition with it. For Grice, metaphors and irony are also similar, in that they both represent blatant violations of the first maxim of quality. In this section, we first present the main features characterizing verbal irony (Section 6.2.1), arguing that they cannot be accounted for by a classical rhetoric or a Gricean account. We then turn to acquisition data and describe the few studies that have addressed children's production of ironic statements (Section 6.2.2), before reviewing the body of literature on children's understanding of irony (Section 6.2.3), and finally discussing the role of linguistic and contextual factors affecting children's comprehension of irony (Section 6.2.4).

6.2.1. What does it take to be ironic?

Wilson (2006, 2012) observed that ironic statements display three distinctive features, none of them shared with metaphors. First, ironic utterances are always used to convey the speaker's negative attitude. Second, irony is most often used to criticize or complain when a situation does not correspond to some norm-based expectations. The negative bias of irony is noticeable from the fact that it is more common to make an ironic remark to criticize a behavior than to praise. For example, while (13) is easily perceived as an ironic comment conveying a criticism of someone who has done something wrong, (14) is more difficult to associate with an ironic comment used to convey that someone has many qualities.

(13) He is such a great guy.
(14) He is such a loser.

The third feature of irony is the specific intonation that is often associated with it, the 'ironic tone of voice'. However, the phonological characteristics of this tone of voice are still a matter for debate in the literature. According to Bryant and Fox Tree (2002: 101), the ironic tone of voice "is thought to be recognized through nasalization, slowed speech rate, prolonged syllables, and other particular prosodic features." Bryant (2010) analyzed in addition the presence of prosodic contrasts (e.g. in mean amplitude and mean syllable duration) between ironic utterances and the utterances immediately preceding them. All utterances from his study came from dialogs spontaneously produced by speakers interacting in dyads. His results indicate that speakers use a prosodic contrast more often when the sequence involves an ironic utterance compared with two adjacent non-ironic utterances. However, the only feature that changed consistently across speakers is speed, as ironic statements are spoken more slowly than preceding speech. Thus, a prosodic contrast between two utterances is an indicator of irony, but the prosodic contours of ironic utterances are variable across speakers.

In classical rhetoric, irony is defined as utterances in which the speaker means the opposite of what he literally says. Sperber and Wilson (1981, 2012) and Wilson (2006) argued, however, that meaning the contrary to what one literally says does not automatically lead to being ironic. For example, if Sarah utters (9) in order to inform Mark that the door of their flat is not closed, the effect achieved is absurd but not ironic.

(15) Look, the door is closed.

Conversely, some utterances are ironic even when the speaker does not mean the contrary of what he says. For example, if Jane addresses (16) to her husband who has just been shouting at her, she does not mean to say that she hates when he is kind to her, but rather that his attitude is precisely not kind.

(16) I love when you are kind to me.

Thus, another definition of irony seems necessary to account for these cases. In the framework of relevance theory, Sperber and Wilson (1981, 2012) argued that the three features of irony described above could be explained in a unified manner by the fact that ironic statements always echo a thought or utterance attributed to someone else with the goal of conveying a dissociative attitude. For example, if (15) were uttered after Mark had assured Sarah that the door was closed, then Sarah's statement would be perceived as ironic, because she would be echoing Mark's previous remark and mocking him. In this framework, the prosody of ironic utterances is also an indication of the speaker's dissociative attitude, because of the contrast introduced with the prosody used in the previous utterance.

The main alternative account to the echoic theory of irony is the pretense theory (Clark & Gerrig, 1984; Currie, 2006; Recanati, 2007). According to this account, the speaker producing an ironic statement is not performing a speech act but merely pretending to do so in order to mock the speakers who would perform it or take it seriously. Thus, recognizing an ironic statement involves the ability to identify that the speaker is pretending to assert something in order to convey a mocking attitude. Wilson (2006) noted, however, that while some cases of irony do involve pretense, this account is not sufficient to explain some cases of irony such as (15), when the ironic intent is clearly dependent on its echoing a previous statement.

In the literature, several models of irony include both an echoic and a pretense component (e.g. Kumon-Nakamura, Glucksberg & Brown, 1995) thus demonstrating that the two accounts are to some extent compatible and even complementary. In addition, in empirical studies, both accounts find some confirmation. For example, Gibbs (1986) assessed the role of echoes for the processing of irony and found that people do indeed process ironic statements faster and recall them better when they include an explicit echo than when the echo is only implicit. Kreuz and Glucksberg (1989) confirmed the importance of echoes, and found in addition that this criterion is related to the normative bias toward criticism. When the ironic statement is used to make a positive comment, it is perceived as more ironic when it echoes a previous remark than when it does not. But when it is a criticism, it is judged to be equally ironic whether it explicitly echoes a previous comment or not. This result tends to confirm that irony is more salient when a criticism is conveyed, and therefore subjects do not need to rely on an explicit source of echo to perceive it as such. It also confirms that the identification of irony relies on a set of contextual and linguistic cues, and that the importance of each of them depends on the presence or absence of other cues.

Finally, empirical studies comparing the way metaphor and irony are processed confirm that these two phenomena are very dissimilar. For example, Colston and Gibbs (2002) have compared the way hearers process statements like (17) when they are uttered in a context that makes them either metaphorical or ironical.

(17) This one is really sharp.

Results indicate that people take significantly less time to read the same statement when it is metaphorical than when it is ironical. This result provides an indication that metaphor and irony do not rely on the same mechanisms and that irony is more complex to process than metaphor. Colston and Gibbs (2002) have also assessed the influence of the capacity to attribute second-order beliefs on the understanding of metaphor and irony. They asked subjects to rate their agreement with statements explicitly mentioning the speaker's belief about another belief as in (18) and found that they agreed more with such statements when the sentence is ironic than metaphorical.

(18) The teacher's remark reflects her multiple beliefs in that she is both referring to her present belief that the scissors are not sharp and her prior belief that the scissors should be sharp.

This indicates that irony, but not metaphor, relies on second-order beliefs. In the same experiment, subjects also agreed more with the fact that the ironic statements are uttered with the goal of mocking than metaphoric statements as in (19), and thus confirming that irony involves a specific speaker's attitude that is not part of the communication of metaphors.

(19) The reason that the teacher possibly refers to her prior belief that the scissors should be sharp is to mock this expectation given that the scissors are not sharp.

Finally, the authors also assessed whether people perceive the fact that irony and metaphor involve a form of pretense as in (20).

(20) The teacher's remark reflects the fact that she is only pretending that the scissors are sharp.

They found that subjects agree significantly more that irony involves pretense than metaphor, thus confirming that pretense is part of people's intuitive conception of irony.

Other processing studies indicate in addition that the non-literal meaning of ironic statements is not secondary compared with their literal meaning, as subjects cannot ignore it even when asked to perform a judgment about the literal meaning of a sentence (Dews & Winner, 1999; Gibbs, 1986). These results thus confirm that in all cases of non-literal language uses such as metaphor, irony but also indirect speech acts (see Chapter 3, Section 3.1) there is no priority of literal over non-literal meaning.

6.2.2. Are children ironic?

Very few studies have addressed children's production of irony. In one of them, Recchia, Howe, Ross, and Alexander (2010) analyzed the production of irony by four- and six-year-old children during interactions taking place at home with their parents. Their data included 40 families, recorded during six or seven 90-minutes sessions. In about half of the observations, children interacted with both their parents while in the other half only mothers were present. For data analysis, the authors merged under the category of irony many different figures of speech such as sarcasm, understatements, rhetorical questions, and hyperboles. However, only sarcasm, defined by the authors as "an utterance in which the literal and the intended meanings of the statements differed in valence (i.e. are opposite to some degree)" (2010: 262), meets the defining criteria of irony presented in the last section. Indeed, while in some cases ironic remarks can include a hyperbole (21) or an understatement (22), Wilson (2012) noted that the latter figures are not intrinsically ironic and rely on distinct pragmatic processes. For the sake of consistency, we therefore only discuss the case of sarcasm.

(21) You are the greatest genius of all times.
(22) Of course, you only made a tiny, insignificant mistake.

Recchia et al. found that parents do use sarcasm with their children and that children from both age groups show some understanding of it by their conversational responses. In addition, six-year-olds use sarcasm a lot more frequently than four-year-olds, and even more frequently than their parents. However, sarcasm is globally less used than the other figures of speech in this dataset. By contrast, Dews and Winner (1997) observed that sarcasm is the main form of irony directed to both adults and children in television programs, thus providing some indication of its salience in the input.

Pexman, Zdrazilova, McConnachie, Deater-Deckard, and Petrill (2009) also studied the production of irony by children aged 3 to 15, while they are interacting with a sibling and a parent during eight-minute sessions. They found that about one-third of the families use verbal irony at least once during the session and that children start to use it by the age of five. They noted in addition that children's production of irony is most closely related to its use in their family rather than to other measures of cognitive and vocabulary development. Finally, Lucariello and Mindolovich (1995) tested six- and eight-year-olds' production of irony in a story continuation task. Their results confirmed that six-year-olds can produce ironic statements when they are familiar with the type of event described in the story (e.g. a birthday party). Eight-year-olds produce more complex forms of irony than six-year-olds, but even at this age, children's ability to produce adult-like forms of irony is still limited, suggesting that the acquisition processes continue until a later age.

In sum, the production studies reviewed in this section indicate that irony emerges in children's speech between the ages of five and six and keeps on developing during several years after that. In the next section, we will address the issue of whether children already have a genuine understanding of the communicative functions and speaker attitude related to irony when they start producing it.

6.2.3. When do children understand irony?

The important body of literature that has investigated children's understanding of irony has produced conflicting results regarding the age at which children master it. While some studies conclude that children do not fully understand irony before the age of 12 or 13 (e.g. Demorest, Silberstein, Gardner & Winner, 1983; Demorest, Meyer, Phelps, Gardner & Winner, 1984), others find that children understand it by the age of six to eight (e.g. Ackerman, 1983; Winner, 1988) and others still find that a form of understanding already emerges between five and six (e.g. Dews et al., 1996; Keenan & Quigley, 1999; Nakassis & Snedeker, 2002).

While part of this discrepancy can be related to methodological differences between the studies (as discussed by Creusere, 1999), such as the measures used to assess comprehension and the salience of the cues contained in the stimuli, Nakassis and Snedeker (2002) noted that these differences are also due to an ambiguity about what understanding irony means. While some studies equate the understanding of irony with the recognition of the speaker's negative attitude, others require that children understand the intended meaning or make second-order belief judgments. These measures target different components of irony, and it is therefore not surprising that children do not show evidence of understanding them at the same age.

In spite of these differences between studies, there is a well-established sequence in the literature between children's understanding of the falsity of the ironic statements and their understanding of the reasons for producing it. Children first understand that the speaker who produces an ironic statement believes something different from what he says around the age of five or six (Ackerman, 1983; Hancock, Dunham & Purdy, 2000). But it is only at the age of six to eight (or even later depending on the salience of the cues) that they understand the speaker's intention to criticize or tease as well as the negative attitude conveyed by irony. An important body of literature has established that the ability to recognize the speaker's intention is related to second-order theory of mind abilities, enabling children to understand that the speaker who produces a false statement for ironic purposes is not lying but wants his addressee to recognize his intention (Filippova & Astington, 2008; Happé, 1993; Sullivan, Winner & Hopfield, 1995; Winner & Leekam, 1991). The sequence between children's understanding of the speaker's belief, intention, and attitude is, however, found only for cases of ironic criticism but not ironic praise (Pexman & Glenwright, 2007). In the latter case, the two components are understood simultaneously, but the recognition of the speaker's attitude is delayed. Pexman and Glenwright noted that this difference could be due to the fact that ironic praises do not allude to norms or expectations and that their falsity is therefore harder to recognize without identifying the speaker's intention.

6.2.4. What are the factors influencing children's understanding of irony?

One of the cues that could help children to identify irony is the specific tone of voice that often goes with it. Several studies have assessed the importance of prosody for children's understanding of irony, with mixed findings. While some of them report that prosody plays a crucial role even for children aged 8 or 10 (e.g. Capelli, Nakagawa & Madden, 1990; Glenwright, Parackel, Cheung & Nilsen, 2013; Groot et al., 1995; Keenan & Quigley, 1999), others find no influence at all of this factor, even for younger children of five or six (e.g. Ackerman, 1983; Demorest et al., 1984; Sullivan et al., 1995; Winner & Leekam, 1991). Nakassis and Snedeker (2002) noted that these conflicting findings could be due to the fact that several positive and negative tones of voice are compatible with irony, and that a proper analysis of this effect must compare them. In their experiment, Nakassis and Snedeker included both a positive and a negative intonation and found that neither of them systematically influences children's understanding of irony. However, while intonation is not intrinsically a facilitating factor, it has an influence when it is related with other factors, more precisely when the information it conveys is not compatible with the literal meaning of the sentence. This result thus confirms the role of contrasts for the recognition of irony.

Irony also implies a normative bias toward negative comments such as criticisms and complaints. Several studies have compared children's understanding of ironic criticism and ironic praise, with the result that children understand ironic criticism better than ironic praise (de Groot et al., 1995; Hancock et al., 2000; Pexman & Glenwright, 2007). Nakassis and Snedeker (2002) reported, however, that children in their study perform equally well with both forms of irony. They attributed this result to the fact that the contextual cues in their study made the ironic intentions extremely clear, thus facilitating comprehension.

Finally, according to relevance theory, irony involves a form of echo of an attributed thought or utterance. Keegan and Quigley (1999) have tested the importance of echoes for 6- to 10-year-old children's understanding of irony. They found that children understand irony better when the ironic statement is an explicit echo of a previous sentence than when it is implicit. However, the effect is found only when the ironic sentences are pronounced with a neutral prosody. De Groot et al. (1995) also tested the role of echo and found that children's understanding of ironic praise is greatly facilitated when the ironic statement explicitly echoes a previous sentence. These results indicate that the role of echoes is greater in the absence of other types of cues (i.e. ironic prosody and normative bias).

To summarize, the developmental studies reviewed above indicate that several factors such as prosody, explicitness of echo, and normative bias all enhance children's understanding of irony. The role of these factors depends on the salience of other cues as well as the measures used to assess comprehension. When all cues are optimal, children can understand irony from the age of 6 but their comprehension continues to develop until 12 or 13 for the subtlest cases.

6.3. Synthesis

The acquisition data presented in this chapter indicate that metaphor and irony are acquired at a different age and rely on different cognitive processes. While children already have some understanding of metaphors at the age of three to four, they do not understand that ironic statements convey a literally false meaning until the age of five or six. It is in addition only later that children understand the speaker's intention and attitude conveyed by irony. The main difference between metaphor and irony is that understanding metaphors does not require a different interpretation process from other utterances, because they rely on the same pragmatic processes of lexical narrowing and broadening. Children already possess the necessary inferential skills to derive metaphorical meanings from a very early age. Their progressive understanding of metaphors is dependent on their possession of the conceptual knowledge that forms the basis of cross-domains mappings and the salience of contextual cues. In contrast, understanding irony rests on specific cognitive processes, as it requires the recognition of the speaker's attitude toward an echoic thought or utterance. Recognizing the speaker's ironic intention involves advanced theory of mind abilities as well as social knowledge about norm-based expectations.

References

Ackerman, B. (1983). Form and function in children's understanding of ironic utterances. *Journal of Experimental Child Psychology, 35*, 487–508.

Asch, S. & Nerlove, H. (1960). The development of double function terms in children. In B. Kaplan, & S. Wapner (eds), *Perspectives in Psychological Theory* (pp. 185–201). New York: International Universities Press.

Barsalou, L. (1987). The instability of graded structure in concepts. In U. Neisser (ed), *Concepts and Conceptual Development* (pp. 101–140). New York: Cambridge University Press.

Bloom, P. (2000). *How Children Learn the Meaning of Words*. Cambridge: MIT Press.

Bryant, G. (2010). Prosodic contrasts in ironic speech. *Discourse Processes, 47*, 545–566.

Bryant, G. & Fox Tree, J. (2002). Recognizing verbal irony in spontaneous speech. *Metaphor and Symbol, 17*, 99–117.

Capelli, C., Nakagawa, N., & Madden, C. (1990). How children understand sarcasm: The role of context and intonation. *Child Development, 61*, 1824–1841.

Carston, R. (2002). *Thoughts and Utterances: The Pragmatics of Explicit Communication*. Oxford: Blackwell.

Carston, R. (2010). Metaphor: Ad hoc concepts, literal meaning and mental images. *Proceedings of the Aristotelian Society, 110*(3), 295–321.

Clark, E. (1973). What's in a word? On the child's acquisition of semantics in his first language. In T. Moore (ed), *Cognitive Development and the Acquisition of Language* (pp. 65–110). New York: Academic Press.

Clark, E. (2003). *First Language Acquisition*. Cambridge: Cambridge University Press.

Clark, H. & Gerrig, R. (1984). On the pretense theory of irony. *Journal of Experimental Psychology: General, 113*, 121–126.

Colston, H. & Gibbs, R. (2002). Are metaphor and irony understood differently? *Metaphor and Symbol, 17*, 57–80.

Creusere, M. (1999). Theories of adults' understanding and use of irony and sarcasm: Applications to and evidence from research with children. *Developmental Review, 19*, 213–262.

Currie, G. (2006). Why irony is pretence. In S. Nichols (ed), *The Architecture of the Imagination* (pp. 111–133). Oxford: Oxford University Press.

de Groot, A., Kaplan, J., Rosenblatt, E., Dews, S., & Winner, E. (1995). Understanding versus discriminating nonliteral utterances: Evidence for a disassociation. *Metaphor and Symbolic Activity, 10*(4), 255–273.

Demorest, A., Silberstein, L., Gardner, H., & Winner, E. (1983). Telling it as it isn't: Children's understanding of figurative language. *British Journal of Developmental Psychology, 1*, 121–134.

Demorest, A., Meyer, C., Phelps, E., Gardner, H., & Winner, E. (1984). Words speak louder than actions: Understanding deliberately false remarks. *Child Development, 55*, 1527–1534.

Dews, S., Winner, E., Kaplan, J., Rosenblatt, E., Hunt, M., Lim, K., McGovern, A., Qualter, A., & Smarsh, B. *et al.* (1996). Children's understanding of the meaning and functions of verbal irony. *Child Development, 67*, 3071–3085.

Dews, S. & Winner, E. (1997). Attributing meaning to deliberately false utterances. In C. Mandell & A. McCabe (eds), *The Problem of Meaning: Behavioral and Cognitive Perspectives* (pp. 377–414). Amsterdam: Elsevier Science.

Dews, S. & Winner, E. (1999). Obligatory processing of literal and nonliteral meanings in verbal irony. *Journal of Pragmatics, 31*, 1579–5799.

Evans, M.-A. & Gamble, L. (1988). Attribute saliency and metaphor interpretation in school-age children. *Journal of Child Language, 15*, 435–449.

Fauconnier, G. (1985). *Mental Spaces*. Cambridge, MA: MIT Press.

Filippova, E. & Astington, J. (2008). Further development in social reasoning revealed in discourse irony understanding. *Child Development, 79*, 126–138.

Gentner, D. (1988). Structure-mapping in analogical development: The relational shift. *Child Development, 59*, 47–59.

Gernsbacher, M. & Robertson, R. (1999). The role of suppression in figurative language comprehension. *Journal of Pragmatics, 31*, 1619–1630.

Gibbs, R. (1986). On the psycholinguistics of sarcasm. *Journal of Experimental Psychology: General, 115*(1), 3–15.

Gibbs, R. (1994). *The Poetics of Mind: Figurative Thought, Language, and Understanding*. Cambridge: Cambridge University Press.

Gibbs, R. (2002). A new look at literal meaning in understanding what speakers say and implicate. *Journal of Pragmatics, 34*, 457–486.

Gibbs, R. (2006). *Embodiment and Cognitive Science*. Cambridge: Cambridge University Press.

Gibbs, R. & Colston, H. (2012). *Interpreting Figurative Meaning*. Cambridge: Cambridge University Press.

Gibbs, R. & Tendahl, M. (2006). Cognitive effort and effects in metaphor comprehension: Relevance theory and psycholinguistics. *Mind & Language, 21*(3), 379–403.

Glenwright, M., Parackel, J., Cheung, K., & Nilsen, E. (2013). Intonation influences how children and adults interpret sarcasm. *Journal of Child Language*, published online.

Glucksberg, S. (2001). *Understanding Figurative Language: From Metaphors to Idioms*. Oxford: Oxford University Press.

Grice, H. P. (1967/1989). *Studies in the Ways of Words*. Cambridge, MA: Harvard University Press.

Hancock, J., Dunham, P., & Purdy, K. (2000). Children's comprehension of critical and complimentary forms of verbal irony. *Journal of Cognition and Development, 12*, 227–240.

Happé, F. (1993). Communicative competence and theory of mind in autism: A test of relevance theory. *Cognition, 48*, 101–119.

Keenan, T. & Quigley, K. (1999). Do young children use echoic information in their comprehension of sarcastic speech? A test of echoic mention theory. *British Journal of Developmental Psychology, 17*, 83–96.

Keil, F. (1986). Conceptual domains and the acquisition of metaphor. *Cognitive Development, 1*, 73–96.

Kövecses, Z. (2002). *Metaphor: A Practical Introduction*. Oxford: Oxford University Press.

Kreuz, R. & Glucksberg, S. (1989). How to be sarcastic: The echoic reminder theory of verbal irony. *Journal of Experimental Psychology: General, 118*(4), 374–386.

Kumon-Nakamura, S., Glucksberg, S., & Brown, M. (1995). How about another piece of pie: The allusional pretense theory of discourse irony. *Journal of Experimental Psychology: General, 124*, 3–21.

Lakoff, G. (1987). *Women, Fire, and Dangerous Things: What Categories Reveal About the Mind.* Chicago: University of Chicago Press.

Lakoff, G. & Johnson, M. (1980). *Metaphors We Live By.* Chicago: University of Chicago Press.

Lucariello, J. & Mindolovich, C. (1995). The development of complex metarepresentational reasoning: The case of situational irony. *Cognitive Development, 10*, 551–576.

Nakassis, C. & Snedeker, J. (2002). Beyond sarcasm: Intonation and context as relational cues in children's recognition of irony. In B. Skarabela, S. Fish, & A. Do (eds), *Proceedings of the Twenty-sixth Boston University Conference on Language Development* (pp. 429–440). Somerville: Cascadilla Press.

Ozçalişcan, S. (2005). On learning to draw the distinction between physical and metaphorical motion: Is metaphor an early emerging cognitive and linguistic capacity? *Journal of Child Language, 32*(2), 291–318.

Pearson, B. 1990. The comprehension of metaphor by preschool children. *Journal of Child Language, 17*(1), 185–203.

Pexman, P. & Glenwright, M. (2007). How do typically developing children grasp the meaning of verbal irony? *Journal of Neurolinguistics, 20*, 178–96.

Pexman, P., Zdrazilova, L., McConnachie, D., Deater-Deckard, K., & Petrill, S. (2009). "That was smooth mom": Children's production of verbal and gestural irony. *Metaphor and Symbol, 24*(4), 237–248.

Pouscoulous, N. (2011). Metaphors: For adults only? *Belgian Journal of Linguistics, 25*, 51–79.

Recanati, F. (2007). Indexicality, context and pretence. In Burton-Roberts, N. (ed), *Pragmatics* (pp. 213–229). Basingstoke: Palgrave Macmillan.

Recchia, H., Howe, N., Ross, H., & Alexander, S. (2010). Children's understanding and production of verbal irony in family conversations. *British Journal of Developmental Psychology, 28*, 255–274.

Searle, J. (1979). Metaphor. In A. Ortony (ed), *Metaphor and Thought* (pp. 83–111). Cambridge: Cambridge University Press.

Sperber, D. & Wilson, D. (1981). Irony and the use-mention distinction. In P. Cole (ed), *Radical Pragmatics.* New York: Academic Press.

Sperber, D. & Wilson, D. (1998). The mapping between the mental and the public lexicon. In P. Carruthers & J. Boucher (eds), *Language and Thought: Interdisciplinary Themes* (pp. 184–200). Cambridge: Cambridge University Press.

Sperber, D. & Wilson, D. (2008). A deflationary theory of metaphor. In Raymond Gibbs (ed), *Cambridge Handbook of Metaphor and Thought* (pp. 84–105). Cambridge: Cambridge University Press.

Sperber, D. & Wilson, D. (2012). *Meaning and Relevance.* Cambridge: Cambridge University Press.

Sullivan, K., Winner, E., & Hopfield, N. (1995). How children tell a lie from a joke: The role of second-order mental state attributions. *British Journal of Developmental Psychology, 13*, 191–204.

Talmy, L. (2000). *Toward a Cognitive Semantics* (2 vols). Cambridge, MA: MIT Press.

Tendahl, M. & Gibbs, R. (2008). Complementary perspectives on metaphor: Cognitive linguistics and relevance theory. *Journal of Pragmatics, 40*, 1823–1864.

Vega Moreno, R. 2007. *Creativity and Convention: The Pragmatics of Everyday Figurative Speech.* Amsterdam: John Benjamins.

Vosniadou, S. (1987). Children and metaphors. *Child Development, 58*, 870–885.

Vosniadou, S. & Ortony, A. (1983). The emergence of the literal-metaphorical-anomalous distinction in young children. *Child Development, 54*, 154–161.

Vosniadou, S., Ortony, A., Reynolds, R., & Wilson, P. (1984). Sources of difficulty in children's understanding of metaphorical language. *Child Development, 55*, 1588–1606.

Wilson, D. (2006). The pragmatics of verbal irony: Echo or pretense? *Lingua, 116*, 1722–1743.

Wilson, D. (2010). Parallels and differences in the treatment of metaphor in relevance theory and cognitive linguistics. *UCL Working Papers in Linguistics, 22*, 41–55.

Wilson, D. (2012). Irony comprehension: A developmental perspective. *Journal of Pragmatics*, available online.

Wilson, D. & Carston, R. (2006). Metaphor, relevance and the 'emergent property' issue. *Mind & Language, 21*, 406–433.

Wilson, D. & Carston, R. (2007). A unitary approach to lexical pragmatics: Relevance, inference and ad hoc concepts. In N. Burton-Roberts (ed), *Pragmatics* (pp. 230–259). Basingstoke: Palgrave.

Winner, E. (1979). New names for old things: The emergence of metaphoric language. *Journal of Child Language, 6*, 469–491.

Winner, E. (1988). *The Point of Words: Children's Understanding of Metaphor and Irony*. Cambridge, MA: Harvard University Press.

Winner, E., McCarthy, M., Kleinman, S., & Gardner, H. (1979). First metaphors. *New Directions in Child Development, 3*, 29–41.

Winner, E. & Leekam, S. (1991). Distinguishing irony from deception: Understanding the speaker's second-order intention. *British Journal of Developmental Psychology, 9*, 257–270.

7

PRAGMATIC INFERENCES

Scalar implicatures

Scalar implicatures are pragmatic inferences related to Grice's maxims of quantity. They are often triggered by the use of lexical items such as quantifiers, numbers, logical connectives, aspectuals, and modals. Current pragmatic theories provide distinct accounts of these implicatures. While some authors like Levinson contend that scalar implicatures represent cases of generalized implicatures leading to default interpretations, Sperber and Wilson argue that they do not represent a natural kind and are derived following the same principles as particularized implicatures. In this chapter, we first present in more details the current theoretical accounts of scalar implicatures and assess their cognitive validity in view of results from processing studies with adult speakers. We then turn to the important body of literature that has tested children's ability to derive scalar implicatures. We conclude that preschoolers already possess the pragmatic ability to derive scalar implicatures and that the problems they encounter in some experimental tasks are due to external linguistic and cognitive factors.

7.1. Scalar implicatures: theoretical accounts and empirical validations

We start this section by comparing the accounts of scalar implicatures provided by neo- and post-Gricean pragmatic theories (Section 7.1.1). We discuss the predictions made by both accounts about the way scalar implicatures are processed. These predictions were tested in a number of processing experiments that we summarize in Section 7.1.2, with the conclusion that the derivation of scalar implicatures is made online during the process of sentence comprehension.

7.1.1. Scalar implicatures: a definition

One of Grice's most crucial contributions to modern pragmatics is the identification of the phenomenon of conversational implicatures as in (1) and (2), in other words pragmatic inferences triggered by utterances not because of some components of their literal meaning but because the speaker is assumed to be rational and to follow a number of rules of conversations (see Chapter 1, Section 1.1.2).

(1) Bill: Would you like to go out for coffee?
Sally: My next class starts in ten minutes.

(2) John: Do you like all of Lisa's friends?
Mary: Some of them are nice.

In (1), due to the maxim of relation, Bill will assume that Sally's reply is a relevant answer to his question, and infer that she does not want to go out for coffee because she does not have time for it. In (2), John will infer Mary does not think that all of Lisa's friends are nice, by assuming that Mary follows the maxim of quantity. Example (2) corresponds to a case of scalar implicature. Such implicatures are triggered by the use of words that are related on a scale such as 'some' and 'all'. The logical interpretation of the weaker words on the scale does not exclude the stronger alternative. For example, the fact that Mary thinks that some of Lisa's friends are nice does not exclude the possibility that she also thinks that all of them are. It is only by assuming that the speaker provides the strongest possible information that this interpretation is rejected. Thus logically, scalar words such as 'some' have a lower-bound interpretation that can be paraphrased as 'some and possibly all'. But during communication, hearers derive an implicature due to the maxim of quantity leading them to have an upper-bound interpretation of scalar words such as 'some' as meaning 'some but not all'.

The implicatures triggered by (1) and (2) share some important properties: they are cancellable, non-detachable, and calculable (e.g. Levinson, 1983). In addition, they do not influence the truth-values of an utterance but its pragmatic felicity. However, there is a crucial difference between them. While the implicature triggered by Sally's reply in (1) would not be derived in all contexts, the implicature triggered by Mary's reply in (2) seems to be relatively robust across contexts due to the use of the quantifier 'some'. The difference between these implicatures corresponds to what Grice called generalized and particularized implicatures. Grice (1989: 37) commented that in the case of generalized conversational implicatures, "one can say that the use of a certain form of words in an utterance would normally (in the absence of special circumstances) carry such-and-such an implicature or type of implicature."

Many scalar implicatures correspond to Grice's definition of generalized implicatures because they rely on the use of words that are semantically situated on a scale, for example, numbers as in example (3), aspectuals as in (4), logical connectives as in (5), and gradable adjectives as in (6). In all cases, the use of a weaker term along the scale pragmatically excludes the interpretation that includes the stronger ones. For example, in (3) the speaker implicates that he does not know more than two of Lisa's friends. In (4), the implicature is that Emma has not finished the puzzle; in (5), that Jim will not get both a train and a construction game; and in (6) that the water is not warm or hot.

(3) I know *two* of Lisa's friends.
(4) Emma has *started* a jigsaw puzzle.
(5) Jim will get a toy train *or* a construction game for Christmas.
(6) The water is *lukewarm*.

In addition to these lexical scales, many other scales can be formed in an ad hoc manner in a given conversational context (Hirschberg, 1985). In that sense, context does play a role in the speaker's derivation of some scalar implicatures and not all of them are generalized in Grice's sense. Another indication that context plays a role in the derivation of generalized scalar implicatures comes from the observation that these implicatures are not generated when they do not contribute to the speaker's discourse goal. There is a well-known distinction between contexts in which only the lower bound of the scalar term, compatible with the logical interpretation, matters while in others it is the upper bound, corresponding to the implicature, that is important for the speaker's goal (Horn, 1984; Levinson, 2000; Sperber & Wilson, 1986/1995). For example, if someone utters (7) and another person answers (8), the scalar implicature indicating that the speaker does not know all of Laura's friends is not relevant, as the speaker's discursive goal is to assert that Laura has friends and the use of 'some' is informative enough in that respect. If on the other hand a speaker gives the same reply in (8) to someone who utters (9), the contrast between the more informative 'all' and the less informative 'some' is relevant and the scalar implicature is therefore generated, leading the hearer to conclude that the speaker does not know all of Laura's friends.

(7) Does Laura have any friends?
(8) I know some of her friends.
(9) Do you know all the people that Laura hangs out with?

Most accounts of scalar implicatures agree that deriving such implicatures involves the following four steps (listed in Barner & Bachrach, 2010; Barner, Brooks & Bale, 2011):

I. Compute basic meaning of a sentence S containing L, a scalar item.
II. Generate a set of alternatives (a_1, a_2, . . . , a_n) to S, called S_{alt}. These are all the sentences that can be generated by replacing L with its scalar alternatives.
III. Restrict the alternatives in S_{alt} by removing any alternative that is entailed by the original utterance S. Call this restricted set $S\star$.
IV. Strengthen the basic meaning of S (containing L) with the negation of all of the members of $S\star$.

In Gricean terms (Breheny, Ferguson & Katsos, 2013b; Papafragou & Skordos, in press), step II involves generating the interpretations that would have been possible if the speaker did not respect the maxim of quantity, by choosing a weak term on a scale. In step III, the hearer eliminates the stronger alternatives on the grounds that the speaker is cooperative and has provided the strongest possible information. This leads the hearer to conclude that the stronger alternatives do not hold.

Neo- and post-Gricean models of pragmatics (see Chapter 1) propose very different accounts of the factors triggering the generation of scalar implicatures. For Levinson (2000), scalar terms generate default implicatures in hearers' minds every time a weaker term on a scale is used. These implicatures result from the application of his Q heuristic stating that "what isn't said, isn't." It follows from this view that if the scalar implicature is not valid in context, it has to be cancelled. In this account, such default pragmatic rules have evolved to optimize the speed of communication. Chierchia (2004, 2006) even suggested that scalar implicatures always occur except in specific grammatical constructions, such as negations or the antecedents of conditionals. They are in this account part of the computational system of grammar and are generated without the intervention of other extra-grammatical modules, contrary to other implicatures.

By contrast, in relevance theory, the necessity to separate generalized from particularized conversational implicatures is contested. In this approach, the same pragmatic principles come into play for all kinds of implicatures (Carston, 1998; Sperber & Wilson, 1986/1995). None of them is generated by default, but their generation always depends on the interaction between the sentence meaning and the context. In addition, Noveck and Sperber (2007) argued that in many cases, the use of scalar words such as 'some' does not lead to the derivation of implicatures but simply to the narrowing of the literal meaning to include in its denotation quantities corresponding to 'at least two and fewer than all'. This narrowing is part of the derivation of the explicit content of utterances and is similar to the derivation of metaphorical meaning (see Chapter 6, Section 6.1). The narrowing is not automatic, but takes place every time it contributes to increasing the relevance of an utterance. According to Noveck and Sperber (2007: 193), it is only in a few cases that 'some' pragmatically implicates 'not all', namely "when the utterance achieves relevance by answering a tacit or explicit question as to whether *all* items satisfy the predicate." Such cases of true scalar implicatures are also said to depend on context rather than a default heuristic.

Katsos and Cummins (2010) underlined that these different theoretical accounts have implications for processing. According to the default interpretation account defended by Levinson (2000) and Chierchia (2004, 2006), generalized implicatures should always be generated in hearers' minds even in neutral contexts, and cancelled when they are not warranted. Pragmatic interpretations should thus be faster to process than logical ones, as the latter require the cancellation of an unwarranted implicature. Because they are generated by default in order to speed communication, it can be assumed that in Levinson's account, generalized implicatures related to lexical scales should be processed faster than other implicatures. By contrast, following the relevance-theoretic account, the same pragmatic principles apply in all cases, and implicatures are always generated only when they are relevant in context. In a neutral context, relevance theory predicts that scalar implicatures are simply not generated. Thus, in this account, pragmatic interpretations of scalar words should take longer to process than logical ones in a neutral context because deriving them induces additional processing cost. However, Noveck and Sperber (2007: 195) emphasized that "contextual factors must be taken into account. For instance, an enriched interpretation may be primed by the context and as a result, may be easier to infer than a literal interpretation." They added that "even when an enriched interpretation of an utterance is not primed, it may require less processing effort than would the literal interpretation because the contextual implications that render relevant the enriched interpretation are more early arrived at than those that would render relevant the literal interpretation." Thus it is only in the absence of such contextual factors that a literal interpretation of scalar words should be more costly than an enriched interpretation. These predictions have been tested in a series of processing experiments, as we now outline.

7.1.2. How are scalar implicatures processed by adult speakers?

One of the aims of processing studies is to determine whether scalar implicatures are always generated by default or not. Recall that according to the default account defended by Levinson and Chierchia, scalar implicatures should be generated by all uses of scalar terms and sometimes cancelled when not warranted in context. In contrast, relevance theory predicts that scalar implicatures need contextual support to be generated, just like any other form of implicatures. When they have to be generated in a neutral context, they are predicted to be more costly than literal meanings. In order to address this issue, Noveck and Posada (2003) had timed subjects while they evaluated the truth or falsity of statements like (10) that are logically true but pragmatically infelicitous because the sentence is underinformative.

(10) Some elephants are mammals.

Subjects who answer that the statement is wrong consider the logical meaning of 'some' to be 'some and possibly all' while subjects who answer that it is true consider the pragmatic upper bound meaning of 'some' as 'some but not all'. They found that subjects take longer to answer 'false' to this statement than 'true'. This indicates that the scalar implicature is not generated by default, as those of the subjects who generated it took longer to respond than those who considered the logical meaning. Bott and Noveck (2004) found in addition that the proportion of subjects answering 'false' and therefore favoring a pragmatic interpretation increases when longer response times are permitted. They concluded that scalar implicatures are not always generated by default and that when they are generated they require an additional processing cost, visible in the longer times that the sentences require to be evaluated.

In order to address more specifically the issue of cognitive load, Dieussaert, Verkerk, Gilliard, and Schaeken (2011) measured the derivation of pragmatic and logical interpretations of sentences containing 'some' in tasks similar to the one described above, but with an increased cognitive load. During the experiment, they alternated the sentence judgment task with a spatial memory task. In this task, three or four dots were shown in a 3×3 matrix and the participant's task was to remember and reproduce their location. In the easy version of the task, three dots were aligned on a vertical or horizontal line. In the hard version of the task, four dots were distributed across the whole matrix. The rationale behind this manipulation is that placing a load on working memory should facilitate automatic responses and inhibit analytic ones. The authors reasoned that if pragmatic interpretations are generated by default they should be increased in the high cognitive load condition. They found, however, that fewer scalar implicatures are generated under high cognitive load, especially for participants with limited working memory span. This result provides some additional confirmation for the relevance-theoretic view that scalar implicatures require more cognitive effort than logical interpretations in neutral contexts.

The studies described above do not, however, provide a full picture of the processing of scalar implicatures, as they represent an indirect measure of processing (i.e. the latencies of replies) and do not give indications about the online processing of sentences containing scalar implicatures. Grodner, Klein, Carbary, and Tanenhaus (2010) argued in addition that the delays found are not necessarily due to the necessity to generate an implicature: "establishing the falsity of the pragmatic interpretation [of sentences like (10)] further requires seeking, and failing to find, a subset of elephants that are not mammals. This additional step is potentially time consuming."

In order to have a more direct measure of processing, online methods such as self-paced reading and eye-tracking must be used. Breheny, Katsos, and Williams (2006) used self-paced reading to assess whether subjects derive scalar implicatures by default in a neutral context. They found that scalar implicatures are only derived when they are warranted by conversational information. In addition, when they are generated, they increase processing cost. The additional processing cost is reflected in the longer reading times of the trigger segment containing the scalar word when the preceding context supports a pragmatically enriched interpretation compared with contexts supporting a literal interpretation. Grodner et al. (2010) argued, however, that with this procedure, the additional reading time is again not necessarily due to the generation of a scalar implicature. In their words: "the longer reading times could also reflect the additional work of constructing the more complex discourse associated with a pragmatic inference. Thus even if the inference arrived immediately, it could have led to elevated reading times."

In order to assess whether participants are able to disambiguate a referent containing a scalar implicature, Huang and Snedeker (2009) used the visual-world paradigm of eye-tracking. Their stimuli included sentences such as (11) that participants heard while looking at a display with four quadrants.

(11) Point to the girl with some/all/two/three of the socks.

Two of the quadrants displayed the pictures of a gender distractor: one boy with two socks and one boy with nothing. The other two quadrants displayed girls: one of them was the target (a girl with e.g. two socks) and the other a picture compatible with the literal meaning of the quantifier but with another object (e.g. a girl with three soccer balls). They found that adult speakers are able to interpret the meaning of quantifiers during the course of sentence comprehension when they contain a specified upper-bound meaning as it is the case for 'all', 'two', and 'three'. With 'some', however, subjects also reached the correct interpretation before the disambiguation point (i.e. the name of the object) but with a delay compared with the other quantifiers. These findings therefore provide additional confirmation for the results obtained with verification judgment tasks: deriving scalar implicatures in cases where the quantifier allows a lower-bounded interpretation induces additional processing cost. Grodner et al. (2010) argued again that some parameters of the study may have induced the observed delay, such as the fact that numbers were used in two of the four conditions thus reducing the acceptability of 'some' and that participants may have had a bias inducing them to initially look at the picture with most objects. Replicating the experiment without these biases, Grodner et al. (2010) found that the interpretation of the pragmatic meaning of 'some' is not delayed compared with expressions that do not require the derivation of a scalar implicature.

The online studies summarized so far all included the use of a quantifier inside a referring expression. Breheny, Ferguson, and Katsos (2013a) argued that this context may represent a confound. While reference is enriched at the explicit level ('what is said'), implicatures are derived at the implicit level ('what is implicated'). In their experiment, Breheny et al. have not asked participants to point to a referent but simply to look and listen. Subjects watched a short video depicting a person transferring quantities of different items to one of two locations. At the end of the video the last image remained on the screen while the participants heard the stimulus sentences, as in (12) and (13):

(12) The man has poured all of the water with oranges into the bowl on tray B and some of the water with limes into the bowl on tray A.

(13) The man has poured some of the water with limes into the bowl on tray A and all of the water with oranges into the bowl on tray B.

In these sentences, participants should be able to predict the target location from the onset of the quantifier 'some' or 'all'. In the baseline condition, the same quantifier is used for both locations and participants should therefore not be able to converge on target before the object noun ('limes' or 'oranges'). By comparing gaze fixations in sentences (12) and (13), Breheny et al. found that subjects' bias to the target picture emerges at the same time when the sentence requires a pragmatic interpretation of 'some' as 'some but not all' and with the quantifier 'all'. They concluded that scalar implicatures are accessed as rapidly as other contextual inferences. They added that even though scalar implicatures are processed very fast, it does not mean that they are generated by default. In fact, several studies (e.g. Bott & Noveck, 2004; Breheny et al., 2006) have demonstrated that implicatures show no evidence of being first generated and then cancelled when they are not warranted in context.

Another issue arising from the theoretical description of scalar implicatures is that if they represent cases of generalized implicatures, then they should be generated differently from particularized implicatures, as predicted by Levinson (2000) but not by Sperber and Wilson (1986/1995). Breheny et al. (2013b) have addressed this question by determining the timecourse with which the hearer has access to particularized quantity implicatures that were not linguistically triggered, as in (14).

(14) The woman has put a spoon into box A and a spoon and a fork into box B.

Upon hearing this sentence, the listener concludes that the woman has put nothing else but a spoon into box A, by assuming that the speaker provides the strongest possible information. In that sense, this implicature is derived from the same principle as the generalized scalar implicatures described above. However, they also differ because they are not related to the use of a particular word. Depending on context, the implicature generated by 'a spoon' could be associated with many different quantities. During the experiment, one participant described the events happening in the video, as in (14), while the other looked at the final image from the video. Breheny et al. found that people are able to process the particularized quantity implicature during the course of sentence interpretation at a similar rate as generalized scalar implicatures (about 200 to 300 ms after the onset of the first cue). This result confirms that the derivation of generalized and particularized quantity implicatures does not differ.

In Gricean pragmatics, one crucial aspect of the derivation of implicatures is that they are generated because the hearer reasons about the speaker's mental states. Breheny et al. (2013b) tested whether the quantity implicature 'but nothing else' triggered by sentences like (14) would still be derived in cases where it was common ground between the speaker and the hearer that the speaker did not have visual access to the whole video. They found that the implicature is not generated in such cases, providing confirmation for the fact that hearers do take the speaker's mental states into account when interpreting utterances and deriving implicatures.

To summarize, the most recent online processing studies demonstrate that access to both particularized and generalized implicatures occur in the course of sentence comprehension, without producing delays compared with sentences that do not require pragmatic inferences. Even though these processes are very rapid and do not lead to additional processing costs, these implicatures are not generated by default but only when they are warranted in context. In the remainder of this chapter, we will discuss children's developing ability to derive such implicatures.

7.2. The acquisition of scalar implicatures

Noveck (2001) was one of the first to test children's ability to derive scalar implicatures in controlled experiments, based on the results of previous studies that had inadvertently included scalar words in their stimuli (e.g. Paris, 1973; Smith, 1980). We start by presenting the puzzling results obtained by Noveck, who concluded that children until the age of nine failed to pragmatically enrich utterances containing a scalar word (Section 7.2.1). We discuss the numerous follow-up studies that have revised and completed this initial picture. We first compare the acquisition of different scalar words (Section 7.2.2) and discuss how some methodological modifications in the design of experiments revealed an early ability to handle scalar implicatures (Section 7.2.3). We then turn to the difference between generalized scalar implicatures conveyed by scalar words like 'some' and 'or' and the particularized implicatures drawn from contextually determined scales (Section 7.2.3). Finally, we discuss the causes for young children's apparent inability to derive scalar implicatures before the age of nine in some experimental settings (Section 7.2.4).

7.2.1. The puzzle of children's logical interpretation of scalar words

In order to assess the acquisition of scalar implicatures by children, Noveck (2001) investigated five-, seven-, and nine-year-olds' agreements and disagreements with statements like (15) made by a puppet.

(15) There might be a parrot in the box.

In his experiment, the statements could be identified as underinformative by reasoning: before presenting the critical statement, the puppet first established that what was in the box was the same thing as what was in two other boxes that the children could see. As both boxes contained parrots, the use of the modal 'might' was an inaccurate way to describe the fact that there had to be a parrot inside the closed box. Similar to the processing experiments described above, children's agreement with this statement would reflect their reliance on a logical interpretation of the modal 'might' as being compatible with the stronger modal 'must'. Children's disagreement would reflect on the other hand that they accessed the pragmatically enriched meaning of 'might' as incompatible with the stronger form 'must'.

Noveck found that at the age of five, 72% of the children agree with statements like (15). However, these children answered some control conditions at chance level, leading Noveck to conclude that they did not show evidence of being competent with the task. At the age of seven, children were competent with the task, as they managed to answer most control questions highly above chance level, but they still preferred the logical interpretation of 'might' (compatible with 'must') in 80% of the cases. Nine-year-olds still preferred the logical interpretation in 69% of the cases, but this score was indistinguishable from predictions based on chance.

This result led Noveck to conclude that by the age of nine, children begin to derive scalar implicatures, even though their performance is still not adult-like, as only 35% of the adults agreed with the statements in this particular task.

In a second experiment, Noveck (2001) increased the training of five- and seven-year-olds with the task in order to ensure that they understood all the parameters correctly. This training increased the proportion of literal interpretations of 'might' for 81% of the five-year-olds, 94% of the seven-year-olds, and even 75% of the adults. This second experiment demonstrated that training could influence the way people reason about a scalar word, but overall the same trend as in the first experiment was replicated. Five-year-olds do not have a global competence with the task and seven-year-olds have a higher probability than adults to derive a logical interpretation of the modal verb rather than generate an implicature.

In a third experiment, Noveck presented children with statements such as (16), similar to those used by Noveck and Posada (2003) and discussed in Section 7.1.2.

(16) Some giraffes have long necks.

In this experiment, 87% of the children (aged 8 and 10) accepted statements such as (16) as true against 41% of the adults. Taken together, these three experiments led Noveck to conclude that children are more logical than adults, and that they are less likely to enrich pragmatically the meaning of scalar words like modals and quantifiers. These results also raised a number of important questions for the acquisition of pragmatics, such as younger children's ability to derive scalar implicatures in some contexts, which were addressed in subsequent studies. We review them in turn in the next sections.

7.2.2. Do all scalar words lead to similar answers?

In his experiments, Noveck tested the acquisition of scalar implicatures through the lens of modals and quantifiers. Scalar implicatures are not however, limited to these words, which raises the question of whether all scalar words would produce the same pattern of results. Chierchia, Crain, Guasti, Gualmini, and Meroni (2001) tested the ability of children aged 3;5 to 6;2 to derive scalar implicatures based on the disjunctive connective 'or'. The logical interpretation of this connective is inclusive ('or and possibly and'), but its pragmatic interpretation is exclusive ('or but not and'). The task involved a modified version of the truth value judgment task (see Chapter 2, Section 2.3.2). In this task, the question was not whether the utterance was true or false as in the original truth value judgment task, because scalar implicatures do not impact on the truth of the sentence but on its pragmatic felicity. In their experiment, children first saw an experimenter acting out a short story. Then they heard a puppet describing what she thought happened in the story as in (17). Children had to say whether they agreed or not with the puppet's statement. In the critical condition, 'or' was used in cases where every boy in the story had chosen both a skateboard and a bike.

(17) Every boy chose a skateboard or a bike.

They found that preschoolers fail to derive scalar implicatures based on disjunction, as they agree with the puppet's statement in about half of the trials. This provides some indication that logical connectives lead to a similar pattern of development as modals and quantifiers.

Another study comparing different types of scales was conducted by Papafragou and Musolino (2003). They compared five-year-olds' ability to derive scalar implicatures belonging to a scale of quantifiers with the Greek equivalents of 'some' and 'all', a scale of numbers with the equivalents of 'two' and 'three' and a scale of aspectuals with the Greek words for 'start' and 'finish'. Similar to Chierchia et al.'s experiment above, after children saw all toy horses jumping over a fence they heard the puppet utter statement (18).

(18) Some of the horses jumped over the fence.

Then the experimenter asked children if the puppet had "answered well" and prompted them to justify their answer. Results indicate that five-year-olds reject the underinformative statement significantly more often when numbers are involved (65% of the trials). No difference was found between the scale of aspectuals and of quantifiers (10% vs 12.5%, respectively). Contrary to the five-year-olds tested in Noveck's experiments above, these children had a very high score on all control questions, confirming that the task was within their reach. When children rejected the statement on the number scale, the justifications that they provided for doing so always correctly appealed to the fact that a more informative alternative should be used (e.g. 'three' instead of 'two'). When children failed to provide the correct answer, their justification either consisted of a reproduction of the statement or (in a minority of cases) of invoking the stronger word on the scale, thus providing some indication that they considered that the weaker term was compatible with the stronger one, as predicted by the logical interpretation.

The specificity of numbers with respect to other scalar words has been confirmed by subsequent acquisition studies (e.g. Hurewitz, Papafragou, Gleitman & Gelman, 2006; Musolino, 2004) which led to the conclusion that numbers have exact meanings that are part of the lexicon and do not give rise to scalar implicatures (e.g. Geurts, 2006). Similar results were found by Papafragou (2006), who compared several aspectuals in Greek roughly corresponding to 'start', 'finish', 'half', and 'halfway' and found that children have a better ability to derive implicatures with 'half' compared with other aspectuals. She concluded that this difference was due to the fact that 'half' has an exact scalar meaning, similar to number words. The alleged difference in the representation of exact scalar words has recently been challenged, and some authors claim that the same pragmatic principles apply to all scalar words. We will discuss this hypothesis in Section 7.2.4.

Another potential difference between the studies reported above comes from the quantifier word used to test children's ability to derive scalar implicatures. In

English, one of the most extensively discussed scales is the one opposing 'some' and 'all', but in many different languages, 'some' can be translated in several ways. Pouscoulous, Noveck, Politzer, and Bastide (2007) argued that in French, the two possible translations of 'some', namely 'certains' and 'quelques' are not equivalent. While both are existential plurals, only 'certains' has a partitive meaning roughly corresponding to 'some of'. Pouscoulous et al. reported results from corpus studies indicating that 'certains' is less frequent than 'quelques' in children's written productions and used less frequently in children's books. It is also less frequent in adult speech. The initial experiments in French by Noveck (2001) used the word 'certains' which, according to these findings, may have reduced children's ability to derive implicatures. This hypothesis has been tested by Pouscoulous *et al.* (2007), who replaced 'certains' by 'quelques' in two experiments involving children aged four, five, seven, and nine. They found that only 32% of four-year-olds follow a logical interpretation of 'quelques' and this rate consistently decreased as children got older (27% for five-year-olds, 17% for seven-year-olds, and none of nine-year-olds). However, Pouscoulous et al. have also changed other important parameters of the task (see Section 7.2.3 for a discussion of the methodological aspects of this study) compared to Noveck's (2001) experiments described above. The exact role of the lexical item used cannot therefore not be assessed for young children. It is only for nine-year-olds that Pouscoulous *et al.* have compared the two words across identical experimental settings. They found that nine-year-olds still favor a logical interpretation of 'certains' in 42% of the cases, while none of them did when 'quelques' was used. Adults on the other hand are not affected by the choice of words and prefer a pragmatic interpretation of the quantifiers in both cases. This last experiment confirms that the choice of words can have a dramatic impact on children's interpretation of scalar words. This difference cannot be due to the semantics of 'certains', as its partitive meaning should encourage children to reach a 'but not all' interpretation. Thus it seems that usage and more precisely children's familiarity with a lexical item plays a crucial role in these tasks. We will come back to this factor in Section 7.2.4.

7.2.3. How does the nature of the task influence children's performance?

One aspect of Noveck's experiments that many subsequent studies have criticized concerns the nature of the experimental task used to assess children's computation of scalar implicatures. Indeed, in these tasks, children had to judge the truth or falsity of statements produced out of context. This does not correspond to the normal communicative situations in which hearers derive implicatures. This problem raises the question of whether children's performance can improve in other experimental settings. Several studies have demonstrated that they do.

A first indication that children may have a more robust understanding of scalar implicatures comes from Chierchia et al. (2001) who asked a group of children (mean age 4;8) to perform a felicity judgment task, involving the presentation of two sentences, one of them containing the underinformative scalar word (19) and the other the appropriate description (20).

(19) Every farmer cleaned a horse or a rabbit.
(20) Every farmer cleaned a horse and a rabbit.

In addition, children were not asked to judge the sentences but to reward with a coin the puppet "who said it better." They found that in 93.3% of the cases children chose the appropriate formulation. Papafragou (2006) noted, however, that felicity judgment tasks can hinder children's ability to derive implicatures because "such tasks are implicitly based on the assumption that participants will [...] take felicity rather than truth to be the basis of their acceptance or rejection of the target sentence. However, it remains an open possibility that children may take the purpose of the task to be the evaluation of the truth of the target statements."

In order to increase children's sensitivity to scalar implicatures, Papafragou and Musolino (2003) provided children with training meant to enhance their ability to detect pragmatic anomalies. The training consisted in presenting children with warm-up stories designed to help them understand that they were required to produce judgments about pragmatic felicity. Children were told that the puppet sometimes said silly things and that they had to help it to say things better. For example, the puppet referred to a dog as "a little animal with four legs" and children were asked to provide a better description. In case they failed to do it, the experimenter gave them the appropriate answer (e.g. 'this is a dog'). They found that children reject the puppet's statement significantly more after this training, in about 50% of the cases for 'some' and 'start' and in about 90% of the cases for 'two'. Thus training did not erase differences between number scales and other scalar words but improved overall performances. Guasti et al. (2005) also inserted a training session during which seven-year-old children were presented with four objects and given two possible descriptions of each of them. Both descriptions were true but one was more informative than the other (e.g. 'grape' vs 'fruit'). Children were also explicitly reminded that there were different ways to describe an object and that some were more appropriate than others. Guasti et al. observed a significant effect of training. Without training, children in their study rejected the logical interpretation of the Italian equivalent of 'some' in only 12% of the cases (in a task similar to the one used by Noveck, 2001), while after training this proportion rose to 52%. Guasti et al. also tested whether the effect of training had durable consequences on children's behavior. They repeated the test without the training session one week after the first test, using a similar procedure but different statements. They found that the rejection rate for underinformative uses of 'some' drops again to 22%, suggesting that training does not have a long-lasting effect on children's performance.

Papafragou and Tantalou (2004) and Papafragou (2006) argued that one additional problem with judgment tasks is that they rely on potential rather than communicated inferences and this does not reflect normal cases of communication.

In order to solve this problem, they designed short dialogs between the experimenter and a puppet as in (21), ascertaining that the scalar implicature was truly part of what the speaker wanted to communicate. Thus the scalar inference was no longer a potential inference as in judgment tasks, but an actual communicated inference. Children were instructed to give a prize to the animal if it had performed the job (e.g. built a school).

(21) Experimenter: Did you build the school?
Animal: I started building it.

Papafragou and Tantalou (2004) reported that five-year-olds overwhelmingly refuse to give a prize to the animal in cases like example (21), on average in 79% of the cases across the three types of scales tested. Using a similar methodology, Papafragou (2006) reported that children perform above chance only with the scalar words 'half' and 'halfway' but not with 'begin' and 'finish', confirming a difference between scales (see the discussion about number scales in Section 7.2.2).

These experiments confirm that children find it easier to evaluate a linguistic production by acting rather than by providing a meta-linguistic judgment. However, this experimental design also has weaknesses, as children can choose to withhold the reward whether or not they compute the scalar implicature (Katsos, 2009). Indeed, if they only understand that the animal started building the school, without strengthening this meaning with the implicature 'but did not finish it' they should still withhold the reward because the animal did not complete the action requested by the experimenter. Thus the task does not truly discriminate between cases where the implicature is and isn't derived.

Pouscoulous et al. (2007) used yet another experimental design, in which children had to demonstrate their understanding of scalar implicatures by acting. In their task, children were presented with five cardboard boxes and plastic tokens. In one condition, two of the boxes contained tokens while the others were empty. In another condition all the boxes contained tokens and in a third condition none of the boxes contained tokens. Children were instructed to act based on statements uttered by the experimenter. In the critical conditions, children heard statement (22) while all the boxes contained tokens and statement (23) while none of the boxes contained a token.

(22) I would like some boxes to contain a token.
(23) I would like some boxes to not contain a token.

In the case of (22), if children follow the logical interpretation, they should leave the boxes as they are. If on other hand they derive a scalar implicature, they should remove part of the tokens (at least one). In the case of (23), if children follow a logical interpretation they should leave the boxes intact but if they derive a scalar implicature they should add at least one token in one of the boxes. Pouscoulous et al. submitted that the negative polarity of (23) should make it more difficult to compute the scalar implicature. Their results indicate that only 32% of the four-year-olds fail to derive the scalar implicatures following statement (22). This number drops to 17% at the age of seven, when children reach adult-like performances (adults fail to derive the implicature in 14% of the cases). Their results also confirm that the negative version (23) is more complex than the positive version, as the percentage of failure to derive a scalar implicature is 41% at the age of four and remains unchanged at the age of seven (adults on the other hand have the same score of 14% of logical interpretations in both cases). This experiment confirms that linguistic complexity is an important factor influencing pragmatic competencies (see also Chapter 3, Section 3.2 for similar conclusion about indirect speech acts).

Another way to assess the derivation of scalar implicatures with an implicit measure is the use of visual world paradigms. Only Huang and Snedeker (2009) included children in one such experiment (as summarized in Section 7.1.2). They found that five year olds are unable to derive scalar implicatures, as they do not converge on the target referent based on the quantifier 'some' before the disambiguation cue arrives. This study has serious limitations, however, and subsequent processing studies with adults (e.g. Grodner et al., 2010) demonstrated that changing some of its parameters suppressed the delay observed. Similar online experiments must also be replicated with children before firm conclusions can be reached.

7.2.4. Is there a difference between generalized and particularized scalar implicatures?

One of the main tenets of the neo-Gricean account of scalar implicatures (Chierchia, 2004, 2006; Levinson, 2000) is that there is a fundamental difference between generalized implicatures triggered by the use of words such as 'some' and 'or' independently of context, and particularized implicatures that are occasion-specific and not derived in the absence of a specific context. These theoretical descriptions of implicatures are not accompanied by direct predictions about their acquisition. Papafragou and Tantalou (2004: 79) noted, however, that "one might expect that generalized SIs [scalar implicatures] would prove easier for children to derive than particularized (context-specific) ones, other things being equal."

Papafragou and Tantalou (2004) compared children's ability to derive implicatures triggered by scalar words such as 'some' and 'all' with their ability to derive similar implicatures based on their world knowledge as in (24).

(24) A: Did you eat the sandwich?
B: I ate the cheese.

In this example, it is part of children's world knowledge that a sandwich contains at least bread and something inside. This example was complemented by visual support, as children saw that an animal had a sandwich made of bread, cheese, and ham. Papafragou and Tantalou also inserted cases of ad hoc scales, including context-specific orderings as in (25).

(25) A. Did you wrap the gifts?
B. I wrapped the parrot.

In such cases, a scenario was set up to build a scale, for example, with an animal assigned the task of wrapping two gifts (a parrot and a doll). Papafragou and Tantalou reported no significant differences in children's ability to respond to the three types of scales.

Katsos (2009) also compared the derivation of particularized and generalized scalar implicatures in children aged 5, 7, 9, and 11. His results indicate that children have a similar rejection rate for both types of implicatures regardless of their age. In his task, participants who rejected the underinformative formulations provided by a character were asked to help him say it better. Again, children's responses in both types of implicatures are qualitatively similar. Adults, however, produced clearer reformulations when the implicature was conveyed by 'some' compared with another word from an ad hoc scale, which might indicate a difference between generalized and particularized implicatures. However, Katsos noted that what becomes more effective with age in the use of generalized implicatures is related to meta-linguistic rather than pragmatic skills.

Finally, Stiller, Goodman, and Frank (2011) constructed ad hoc scales using a simple design involving differences in the number of features between images, instead of linguistic stimuli. For example, they presented children with a face with glasses and a hat (two features corresponding to 'all'), a face with only glasses (one feature corresponding to 'some'), and a face without any of the two features. They asked three- and four-year-olds to point to a correct face following the stimulus sentence like (26).

(26) My friend has glasses.

They found that in both age groups children correctly point to the face with only glasses above chance level, but with a lower frequency than adults. In addition, when the three faces were not related in a scalar manner, both children and adults failed to derive an implicature. They concluded that young children already have some ability to draw implicatures and that the difficulties evidenced by previous work are due to the particular linguistic items used in the experiments. We elaborate on the potential explanations of the sources of difficulty of scalar implicatures in the next section.

7.2.5. What are the factors explaining young children's apparent failure to derive scalar implicatures in many experimental settings?

Even in studies including an experimental design minimizing the effort of generating implicatures, children are often not shown to reach adult-like performances before the age of six or seven. The question is then if children genuinely lack the pragmatic ability to derive implicatures or if some other factors explain these difficulties. One indication that young children do not lack the pragmatic ability to derive scalar implicatures comes from the results of studies by Chierchia et al. (2001) presented above and Gualmini, Crain, Meroni, Chierchia, and Guasti (2001). In these experiments, when four-year-olds were asked to choose between the underinformative and the informative version of a statement, they overwhelmingly chose the corrective informative statement.

In Section 7.1.1, we presented the four steps involved in the derivation of scalar implicatures. Recall that step II involved the generation of a set of alternatives ordered on a scale of informativeness. The experiments by Chierchia et al. (2001) and Gualmini et al. (2001) suggest that children can recognize which of two statements is optimally informative when explicitly provided with the alternatives. This result led the authors to conclude that what prevents children from deriving scalar implicatures in other experimental tasks is that they do not have yet a conventional entry in their mental lexicon containing the scalar word as well as the stronger alternatives.

The importance of accessing alternatives for children's ability to derive scalar implicature has received further confirmation in later studies. Barner et al. (2011) presented four-year-olds with a set of three reading animals and asked the following questions:

(27) Are some of the animals reading?
(28) Are only some of the animals reading?
(29) Are the cat and the dog reading?
(30) Are only the dog and the cat reading?

They reasoned that if children's difficulty with scalar implicatures is due to a failure to access alternatives, then they should not be sensitive to the addition of 'only' in (28) because the scale between 'some' and 'all' is context independent. They should on the other hand be able to answer correctly to (30) because the set of alternatives are contextually specified. They found that children agree with the underinformative statements in (27) and (28) in about 66% of the trials, regardless of the linguistic form used. In contrast, children answer correctly to (29) in 93% of the trials and to (30) in 86% of the trials. Children's high performance in (29) is due to the fact that the need to generate alternatives is eliminated. In (30), children's high performance is due to the fact that the set of animals was visually displayed. Thus, even though children understand from an early age that 'some' and 'all' refer to different set relations (Barner, Chow & Yang, 2009) they still need to learn that they belong to the same scale, and this is what prevents them from drawing scalar implicatures containing these quantifiers. Barner and Bachrach (2010) extended this explanation to children's better performance with number words compared to other scales. According to them, deriving scalar implicatures from numbers is easier because one of the first things that children learn about numbers is that they are ordered on a scale.

Skordos and Papafragou (2012) also tested the role of alternatives by designing a task condition in which statements containing 'some' and 'all' were mixed so that lexical contrasts could be established. They found that children are much more prone to derive implicatures when items are presented in this order than when all the sentences constraining 'some' are presented before the sentences containing 'all'. They also found that children have a better performance when the sentences containing 'some' alternated between felicitous and underinformative uses of 'some' compared to when all underinformative uses were presented first. This indicates that the lexical contrast between 'all' and 'some' facilitates children's ability to derive implicatures. There is in addition a usage effect in which contrasting felicitous with underinformative uses of the same item also increases children's awareness and enhances their ability to correctly derive the scalar implicature.

Another line of explanation for children's failure in some of the experimental tasks was proposed by Davies and Katsos (2010) and Katsos and Bishop (2011). They submit that even though children may be sensitive to violations of the quantity maxim (as required in step II of the derivation procedure), they are tolerant to pragmatic infelicities and therefore do not reject underinformative statements in binary judgment tasks. They found that when children are given a magnitude estimation scale rather than a binary task, they penalize overinformative utterances and rate them lower than optimal ones. This hypothesis gains plausibility in view of the fact that children around the age of three are not overinformative when they answer questions (e.g. Ferrier, Dunham & Dunham, 2000) and are also able to modulate their referential acts depending on the information needs of their addressee (see Chapter 8, Section 8.1).

7.3. Synthesis

In this chapter, we have discussed how one specific type of implicatures involving scalar words is processed by adult speakers and progressively mastered by children. Results from processing experiments indicate that adult speakers do not generate scalar implicatures by default but only when they are warranted by context. In such cases, these implicatures do not involve additional processing cost. We reviewed the body of literature indicating that young children under the age of six or seven lack a robust ability to derive scalar implicatures. We argued that children's failure does not reflect a pragmatic inability to derive implicatures but their lack of linguistic knowledge about the way words are ordered on a scale as well as their tolerance towards pragmatic infelicities.

References

Barner, D. & Bachrach, A. (2010). Inference and exact numerical representation in early language development. *Cognitive Psychology*, *60*, 40–62.

Barner, D., Brooks, N., & Bale, A. (2011). Accessing the unsaid: The role of scalar alternatives in children's pragmatic inference. *Cognition*, *188*, 87–96.

Barner, D., Chow, K., & Yang, S. (2009). Finding one's meaning: A test of the relation between quantifiers and integers in language development. *Cognitive Psychology, 58*, 195–219.

Bott, L. & Noveck, I. (2004). Some utterances are underinformative: The onset and time course of scalar inferences. *Journal of Memory and Language, 51*, 437–457.

Breheny, R., Katsos, N., & Williams, J. (2006). Are scalar implicatures generated by default? *Cognition, 100*, 434–463.

Breheny, R., Ferguson, H.J., & Katsos, N. (2013a). Investigating the timecourse of accessing conversational implicatures during incremental sentence interpretation. *Language and Cognitive Processes, 28*(4), 443–467.

Breheny, R., Ferguson, H.J., & Katsos, N. (2013b). Taking the epistemic step: Toward of model of on-line access to conversational implicatures. *Cognition, 126*(3), 423–440.

Carston, R. (1998). Informativeness, relevance and scalar implicature. In R. Carston & S. Uchida (eds), *Relevance Theory: Applications and Implications* (pp. 179–236). Amsterdam: John Benjamins.

Chierchia, G., Crain, S., Guasti, M.T., Gualmini, A., & Meroni, L. (2001). The acquisition of disjunction: Evidence for a grammatical view of scalar implicatures. In A.H.-J. Do, L. Dominguez, & A. Johansen (eds), *Proceedings of the 25th Boston University Conference on Language Development* (pp. 157–168). Somerville, MA: Cascadilla Press.

Chierchia, G. (2004). Scalar implicatures, polarity phenomena, and the syntax/pragmatics interface. In A. Belleti (ed), *Structures and Beyond* (pp. 39–103). Oxford: Oxford University Press.

Chierchia, G. (2006). Broaden your views: Implicatures of domain widening and the logicality of language. *Linguistic Inquiry, 37*(4), 535–590.

Davies, C. & Katsos, N. (2010). Over-informative children: production/comprehension asymmetry or tolerant of pragmatic violations? *Lingua, 120*(8), 1956–1972.

Dieussaert, K., Verkerk, S., Gilliard, E., & Schaeken, W. (2011). Some effort for some: Further evidence that scalar implicatures are effortful. *The Quarterly Journal of Experimental Psychology, 64*, 2352–2367.

Ferrier, S., Dunham, P., & Dunham, S. (2000). The confused robot: Two-year-olds' responses to breakdowns in conversation. *Social Development, 9*(3), 337–347.

Geurts, B. (2006). Take 'five': The meaning and use of a number word. In S. Vogeleer & L. Tasmowski (eds), *Non-Definiteness and Plurality* (pp. 311–329). Amsterdam: John Benjamins.

Gualmini, A., Crain, S., Meroni, L., Chierchia, G., & Guasti, M.T. (2001). At the semantics/pragmatics interface in child language. *Proceedings of Semantics and Linguistic theory XI*. Ithaca, NY: CLC Publications, Department of Linguistics, Cornell University.

Guasti, M.T., Chierchia, G., Crain, S., Foppolo, F., Gualmini, A., & Meroni, L. (2005). Why children and adults sometimes (but not always) compute implicatures. *Language and Cognitive Processes, 20*(5), 667–696.

Grice, H.P. (1989). Logic and conversation. In *Studies in the Way of Words* (pp. 22–40). Cambridge, MA: Harvard University Press.

Grodner, D.J., Klein, N.M., Carbary, K.M., & Tanenhaus, M.K. (2010). "Some," and possibly all, scalar inferences are not delayed: Evidence for immediate pragmatic enrichment. *Cognition, 116*, 42–55.

Hirschberg, J. (1985). *A Theory of Scalar Implicature*. Doctoral dissertation, University of Pennsylvania.

Horn, L. (1984). Toward a new taxonomy for pragmatic inference. In D. Schiffrin (ed), *Meaning, Form and Use in Context: Linguistic Applications, Proceedings of GURT '84* (pp. 11–42). Washington, DC: Georgetown University Press.

Huang, Y.T. & Snedeker, J. (2009). Online interpretation of scalar quantifiers: Insight into the semantic-pragmatics interface. *Cognitive Psychology, 58*, 376–415.

Hurewitz, F., Papafragou, A., Gleitman, L., & Gelman, R. (2006). Asymmetries in the acquisition of numbers and quantifiers. *Language Learning and Development, 2*, 77–96.

Katsos, N. (2009). Neither default nor particularised: Scalar implicature from a developmental perspective. In U. Sauerland, & K. Yatsushiro (eds), *Experimental Semantics and Pragmatics* (pp. 51–73). London: Palgrave Macmillan.

Katsos, N. & Bishop, D. (2011). Pragmatic tolerance: Implications for the acquisition of informativeness and implicatures. *Cognition, 120*, 67–81.

Katsos, N. & Cummins, C. (2010). Pragmatics: From theory to experiment and back again. *Language and Linguistics Compass, 4/5*, 282–295.

Levinson, S. (1983). *Pragmatics*. Cambridge, UK: Cambridge University Press.

Levinson, S. (2000). *Presumptive Meanings*. Cambridge, MA: MIT Press.

Musolino, J. (2004). The semantics and acquisition of number words: Integrating linguistic and developmental perspectives. *Cognition, 93*(1), 1–41.

Noveck, I. (2001). When children are more logical than adults. *Cognition, 86*, 253–282.

Noveck, I. & Posada, A. (2003). Characterising the time course of an implicature. *Brain and Language, 85*, 203–210.

Novek, I. & Sperber, D. (2007). The why and how of experimental pragmatics. In N. Burton Roberts (ed), *Pragmatics* (pp. 184–212). Basingstoke: Palgrave.

Papafragou, A. (2006). From scalar semantics to implicature: Children's interpretation of aspectuals. *Journal of Child Language, 33*, 721–757.

Papafragou, A. & Musolino, J. (2003). Scalar implicatures: Experiments at the semantics/pragmatics interface. *Cognition, 86*, 253–282.

Papafragou, A. & Skordos, D. (in press). Implicature. In J. Lidz, W. Snyder, & J. Pater (eds), *The Oxford Handbook of Developmental Linguistics*. Oxford: Oxford University Press.

Papafragou, A. & Tantalou, N. (2004). Children's computation of implicatures. *Language Acquisition, 12*(1), 71–82.

Paris, S.G. (1973). Comprehension of language connectives and propositional logical relationships. *Journal of Experimental Child Psychology, 16*(2), 278–291.

Pouscoulous, N., Noveck, I., Politzer, G., & Bastide, A. (2007). A developmental investigation of processing costs in implicature production. *Language Acquisition, 14*, 347–376.

Skordos, D. & Papafragou, A. (2014). Scalar inferences in 5-year-olds: The role of alternatives. In W. Orman & M. Valleau (eds), *Proceedings of the 38th Annual Boston University Conference on Language Development* (pp. 438–450). Somerville: Cascadilla Press.

Smith, C.L. (1980). Quantifiers and question answering in young children. *Journal of Experimental Child Psychology, 30*(2), 191–205.

Sperber, D. & Wilson, D. (1986/1995). *Relevance: Communication and Cognition*. Oxford: Blackwell.

Stiller, B., Goodman, N., & Frank, M. (2011). Ad hoc scalar implicatures in adults and children. *Proceedings of the 33rd Annual Meeting of the Cognitive Science Society*, Boston, MA.

8

DISCOURSE PRAGMATICS

Referring expressions and connectives

Sentences forming a text or a discourse are linked together coherently, and such coherence is often reflected in the use of linguistic items known as cohesive ties. In this chapter, we focus on the acquisition of two such ties, namely referring expressions and discourse connectives. In Section 8.1, we discuss how children become able to choose referring expressions conveying the appropriate level of informativeness given the common ground between the speaker and his audience, and assess their ability to use perceptual and linguistic cues of common ground. In Section 8.2, we turn to the acquisition of discourse connectives and discuss the cognitive and social factors influencing the order of acquisition between connectives conveying various coherence relations. We also discuss children's growing ability to use the processing instructions conveyed by connectives during reading. In both cases, we argue that children display an early sensitivity to their audience's informational needs as well as an implicit ability to link sentences together coherently long before they master the linguistic means to express discourse coherence.

8.1. The development of referential communication

We argued in Chapter 2 (Section 2.2.1) that children use their pragmatic skills from a very early age in order to assign the correct label to an unknown referent during word learning. In this section, we address another aspect of referential communication, related to the choice of referring expressions. From a pragmatic perspective, one of the difficulties of producing the correct referring expression in context is that this requires the ability to evaluate which linguistic and contextual elements are accessible to the hearer, in other words what is part of the common ground. In Section 8.1.1, we introduce the notion of common ground and the scales of accessibility for referring expressions. We go on to discuss children's ability to integrate information from two different sources into the common ground: perception (Section 8.1.2) and prior discourse (Section 8.1.3). We conclude that between the age of two and three, children show evidence of taking both sources of evidence into account when producing referential acts.

8.1.1. Common ground and accessibility

In order for referential communication to be effective, speakers must take into account the information that they share and do not share with their audience. For example, it would be appropriate to request a book by uttering (1) only if there was just one possible and salient book in the linguistic and perceptual environment shared by the speaker and the listener.

(1) Give me the book.

In other words, successful referential communication requires the ability to evaluate what is part of the common ground between speaker and hearer. In Clark's definition (1992: 3), the common ground between speaker and hearer corresponds to "the sum of their mutual knowledge, mutual beliefs and mutual suppositions." Clark and Marshall (1981) suggested that mutual knowledge can result from community membership, physical copresence, linguistic copresence, and indirect copresence. The latter corresponds to cases when a speaker assumes that a hearer indirectly knows something as a result of his physical or linguistic copresence. Ariel (1985) also contended that what is part of the common ground or, in other words, what is 'given' between speaker and hearer, comes from three different sources: shared knowledge, the physical situation, and textually evoked elements. All three sources of information can be marked linguistically by specific forms: shared knowledge is conveyed by definite noun phrases (NPs) as well as 'it' clefts and some connectives like 'after all'; the physical situation is linguistically marked by demonstrative pronouns as well as first and second person pronouns; and textually evoked elements are marked by third person pronouns. Ariel argued in addition that the three sources of givenness also correspond to three types of contexts: general knowledge stored in long-term memory for shared knowledge, and immediate perceptual and linguistic elements stored in short-term memory. In other words, while linguistic and perceptual givenness are highly accessible, facts pertaining to shared knowledge are less accessible, as they must be retrieved from long-term memory.

Several authors have elaborated on the idea that linguistic expressions can encode different degrees of accessibility, and designed scales of accessibility associated with referring expressions (Ariel, 1988, 2001; Givón, 1983; Prince, 1981). For example, Gundel, Hedberg, and Zacharski (1993) proposed the following scale of accessibility (ranging from highest to lowest accessibility) with its corresponding linguistic expressions:

1. In focus (it, he, she)
2. Activated (that, this)
3. Familiar (that man)
4. Uniquely identifiable (the man)
5. Referential (this man)
6. Type identifiable (a man)

In this model, using the appropriate referring expression on the scale requires pragmatic abilities to evaluate the appropriate level of informativeness, following Grice's maxims of quantity. It also requires the cognitive ability to take the listener's perspective and assess whether a referent is accessible to him based on the perceptual context, immediate preceding discourse and world knowledge.

Children's ability to use referring expressions encoding the appropriate degree of accessibility has long been a domain of interest in studies of language and cognitive development. Early studies, summarized by Yule (1997), concluded that preschool children were not mature enough to take the listener's perspective, causing egocentric errors in the production of referring expressions, as well as misinterpretations of ambiguous referring expressions like pronouns. In addition, children's frequent use of reduced or omitted forms to introduce new referents in discourse led to the hypothesis that they may have an immature pragmatic system (e.g. Schaeffer, 2000; Van Hout, Harrigan & de Villiers, 2010). A recent body of literature suggests, however, that children between the age of two and three are already able to take the listener's perspective in many different situations and to adapt their communicative behavior accordingly, casting some doubt on the affirmation that their early linguistic behavior truly reflects lack of pragmatic skills. We outline these studies and present some lines of explanations for the results of earlier studies in the next sections.

8.1.2. Children's use of perceptual cues of accessibility

Even before they are able to produce referring expressions linguistically, several studies have demonstrated that children show sensitivity to the informational needs of their addressee depending on their knowledge state through their pointing behavior. In one of them, Liszkowski, Carpenter, and Tomasello (2008) found that 12-month-olds respond to an adult's searching behavior differently when the adult knows the location of the searched object, for example, because they witnessed it falling, than when the adult is ignorant of its location. In the latter case, children point more often to the object, showing some understanding about others' knowledge and ignorance. Begus and Southgate (2012) also found that at the age of 16 months, children point to novel objects more often when interacting with a knowledgeable than with an ignorant partner. By the age of two, Moll and Tomasello (2006) reported that children are able to understand that the content of what another person sees may be different from what they see. In their experiment, children saw two objects, but only one of them was also visible for an adult sitting in front of them. When children were asked to help the adult finding an object he was looking for, they passed the object that was hidden from the adult's perspective. Children thus showed evidence of understanding that someone is likely to be looking for something that is not accessible from his perspective.

Other studies have found that in addition to their pointing behavior, young children also modify their verbal behavior based on the perceptual common ground. For example, O'Neill (1996) investigated the sensitivity of two-year-olds to their parent's knowledge state when requesting help to retrieve a toy. In this experiment, children were presented with a toy that was subsequently put into one of two containers placed on a high shelf. In one condition, parents witnessed these actions, while in another condition they were ignorant of these events, either because they had left the room or covered their eyes and ears. Results indicate that children name the toy and its location and gesture toward it much more when their parent did not witness the events than when they did. In a second experiment, children also gestured much more toward the location of a sticker that they wanted to retrieve when their parent was ignorant of its location. In a follow-up experiment, O'Neill and Topolovec (2001) varied the object's position so that it was either possible or impossible for the child to produce an unambiguous request based on pointing gestures alone. In one experiment, the objects were two identical boxes with a different picture of a vehicle. They found that children aged 2;8 are more likely to name the picture on the box when their referential gesture cannot unambiguously specify the box they want. In another experiment, O'Neill and Topolovec placed stickers under different animal figures (a duck, a pig, etc.) in order to make it easier for children to verbally refer to the correct location by using the animal's name. They found that at age 2;9 but not at 2;3 children show evidence of realizing the inefficacy of their pointing gesture and adapt their communicative strategies accordingly. Thus it seems that when children approach their third birthday, they become able to modulate the amount of linguistic information provided to disambiguate a referent designated by a pointing gesture.

Another set of studies has investigated children's ability to modulate their choice of referring expressions based on the perceptual availability of an object for their interlocutor. Matthews, Lieven, Theakston, and Tomasello (2007) reported that three- and four-year-olds' choices of referring expressions are dependent on the perceptual availability of the intended object for their addressee. At the age of three, children preferentially use full nouns when the object is not accessible for their addressee and by the age of four, they correctly use pronouns to refer to accessible objects for their addressee rather than null referents as three-years-olds do. Three- and four-year-olds also modulate their answers to predicate-focus questions, as in (2), after witnessing scenes in which an agent performed an action on a patient, for example, a monkey stroking a lion (Salomo, Graf, Lieven & Tomasello, 2011).

(2) What is the monkey doing?

In this experiment, the patient on whom the action was performed was sometimes perceptually accessible to the questioner when the question was asked and sometimes not. Children from both age groups were sensitive to perceptual accessibility, as they tended to use more informative referring expressions in the forms of full lexical nouns when the patient was not accessible.

We argued in Chapter 2 (Section 2.2.1) that joint attention played a crucial role for children's lexical development. Recent studies indicate that children also take joint attention into account when producing referring expressions. Skarabela, Allen, and Scott-Phillips (2013) analyzed a videotaped corpus of naturalistic interactions of four children acquiring Inuktitut between the age of 2 and 3;6. They found that children tend to omit referents when there is joint attention with their listeners and use full nouns in the absence of joint attention. This result indicates that children's omission of referents is not due to lack of pragmatics skills but on the contrary reflects children's awareness of the maxim of quantity as well as their ability to modulate the informativeness of their referring expressions depending on their perception of the listener's need for information. These results also imply that children's tendency to use of null subjects, which led many authors to conclude that children were pragmatically immature in early studies of referential communication, may in fact be due to other limitations in children's linguistic development. A likely possibility is that these omissions are due to an immaturity of the syntactic system, as suggested by some syntactic theories of language acquisition (e.g. Hyams & Wexler, 1993; Rizzi, 2005).

The studies summarized above tested young children's ability to produce simple referential expressions with full nouns or pronouns. But in some cases, producing an unambiguous referential expression requires the production of a complex NP. Nadig and Sedivy (2002) elicited the production of referential expressions by five- and six-year-olds in a situation where they were asked to request a confederate to pick an object in three different conditions. In the first condition, two similar objects with one feature differentiating them, for example, a big and a small glass, were placed in such a way as to make them visible for both the child and the confederate, thus creating a situation of common ground. In the second condition, named the privileged condition, one of the two objects was only visible for the participant but not the confederate, and in the third control condition subjects saw an unrelated control object. Results indicate that children aged five to six can identify information that is part of the common ground, as they produce more scalar adjectives such as 'big', 'small' in the common ground condition than in the privileged condition (74.7% of the trials vs only 50%). However, children were not yet adult-like in their production of adjectives, as a control group of adults produced scalar adjectives in 100% of the trials in the common ground condition.

In a second experiment, Nadig and Sevidy used eye-tracking to measure the time course of children's processing of common ground information. In this experiment, the conditions of the first experiment were replicated but the communicative situation was reversed. This time it was the confederate who provided information and the children had to select the appropriate referent. In the common ground condition, children's eye-gazes alternated between the target object and the competitor object (as well as their partner's face for help) during the first two seconds, indicating that the children realized that the speaker could potentially refer to one of the two objects that were part of the common ground. In the privileged condition, however, children only rarely looked at the competitor object, confirming that they realized that the speaker could not refer to an object that was not visible for him. In addition, children's convergence on the target referent differed very quickly between the privileged and the common ground conditions, suggesting that children use common ground information very quickly during the processing of referring expressions.

As the age group tested by Nadig and Sedivy in their offline experiment did not reach adult-like performances, Bahtiyar and Küntay (2008) have replicated their experiment with Turkish-speaking children aged five to six and nine to ten. Results confirm that both age groups have some sensitivity to the common ground condition, as they use more disambiguating adjectives in this case. However, an age-related progression was observed between the two groups and also between the older group and a control group of adults, indicating that children continue to develop their referential strategies over a long period. This result is not surprising in view of the fact that young children do not yet understand that many words are ordered along a scale, thus hindering their ability to succeed at many tasks involving scalar implicatures (see Chapter 7, Section 7.2.4). Bahtiyar and Küntay also reported that preschoolers' production of discriminative adjectives increased when they were instructed to convey polite requests. The rationale for this instruction is that young children performing the task may be simply labeling an item, a task for which the information needs of their addressee are not salient, whereas when they produce a request they are performing a communicative task, rendering the needs of their addressee more salient. The instruction to perform 'polite requests' may also have increased children's integration of their addressee's needs, as being polite requires taking the perspective of the addressee. Thus the type of task that children are performing strongly influences their ability to take informational needs into account. Finally, children's production of referring expressions can also improve under some conditions, as Matthews, Lieven, and Tomasello (2007) reported that providing feedback to two-, three-, and four-year-old children about their ambiguous referential acts led to an improvement in their referential strategies in later sessions.

8.1.3. Children's use of linguistic cues of accessibility

In addition to the role of perceptual salience, several studies have also investigated children's ability to integrate prior discourse into the common ground. In one of them, Campbell, Brooks, and Tomasello (2000) tested two-, three-, and four-year-old children's sensitivity to the fact that their addressee had previously mentioned a referent. In their experiment, children sat with an adult who commented on a video. Then a second adult came in the room. In one condition, the second adult had overheard the name of the character discussed in the video and asked the question in (3). In another condition, the second adult did not overhear the character's name and asked a neutral question as in (4).

(3) That was the clown? Oh, what happened?
(4) That sounds like fun. What happened?

The authors reasoned that if children are sensitive to previous mentions in discourse, they should react differently in each condition, even though the question is asked in a similar format. More specifically, children should use more pronouns to answer question (3) because of the common ground situation and more full names to answer question (4) because of the lack of common ground. They report that at the age of two, children are already more likely to simply name the referent when their addressee has not heard it before. At the ages of three and four, children become able to use fewer full nouns when the adult has overheard the name of the character. At the age of four, the difference is also reflected by a correct alternation between full nouns when there is no common ground and pronouns when there is common ground. In another experiment Wittek and Tomasello (2005) reported that children aged 2;6 and 3;6 answer differently to questions when the referent is mentioned in the question as in (5) and when it is not mentioned as in (6). When the referent is mentioned, children of both age groups tend to use null referents or pronouns. But when the question is formulated without mentioning the referent as in (6) they tend to answer with full nouns.

(5) Where is the pencil?
(6) What do we need?

They did not, however, replicate this finding with two-year-olds, indicating that this sensitivity emerges in the course of children's third year.

Another way to test children's incorporation of prior discourse into the common ground is to ask them to continue a story in which characters have already been introduced. Serratrice (2013) presented four-year-olds with a picture containing either one or two animate characters while starting a story with one sentence about them, as in (7).

(7) Woody said hello to Bo Peep and outside the bakery and then …

Children then had to continue the story based on a second picture in which only one character was present. Results indicate that when only one character is visually depicted in the first scene and linguistically mentioned, children overwhelmingly refer to it with a pronoun in the second picture. But when two characters are present in the first picture and mentioned as in (7), children use significantly fewer pronouns, even when the two characters differ in gender, and a pronoun would therefore be sufficiently informative to disambiguate the referents. This result indicates that children, like adults (e.g. Fukumura, van Gompel & Pickering, 2010; Fukumura, van Gompel, Harley & Pickering, 2011), are affected by similarity interferences in their choice of referring expressions. In this particular case, the similarity between two animate agents is more accessible than the difference in gender between them, and leads children to choose an overinformative form. In a second experiment, Serratrice specifically tested the role of animacy in this effect by including in the first scene one agent performing an action on an inanimate referent (e.g. 'Woody fixed his bike'). In this condition, children used pronouns in 80% of the cases to describe the second picture, a rate similar to the one found when only one referent is present in the first scene.

In addition to these production studies, experiments that have tested children's comprehension of pronouns also lead to the conclusion that they have an early ability to build a discourse model and incorporate linguistic information into the common ground. Song and Fisher (2007) tested the interpretation of pronouns by children aged 2;6 using eye-tracking and reported that children's interpretation of ambiguous pronouns is affected by prior discourse. More specifically, children look longer at the character that was most salient (i.e. the one mentioned first and placed in subject position) in preceding discourse. Sekerina, Stromswold, and Hestvik (2004) also reported that four- to seven-year-olds are able to perceive the ambiguity of pronouns that could potentially refer to two characters from previous discourse. More importantly, children show an implicit understanding of this ambiguity through the alternation of their gaze fixations between the two characters in an eye-tracking experiment but not in an offline task involving pointing to a picture. In the latter case, they choose a referent even when there is an ambiguity. This result further confirms that though children may first go through a phase of implicit knowledge this is not consistently reflected by their explicit pointing and linguistic behavior, as we discussed in the case of theory of mind development (see Chapter 5). This result also explains why young children appeared blind to ambiguities in early referential tasks that were mostly based on offline measures.

So far we have discussed the role of perceptual salience and prior discourse for children's referential choices. According to Ariel, givenness in discourse can also come from world knowledge. To the best of our knowledge, this factor has not been included in developmental studies yet, probably because it is harder to control for than the other factors, especially with young children. O'Neill and Happé (2000) had, however, tested 22-month-old children's ability to initiate topics of conversation based on the perceptual salience of objects. Their experiment was meant to assess whether young children at the one- or two-word stage perceive which aspects from the environment can be of shared interest with their audience and constitute good topics of conversation. For example, they showed children three identical plastic ducks one after the other and then a fourth much larger plastic duck. They reported that children all direct their attention to the same aspect of the toys showed to them (i.e. what is new) and produce similar words about them. In addition, their intervention occurred at the same time during the trials. These results confirm that very young children already know what other people typically talk about and pay attention to.

Another question stemming from our discussion is whether the ability to build common ground either based on perception or linguistic cues arise simultaneously or sequentially in development. Studies that have compared the two factors do not lead to consensual results. While some of them argue that the ability to take prior discourse mentions into account precedes the ability to integrate perceptual availability (Campbell et al., 2000; Wittek & Tomasello, 2005), others (Salomo et al., 2011) report that perceptual salience dominates when a conflict arises between the two factors. However, in their discussion, the authors of these studies admit that children's reliance on one or the other factor is partly dependent on settings of the task. Hughes and Allan (2013) compared the role of six features of accessibility for children's referential choices in naturalistic data and reported that prior mention, physical presence, and shared attention are all important for determining children's referential choices between the age of two and three and that these features are often interrelated. Similarly, Salazar Orvig et al. (2010) reported that French-speaking children's use of third person anaphoric pronouns between the age of 1;10 to 3;0 occurs mostly when the object is in the interlocutor's focus of attention and at the same time has been previously mentioned in the discourse, thus providing further confirmation for the importance of these two factors.

Taken together, the studies summarized in this section indicate that between the age of two and three, children become able to take the perspective of their listener based on perceptual cues such as physical copresence and joint attention as well as based on linguistic cues from prior discourse. When the referential disambiguation involves a complex NP, for example, when it is determined by the presence of a scalar adjective, children's performance continues to improve until late childhood. Several factors explain the discrepancy between this new set of findings and earlier studies that reported young children's lack of pragmatic skills in referential tasks. First, many early studies focused on the ability to produce complex NPs to disambiguate referents instead of more simple communication situations. Second, most studies relied on offline tasks to evaluate children's understanding of the ambiguity caused by some uses of pronouns, and therefore missed young children's early implicit ability to identify such problems. Lastly, earlier production studies lacked access to multimodal datasets, and therefore failed to notice that children often omit referents in contexts where it is pragmatically appropriate to do so because of joint attention between speaker and hearer.

8.2. Structuring discourse with connectives

In this section, we investigate children's growing ability to produce and understand coherence relations between sentences within a text, as well as their ability to use the lexical items encoding these relations, namely discourse connectives like 'if', 'but', and 'because'. We first discuss how connectives are used and processed by adult speakers (Section 8.2.1) and go on to address three questions for the acquisition of connectives. First, the order of acquisition between different coherence relations and the connectives encoding them (Section 8.2.2); second, the acquisition of subtle semantic distinctions separating connectives encoding the same coherence relation, such as the distinction between objective and subjective causality (Section 8.2.3); and finally the age at which children become able to effectively use the processing instructions conveyed by connectives during reading (Section 8.2.4).

8.2.1. Connectives and coherence relations

Discourse connectives form a functional category intersecting several grammatical categories such as conjunctions and adverbs. Their function is to convey coherence relations between units of text or discourse (e.g. Halliday & Hasan, 1976; Mann & Thompson, 1988; Sanders, Spooren & Noordman, 1992; Knott & Dale, 1994). Some examples are additive (8), temporal (9), causal (10), and adversative (11) relations.

(8) Ian likes to play the piano *and* to run marathons in his free time.
(9) John was surprised *when* he met Peter at the race.
(10) Mary is happy *because* she won the competition.
(11) Irvin likes fish *but* David prefers meat.

Even though a specific connective is used to convey each coherence relation in (8) to (11), a one-to-one mapping cannot be established between connectives and coherence relations. First, in many languages, coherence relations such as causality can be conveyed by several connectives. For example, in English, 'because', 'since', and 'as' can all be used to convey a causal relation. These connectives are not semantically equivalent however, and the distinction between them lies mainly on the degree of subjectivity of the relations they are prototypically conveying. While 'since' and 'as' are specifically used to convey claim-argument relations as in (12), that are taking place in the speaker's mind and are therefore subjective, 'because' can be used to convey both subjective argument-claim relations and objective consequence-cause relations taking place in the outside world, as in (13). In English, the connective 'because' is therefore semantically underspecified between objective and subjective causality, but in many other languages such as Dutch,

German, French, Portuguese, and Mandarin Chinese (see Stukker & Sanders, 2012 for a review) a specific connective is used in each case.

(12) Sarah cannot be at home, because she phoned from work five minutes ago.
(13) The door slammed because there is high wind.

A second reason why coherence relations and connectives do not have a one-to-one mapping is that some connectives can convey several coherence relations depending on context. For instance in English, 'since' sometimes conveys a temporal relation and sometimes a causal one. Lastly, in many cases, coherence relations can be understood by inference even in the absence of a connective explicitly marking them. For example, in (10), because of the semantics of the related segments and more specifically because of world knowledge, a causal relation between winning the competition and being happy remains accessible by inference even when the connective 'because' is removed, as in (14).

(14) Mary is happy. She won the competition.

Even though the use of connectives is not compulsory to indicate coherence relations, processing studies indicate that coherence relations that are explicitly conveyed by connectives are not processed in the same way as sentences where the relation is left implicit. When a connective is used, the second segment of a coherence relation is read faster compared with sentences without a connective (Millis & Just, 1994; Sanders & Noordman, 2000) and readers have a better understanding and memory of textual content (Caron, Micko & Thuring, 1988; Sanders, Land & Mulder, 2007). They are in addition also more likely to draw inferences when the relation between events is explicitly stated (Millis, Golding & Barker, 1995). Finally, when two sentences are not coherently related, the use of a connective hinders subjects' ability to detect the lack of coherence (Ferstl & von Cramon, 2001).

Processing studies have also revealed differences of complexity between several uses of connectives. The most notorious case concerns the difference between objective and subjective causal relations presented above. Traxler, Sanford, Aked, and Moxey (1997) compared the reading times of identical segments introduced by the English connective 'because', when the relation conveyed was either objective or subjective, as indicated by the semantic content of the first segment, as in (15) and (16), respectively.

(15) Heidi felt proud and happy, because she won first prize at the art show.
(16) Heidi could draw, because she won first prize at the art show.

They found that subjective relations lead to a longer reading time compared to objective relations. Traxler, Bybee, and Pickering (1997) reported in addition that this effect occurs before the end of the sentence, at the words 'won first prize' in examples (15) and (16). The authors conclude that at this point, the subjective interpretation is reached based on the semantic content of the related segments. Canestrelli, Mak, and Sanders (2013) replicated this experiment in Dutch, a language that encodes the distinction between objective and subjective causality in two specific connectives ('omdat' and 'want'). They reported that the slowdown induced by subjective relations occurs at the words immediately after the subjective connective 'want' instead of later on during the sentence. They concluded that 'want' gives processing instructions about subjectivity, producing an earlier effect, thus confirming that connectives provide processing instructions that are immediately integrated in the course of sentence processing.

In order to account for the variations in cognitive complexity between coherence relations, Sanders et al. (1992) proposed a set cognitive primitives to categorize coherence relations and rank them in terms of cognitive complexity. For all primitives, two possible values can be assigned, one of which being cognitively simple and the other one being more complex. The first primitive, called basic operation, distinguishes between additive (simple) and causal (complex) relations. The second primitive is polarity, and distinguishes between positive (simple) and negative (complex) relations. The third primitive, temporality, distinguishes between temporally non-ordered (simple) and ordered (complex) relations. All connectives thus receive a value from all primitives. For example, the connective 'because' is causal, positive, and can be both temporal and non-temporal in some of its uses. Sanders et al.'s model thus predicts that some combinations are cognitively more complex than others but also that some are of a similar level of complexity. For example, while non-temporal/additive/positive relations (corresponding to the connective 'and') are the easiest combination, no order emerges between temporal/positive/additive relations and non-temporal/negative/additive ones, because both contain two cognitively simple values and one complex value. We will discuss the validity of this model for developmental data in Section 8.2.2.

8.2.2. The order of acquisition between discourse connectives

From a developmental perspective, the cognitive model advocated by Sanders et al. predicts that some coherence relations should be cognitively more complex than others for children to acquire. The first study chronologically that has assessed the order of acquisition between connectives was conducted by Bloom, Lahey, Hood, Lifter, and Fliess (1980). They compared the order of emergence between coherence relations expressed with and without connectives in four children recorded between the age of 1;7 and 3;0. They found a fixed order of emergence between four coherence relations. All children start by producing additive relations, followed by temporal relations, then causal relations, and lastly adversative relations. The same regularity was not found, however, in the order of emergence of the corresponding connectives. While all children started by producing the connective 'and', the order of emergence between the other connectives found in their corpus, namely 'and then', 'because', 'when', 'if', 'so', and 'but' was variable across children. Bloom et al. explained the regularity in the emergence of coherence relations on the basis of cumulative conceptual complexity. More specifically, they argued that a form of addition is included in all temporal, causal, and adversative relations because in all cases two events or states are joined. Similarly, all causal relations are also partly additive and partly temporal. More generally, a more complex relation subsumes the simpler ones and children master them when they have reached the corresponding conceptual development. This approach does not explain, however, why the acquisition of the connectives used to convey these relations is not coherent across children.

This problem can be solved by adopting a multidimensional approach to cognitive complexity, as advocated by Sanders et al. (1992). This model explains why some limited variability should be expected in the order of acquisition between connectives, as some relations are equal in terms of cognitive complexity. However, for each primitive, one alternative is deemed to be easier than the other and should lead to a fixed order of acquisition. Evers-Vermeul and Sanders (2009) assessed this order of acquisition for 12 Dutch speaking children recorded over several years at ages ranging from 1;5 for the youngest child at the beginning of the study and 5;6 for the older child at the end of the study. Data were collected from several different corpora. Results confirm that all children produced an additive connective before a causal one, and all children but one also produced a positive connective before a negative one. Finally, all children produced temporally non-ordered connectives before ordered ones, confirming the differences of cognitive complexity between the two possible values for all three primitives.

In addition to cognitive complexity, other linguistic and social factors may also play a role in the order of acquisition between connectives, such as the syntactic complexity of the clauses in which connectives are used and their frequency in the input. Evers-Vermeul and Sanders (2009) demonstrated the syntactic complexity of the clauses (defined following the criteria of Diessel, 2004) is also an important factor accounting for the order of acquisition between connectives that express a similar coherence relation as well as between different uses of the same connective. For example, in Dutch, Evers-Vermeul and Sanders note a sequence of acquisition between the two causal connectives 'want' and 'omdat'. The former is used earlier because it is a coordinative conjunction while the latter is a subordinating conjunction. However, these two connectives are not semantically equivalent (see Section 8.2.3) and children at first mistakenly use 'want' for the relations that should be conveyed by 'omdat'. Van Veen, Evers-Vermeul, Sanders, and van den Bergh (2011) studied the role of parental input for the acquisition of German connectives (focusing on the connectives 'aber', 'damit', 'und', 'weil', and 'wenn') by a child recorded between 1;11 and 2;11. They compared the effect of age, submitting that an increase in age corresponded to an increase in cognitive abilities, with the short term effects of parental input during the space of one recording and the long-term effects of this input by cumulative usage of a connective over the recordings. They reported that all three factors play a role for the acquisition of connectives.

The studies reported so far all document the emergence of connectives in children's speech between the age of two and three. Both Bloom et al. (1980) and Evers-Vermeul and Sanders (2009) noted in addition that implicit coherence relations between sentences occur before the correct connectives to express them are acquired. In other words, when children start to produce multiple sentences between the age of two and three, these sentences are already linked together with identifiable coherence relations. This suggests that children already possess the ability to manipulate coherence relations before they acquire the meaning of connectives that are used to mark them explicitly. By contrast, several comprehension experiments indicate that children do not fully master the use of connectives until late childhood. For example, Cain, Patson, and Andrews (2005) used a cloze test to compare eight and ten-year-olds ability to use additive, causal, adversative, and temporal connectives. They found that 10-year-olds outperform 8-year-olds with causal, temporal, and adversative connectives but not with additive connectives, indicating that three out of the four types of connectives studied still develop between the age of 8 and 10. Crosson, Lesaux, and Martiniello (2008) also reported that nine-year-olds perform less well with causal, temporal, and adversative connectives compared to additive connectives. Cain and Nash (2011) used a sense judgment task for temporal, causal, and adversative connectives and reported that 10-year-olds but not 8-year-olds reach adult-like performances, even though 8-year-olds showed some ability to discriminate correct from incorrect uses for all three relations. In short, results from these studies reveal that children do not fully master the usage of frequently used connectives to express relations of causality, temporality, and adversity until late childhood, many years after they first appear in their productions.

8.2.3. The acquisition of objective and subjective relations

In addition to learning how to use connectives to express various coherence relations, children must also learn the subtle differences of meaning between connectives expressing a single coherence relation, such as the difference between objective and subjective causal relations discussed in Section 8.2.1. Several studies have investigated the order of acquisition between objective and subjective causal relations (Kyratzis, Guo & Ervin-Tripp, 1990; Spooren & Sanders, 2008; Zufferey, 2010; Evers-Vermeul & Sanders, 2011).

In Dutch, Spooren and Sanders (2008) designed two elicitation tasks to analyze the production of causal relations by children from two age groups: 6–7-year-olds and 11–12-year-olds. All sequences of causally related sentences were analyzed, independently of the presence of connectives. Results indicate that the use of subjective relations did not differ between the two groups. These experiments also highlighted the role of context for the production of domains of use. In one of the tasks, children were asked to describe a picture, with the effect of strongly biasing them toward the production of objective relations. Another task, involving argumentation, biased children toward subjective relations. Given that the younger age group from this study already produced both types of relations, Evers-Vermeul and Sanders (2011) conducted two additional elicitation tasks in Dutch with three-, four- and five-year-old children, again designed to bias the production of causal relations toward one specific domain of use. Results indicate that children as young as three are already able to produce all kinds of relations when the task they have to perform encourages them to do so. However, both three- and four-year-olds produced significantly less subjective relations than five-year-olds.

As three-year-old Dutch-speaking children are already able to produce all kinds of relations, Evers-Vermeul and Sanders (2011) have also studied 12 younger children's productions in a series of longitudinal Dutch corpora available through the CHILDES database. The recordings included the period of 2;0 to 3;6 on average. In this experiment, causal relations were studied only when they were marked by four specific connectives: 'omdat', 'want', 'dus', and 'daarom'. The connectives 'omdat' and 'want' indicate backward causal relations, that is, relations with the consequence presented first in the sentence and the cause following the connective, while 'dus' and 'daarom' are forward causal connectives, with segments presented in reversed order. The conclusions from this analysis are that children are able to produce objective and subjective causal connectives by the age of three, and that subjective relations are systematically produced later than objective relations. In another longitudinal corpus study in French, Zufferey (2010) analyzed productions of the causal connective 'parce que' by four children. Three of the children were recorded between the age 2;3 and 3;4. The fourth child was recorded between the age of 2;8 and 4;3. These results indicate that French-speaking children are also able to produce objective and subjective relations by the age of three, and that the onset of production for subjective relations is delayed with respect to objective relations.

All the studies mentioned above have investigated the emergence of children's spontaneous production of connectives in naturalistic data. Van Veen (2011) addressed the question of children's comprehension of objective and subjective relations using the visual world paradigm of eye-tracking. In her experiment, children were presented with two pictures on a computer screen, and heard a stimulus sentence that contained either an implicit objective or an implicit subjective relation with one of them. For example, children saw a picture of a pig standing in some mud plus an additional distraction picture featuring the same pig and heard sentences like (17).

(17) The pig will get dirty.

In this case, there is an objective relation (taking place in the real physical world) between the fact of standing in the mud and that of getting dirty. Preferential looking time was measured for two groups of children: 2;0 and 3;4 year-olds, as well as an adult control group. This study revealed that while both groups of children displayed a similar behavior with objective relations, the 3;4 group performed better that the 2;0 group with subjective relations. More specifically, while children from both age groups did manage to relate the correct pictures to the verbal stimuli even in the subjective condition, three-year-old children were faster and more accurate than two-year-olds. This was not the case for objective relations, for which both groups got comparable results. Crucially, the performance of three-year-olds was not yet comparable to that of adults in both conditions, indicating that some further developments must be taking place at a later age. This study indicates, however, that young children already have some ability to distinguish between objective and subjective relations before they master the connectives to express them.

8.2.4. When do children use the processing instructions of connectives?

In Section 8.2.1, we reported studies indicating that adult readers use the processing instructions provided by connectives, and did so very early in the course of sentence processing, as soon as either the connective or the semantic content of the relation provided them a cue about interpretation. The question we address in this section is whether young readers by the age of eight already use the meaning of connectives as processing instructions the way adults readers do, even though they do not systematically choose the correct connective to express a relation until the age of ten in offline tasks.

Several self-paced reading studies have measured the reading times of segments following connectives by young readers. Mouchon, Fayol, and Gaonac'h (1995) reported that from the age of eight, children read a segment faster when it is preceded by the connectives 'mais' and 'soudain' compared with an implicit relation. Cain and Nash (2012) tested 8- and 10-year-olds' reading of sentences containing a temporal, causal, and adversative connective related with a correct, incorrect, or neutral ('and') connective. They reported longer reading times of the clause following the connective when an incorrect or neutral connective is used compared to a correct connective. The authors suggest that the longer reading times for incorrect connectives may be due to the processing cost associated with trying to repair the disruption of coherence caused by the clash between the meaning of the connective and the semantic content of the segments. When the neutral 'and' connective is used, the interpretation of a stronger causal, temporal, or adversative reading relation remains possible by inference. Cain and Nashed submit that the longer reading time observed after 'and' may be due to the extra cost associated with having to construct the semantically underdetermined relation by inference. This hypothesis is compatible with results from Noveck and Chevaux (2002), who also found that strengthening the meaning of 'and' with a temporal meaning (i.e. 'and then') or a causal meaning (i.e. 'and so') in context induced additional processing cost.

In sum, these studies indicate that young readers are able to use the processing instructions conveyed by commonly used connectives like 'before', 'because', and 'but' during reading. Zufferey and Sanders (2014) assessed whether young readers were also able to use subtle semantic distinctions such as the one separating objective from subjective causality, the way adult readers have been shown to do (see Section 8.2.1). They tested children aged 8–11, and presented them with subjective causal relations correctly conveyed by 'want', or incorrectly conveyed by 'omdat'. They reasoned that if children have adult-like behavior, they should slowdown immediately after 'want' because of the subjectivity effect, and then proceed smoothly with the rest of the sentence. The use of 'omdat' should not lead to a slowdown immediately after the connective but to longer reading times at the end of the sentence because of the disruption of coherence caused by the incorrect use of connective (both effects were reported for adults by Canestrelli et al., 2013). None of the two effects occurred, however, suggesting that children do not yet fully master the subtle processing instructions of subjectivity by the age of 11.

8.3. Synthesis

In this chapter, we reviewed children's growing ability to take common ground into account in order to produce adequately informative referential expressions, as well as their emergent use and understanding of coherence relations and the linguistic means to convey them. In both cases, results demonstrate that children's discourses are not limited by lack of pragmatic skills, as they modulate the informativeness of their pointing gestures and vocal productions depending on the needs of their addressee, and produce conjoined sentences that are coherently related, albeit often implicitly. These results thus provide some confirmation that pragmatic competencies are operational early, but that the use of appropriate linguistic forms such as pronouns and connectives to express them spans over a long period of time, because of the need to understand the sometimes complex procedural instructions that they encode.

References

Ariel, M. (1985). The discourse functions of given information. *Theoretical Linguistics, 12*, 99–113.

Ariel, M. (1988). Referring and accessibility. *Journal of Linguistics, 24*, 65–87.

Ariel, M. (2001). Accessibility theory: an overview. In T. Sanders, J., Schilperoord, & W. Spooren (eds), *Text Representation: Linguistic and Psycholinguistic Aspects* (pp. 29–88). Amsterdam: John Benjamins.

Bahtiyar, S. & Küntay, A. (2008). Integration of communicative partner's visual perspective in patterns of referential requests. *Journal of Child Language, 36*(3), 529–555.

Begus, K. & Southgate, V. (2012). Infant pointing serves an interrogative function. *Developmental Science, 15*(5), 611–617.

Bloom, L., Lahey, M., Hood, L., Lifter, K., & Fiess, K. (1980). Complex sentences: Acquisition of syntactic connectives and the semantic relations they encode. *Journal of Child Language, 7*, 235–261.

Cain, K. & Nash, H. (2011). The influence of connectives on young readers' processing and comprehension of text. *Journal of Educational Psychology, 103*(2), 429–441.

Cain, K., Patson, N., & Andrews, L. (2005). Age- and ability-related differences in young readers' use of conjunctions. *Journal of Child Language, 32*, 877–892.

Campbell, A., Brooks, P., & Tomasello, M. (2000). Factors affecting young children's use of pronouns as referring expressions. *Journal of Speech, Language, and Hearing Research, 43*, 1337–1349.

Canestrelli, A., Mak, W., & Sanders, T. (2013). Causal connectives in discourse processing: How differences in subjectivity are reflected in eye-movements. *Language and Cognitive Processes, 28*(9), 1394–1413.

Caron, J., Micko, H. C., & Thuring, M. (1988). Conjunctions and the recall of composite sentences. *Journal of Memory and Language, 27*, 309–323.

Clark, H. (1992). *Arenas of Language Use*. Chicago: University of Chicago Press.

Clark, H. & Marshall, C. (1981). Definite reference and mutual knowledge. In A. Joshi, B. Webber, & I. Sag (eds), *Elements of Discourse Understanding* (pp. 10–63). Cambridge: Cambridge University Press.

Crosson, A., Lesaux, N., & Martiniello, M. (2008). Factors that influence comprehension of connectives among language minority children from Spanish-speaking backgrounds. *Applied Psycholinguistics, 29*, 603–625.

Diessel, H. (2004). *The Acquisition of Complex Sentences*. Cambridge: Cambridge University Press.

Evers-Vermeul, J. & Sanders, T. (2009). The emergence of Dutch connectives: How cumulative cognitive complexity explains the order of acquisition. *Journal of Child Language, 36*, 829–854.

Evers-Vermeul, J. & Sanders, T. (2011). Discovering domains: On the acquisition of causal connectives. *Journal of Pragmatics, 43*, 1645–1662.

Ferstl, E. & von Cramon, D. (2001). The role of coherence and cohesion in text comprehension: An event-related fMRI study. *Cognitive Brain Research, 11*, 325–340.

Fukumura, K., van Gompel, R., & Pickering, M. (2010). The use of visual context during the production of referring expressions. *The Quarterly Journal of Experimental Psychology, 49A*, 991–1004.

Fukumura, K., van Gompel, R., Harley, T., & Pickering, M. (2011). How does similarity-based interference affect the choice of referring expression? *Journal of Memory and Language, 65*, 331–344.

Givón, T. (1983). *Topic Continuity in Discourse: A Quantitative Cross-Language Study*. Amsterdam: John Benjamins.

Gundel, J., Hedberg, N., & Zacharski, R. (1993). Cognitive status and the form of referring expressions in discourse. *Language, 69*(2), 274–307.

Halliday, Michael & Ruqaiya Hasan. (1976). *Cohesion in English*. London: Longman.

Hughes, M. & Allan, S. (2013). The effect of individual discourse pragmatic features on referential choice in child English. *Journal of Pragmatics, 56*, 15–30.

Hyams, N. & Wexler, K. (1993). On the grammatical basis of null subjects in child language. *Linguistic Inquiry, 24*(3), 421–459.

Knott, A. & Dale, R. (1994). Using linguistic phenomena to motivate a set of coherence relations. *Discourse Processes, 18*, 35–62.

Kyratzis, A., Guo, J., & Ervin-Tripp, S. (1990). Pragmatic conventions influencing children's use of causal constructions in natural discourse. In K. Hall, J. Koenig, M. Meacham, S. Reinman, & L. Sutton (eds), *Proceedings of the Sixteenth Annual Meeting of the Berkeley Linguistics Society* (pp. 205–214). Berkeley, CA: Berkeley Linguistic Society.

Liszkowski, U., Carpenter, M., & Tomasello, M. (2008). Twelve-month-olds communicate helpfully and appropriately for knowledgeable and ignorant partners. *Cognition, 108*(3), 732–739.

Mann, W. & Thompson, S. (1988). Rhetorical strucutre theory: Toward a functional theory of text organization. *Text*, (8), 243–281.

Mann, W. & Thompson, S. (1992). Relational discourse structure: A comparison of approaches to structuring text by 'contrast'. In S. Hwang, & W. Merrifield (eds), *Language in Context: Essays for Robert E. Longacre* (pp. 19–45). Dallas: SIL.

Matthews, D., Lieven, E., Theakson, A., & Tomasello, M. (2006). The effect of perceptual availability and prior discourse on young children's use of referring expressions. *Applied Psycholinguistics, 27*, 403–422.

Matthews, D., Lieven, E., & Tomasello, M. (2007). How toddlers and preschoolers learn to uniquely identify referents. *Child Development, 78*, 1744–1759.

Millis, K., Golding, J., & Barker, G. (1995). Causal connectives increase inference generation. *Discourse Processes, 20*, 29–49.

Millis, K. & Just, M. (1994). The influence of connectives on sentence comprehension. *Journal of Memory and Language, 33*, 128–147.

Moll, H. & Tomasello, M. (2006). Level I perspective taking at 24 months of age. *British Journal of Developmental Psychology, 24*, 603–613.

Mouchon, S., Fayol, M., & Gaonac'h, D. (1995). On-line processing of links between events in narratives: study of children and adults. *Current Psychology of Cognition, 14*, 171–193.

Nadig, A. & Sedivy, J. (2002). Evidence of perspective-taking constraints in children's online-reference resolution. *Psychological Science, 13*, 329–336.

Noveck, I. & Chevaux, F. (2002). The pragmatic development of and. *Proceedings of the Twenty-sixth Annual Boston University Conference on Language Development*. Sommerville, MA: Cascadilla Press.

O'Neill, D. (1996). Two-year-old children's sensitivity to a parent's knowledge state when making requests. *Child Development, 67*, 659–677.

O'Neill, D. & Happé, F. (2000). Noticing and commenting on what's new: Differences and similarities among 22-month-old typically developing children, children with Down syndrome, and children with autism. *Developmental Science, 3*, 457–478.

O'Neill, D. & Topolovec, J. (2001). Two-year-old children's sensitivity to the referential (in)efficacy of their own pointing gestures. *Journal of Child Language, 28*, 1–28.

Prince, E. (1981). Toward a taxonomy of given/new information. In P. Cole (ed), *Radical Pragmatics* (pp. 223–254). New York: Academic Press.

Rizzi, L. (2005). Grammatically-based target inconsistencies in child language. In K. Deen, J. Nomura, B. Schulz, & B. Schwartz, (eds), *The Proceedings of the Inaugural Conference on Generative Approaches to Language Acquisition: North America*. University of Connecticut Occasional Papers in Linguistics, 4, 19–49.

Salazar Orvig, A., Marcos, H., Morgenstern, A., Hassan, R., Leber-Marin, J., & Parès, J. (2010). Dialogical beginnings of anaphora: The use of third person pronouns before the age of 3. *Journal of Pragmatics, 42*(7), 1842–1865.

Salomo, D., Graf, E., Lieven, E., & Tomasello, M. (2011). The role of perceptual availability and discourse context in young children's question answering. *Journal of Child Language, 38*, 918–931.

Sanders, T., Land, J., & Mulder, G. (2007). Linguistic markers of coherence improve text comprehension in functional contexts. *Information Design Journal, 15*(3), 219–235.

Sanders, T. & Noordman, L. (2000). The role of coherence relations and their linguistic markers in text processing. *Discourse Processes, 29*, 37–60.

Sanders, T., Spooren, W., & Noordman, L. (1992). Toward a taxonomy of coherence relations. *Discourse Processes, 15*, 1–35.

Schaeffer, J. (2000). *The Acquisition of Direct Object Scrambling and Clitic Placement: Syntax and Pragmatics*. Amsterdam: John Benjamins.

Sekerina, I., Stromwold, K., & Hestvik, A. (2004). How do adults and children process referentially ambiguous pronouns? *Journal of Child Language, 31*(1), 123–152.

Serratrice, L. (2013). The role of number of referents and animacy in children's use of pronouns. *Journal of Pragmatics, 56*, 31–42.

Skarabela, B., Allan, S., & Scott-Phillips, T. (2013). Joint attention helps to explain why children omit new referents. *Journal of Pragmatics, 56*, 5–14.

Song, H.-J. & Fisher, C. (2007). Discourse prominence effects on 2.5-year-old children's interpretation of pronouns. *Lingua, 117*(11), 1959–1987.

Spooren, W. & Sanders, T. (2008). The acquisition order of coherence relations: On cognitive complexity in discourse. *Journal of Pragmatics, 40*, 2003–2026.

Stukker,, N. & Sanders, T. (2012). Subjectivity and prototype structure in causal connectives: A cross-linguistic perspective. *Journal of Pragmatics, 34*(2), 169–190.

Traxler, M., Bybee, M., & Pickering, M. (1997). Influence of connectives on language comprehension: Eye-tracking evidence for incremental interpretation. *Quarterly Journal of Experimental Psychology Section A: Human Experimental Psychology, 50*, 481–497.

Traxler, M., Sanford, A., Aked, J., & Moxey, L. (1997). Processing causal and diagnostic statements in discourse. *Journal of Experimental Psychology: Learning, Memory and Cognition, 23*, 88–101.

van Hout, A., Harrigan, K., & de Villiers, J. (2010). Asymmetries in the acquisition of definite and indefinite NPs. *Lingua, 120*(8), 1973–1990.

Van Veen, R. (2011). *The Acquisition of Causal Connectives.* Unpublished PhD Thesis, University of Utrecht, the Netherlands.

Van Veen, R., Evers-Vermeul, J., Sanders, T., & van den Bergh, H. (2009). Parental input and connective acquisition. A growth curve analysis. *First Language, 29*(3), 266–288.

Wittek, A. & Tomasello, M. (2005). Young children's sensitivity to listener knowledge and perceptual context in choosing referring expressions. *Applied Psycholinguistics, 26*, 541–558.

Yule, G. (1997). *Referential Communication Tasks.* Mahwah, NJ: Lawrence Erlbaum.

Zufferey, S. (2010). *Lexical Pragmatics and Theory of Mind: The Acquisition of Connectives.* Amsterdam: John Benjamins.

Zufferey, S. & Sanders, T. (2014). The acquisition of objective and subjective causality. *Paper Presented at the 13th International Congress for the Study of Child Language (IASCL)*, Amsterdam, the Netherlands.

PART IV

The acquisition of pragmatics under specific constraints

9

PRAGMATIC IMPAIRMENTS IN AUTISM SPECTRUM DISORDERS

Autism is a neurodevelopmental disorder characterized by core impairments in the domains of social interaction as well as language and communication. For this reason, autism has been a thoroughly studied pathology in relation to atypical pragmatic development. In this chapter, we start by reviewing the linguistic and pragmatic impairments associated with autism in Section 9.1. We then discuss two psychological theories that have often been called upon in the literature to explain the communicative and social impairments in autism, namely the hypothesis of a deficit in theory of mind abilities (Section 9.2) and of weak central coherence (Section 9.3). We argue that in addition to their lack of attunement to social cues, autism spectrum disorders (ASDs) subjects' pragmatic impairments can also be related to deficits in the structural domains of language that have until recently been overlooked.

9.1. Language and communicative profile

It should be noted first that the clinical picture of autism can be more or less severe, ranging from deep to high-functioning autism (hereafter HFA). Because of this high heterogeneity, autism is now commonly referred to as ASDs. Traditionally, research on language and communication in autism concluded that the language of high functioning individuals with autism was relatively spared, and that these good linguistic skills strikingly contrasted with their generalized inability to use language for communication. More recent investigations using fine-grained measures of language assessment have revealed, however, that even high-functioning ASD subjects suffer from subtle forms of language impairment. In this section, we first present the linguistic profile of autism (Section 9.1.1) before turning to pragmatic impairments (Section 9.1.2).

9.1.1. Structural domains of language

The linguistic skills of the ASD population are quite variable. At the lower end of the spectrum, 15% of the subjects diagnosed with ASD remain non-verbal at the age of nine (Gotham, Bishop & Lord, 2010). In contrast, at least some subjects with ASD do not have any deficit in the structural domains of language such as syntax or phonology in adulthood (Kelley, Paul, Fein & Naigles, 2006). At the higher end of the spectrum, a distinction between HFA and another form of neurodevelopmental disorder involving impairments in social interactions, called Asperger syndrome, has traditionally been established based on early language skills. More specifically, Asperger syndrome was distinguished from the rest of the ASD population because of the absence of clinically significant delays in early language development.[1] In the most recent version of the *Diagnostic and Statistic Manual for Mental Disorders* (*DSM-V*, American Psychological Association, 2013), Asperger syndrome has, however, been included in the ASD spectrum as a variant of HFA, because the linguistic skills of these two sub-groups are often undifferentiated in adulthood. In addition, the diagnosis of Asperger syndrome relies mostly on caregiver reports about early language development, which have been found to be unreliable indicators of actual linguistic skills (Hus, Taylor & Lord, 2011).

While the standard view held for a long time was that verbal children with ASD did not suffer from impairments in the structural domains of language such as phonology and syntax, this conclusion has been recently challenged in the literature. Kjelgaard and Tager-Flusberg (2001) reported impairments of vocabulary, syntax, and semantics in a sub-group of children with ASD. Studies specifically targeting more fine-grained aspects of language development have also reported a range of impairments.

In the domain of phonology, Sheinkopf, Mundy, Oller, and Steffens (2000) reported that even in the very early stages of vocalizations, children with ASD have atypical phonation, in other words impairment in vocal quality. Later on during development, electrophysiological studies have revealed that verbal autistic children retain auditory input abnormalities (Rapin & Dunn, 2003). General deficits have also been found in the area of prosody (McCann, Peppé, Gibbon, O'Hare, & Rutherford, 2007), and more specifically in the production and perception of stress (Paul, Augustyn, Klin & Volkmar, 2005).

Specific impairments in complex syntax have also been reported, in the areas of question formation (Eigsti, Bennetto & Dadlani, 2006), tense marking (Roberts, Mabel, Rice & Tager-Flusberg, 2004), passives and bindings (Perovic, Nadya & Wexler, 2013), and relative clauses (Durrleman & Zufferey, 2013). Many of these phonological and syntactic deficits have also been attested in children with specific language impairment (SLI), for example, problems with tense marking (Leonard, 1998; Rice, Wexler & Hershenberger, 1998), which lead to the hypothesis that some children with ASD may suffer from SLI in addition to autism. Despite these similarities, the comparison between autism and SLI has not yet provided conclusive evidence that the linguistic impairments of both populations should be treated as one and the same thing. First of all, data on syntax in autism remains scarce, and as Phillips (2005) observed, problems with verb inflections have been found in many other developmental language disorders presumed to have different genetic causes than those for autism. Moreover, genetic comparisons between autism and SLI led to controversial results (Whitehouse, Barry & Bishop, 2008).

The lexicon of children with ASD is deviant in several respects. First, children with ASD have a tendency to use words in an idiosyncratic and excessively limited fashion. Second, they tend to invent words or to assign new meanings to existing words. For example, Attwood (2006: 205) reported that one child coined the word 'snook' to refer to chocolate flakes found in an ice cream and another one coined the word 'clink' to designate a magnet. Lastly, they name objects based on personal associative criteria. When they reach adulthood, the lexicon of HFA subjects still remains well below chronological age level (Howlin, 2003). This delay is similar for subjects diagnosed with HFA and those diagnosed with Asperger syndrome, confirming the similarity of linguistic competencies between the two populations in adulthood.

In sum, the functional aspects of language are not fully spared in the ASD population, even at the higher end of the spectrum. It has often been argued, however, that ASD subjects' impairments in the structural aspects of language are more variable and always less severe than in the domain of pragmatics. Frith (2003: 118) observed, for example, that "whatever the level of syntactic or semantic skill in autism, the level of pragmatic skill will be lower." We now turn to the description of these pragmatic impairments.

9.1.2. Nature and extent of pragmatic impairments in ASD

Already during the preverbal period, parents of children with ASD notice that their child does not produce proto-declarative pointing to call their attention to something. This seems to indicate that contrary to normally developing children, children with ASD do not use language to share their interest for an object. On the other hand, they use proto-imperative pointing in order to ask for something, just like the other children. This observation finds some confirmation in a study conducted by Wetherby and Prutting (1984) on the use of speech acts by ASD and typically developing children. Their results show that while children with ASD use requests in order to ask for an object or an action just like the other children, other types of requests such as requests for information are completely absent from their production.

When they become verbal, children with ASD exhibit many forms of pragmatic impairments. At a social level, they often have difficulties conducting a conversation. While at a basic level such as turn taking, they seem to have globally intact abilities (Tager-Flusberg, 2001), they are often incapable of maintaining a topic of conversation across several turns or to change topic in an appropriate way. For instance, they often use fixed expressions like 'by the way', 'talking of', or 'well, anyway' without introducing a new topic of conversation (Frith, 2003: 128). Volden (2004) also found that subjects with ASD were more likely than controls to produce bizarre topic shifts or to discontinue the interaction. They also have many difficulties following rules of politeness, notably because they mix the various levels of politeness in an inappropriate manner. For example, Baltaxe (1977) studied German-speaking ASD teenagers and found that they were mixing the polite and familiar forms ('Sie' and 'du') inappropriately. They also use the pronoun 'we' less than controls (Hobson, Lee & Hobson, 2010). Moreover, they sometimes use an excessively polite language. Frith (2003: 133) related the case of a young boy who often started his phone calls to his favorite aunt by "It's M. C. Smith, your nephew, calling." In sum, subjects with ASD suffer from deficits in the domains of pragmatic abilities related to social norms, which corroborates the fact that one of the main diagnostic criteria for autism is impaired social interactions.

From a cognitive perspective, many contemporary pragmatic theories emphasize that pragmatic enrichment does not only occur at the level of implicit meaning such as non-literal language uses and conversational implicatures, as Grice had initially argued, but also at the explicit level (see Chapter 1, Section 1.1.2). This raises the question of whether ASD children are impaired across all layers of explicit and implicit pragmatic enrichment or whether these impairments are limited to the implicit cases. Results from the literature tend to indicate that the areas of impairment found in autism cannot be related to their degree of implicitness alone. While de Villiers, Brooks, and Stainton (2007) reported from the analysis of a corpus of natural interactions with ASD subjects that enrichment at the explicit level, for example, assigning a referent to indexical pronouns, enriching the utterance by adding null complements and resolving polysemy, is relatively spared, other studies have evidenced deficits in the ability to disambiguate homographs in context (e.g. Jolliffe & Baron-Cohen, 1999). Other areas of enrichment at the explicit level have also been found to be impaired. For example, in current pragmatic theories such as relevance theory, metaphors are considered to be a case of lexical adjustment leading to the formation of an ad hoc concept, occurring at the explicit level of utterance interpretation (See Chapter 6, Section 6.1). Children with ASD have repeatedly been found to be less able than controls to understand metaphors (Gold & Faust, 2010; Happé, 1993; MacKay & Shaw, 2004; Rundblad & Annaz, 2010). The derivation of scalar implicatures, which some authors also consider as a case of lexical adjustment (e.g. Noveck & Sperber, 2007) is, however, spared, at least the derivation of generalized implicatures (see Chapter 7) related to scalar words such as 'or' and 'some' (Chevallier, Wilson, Happé & Noveck, 2010; Pijnacker, Hagoort, Buitelaar, Teunisse & Geurts, 2009). Evidence is still lacking about ASD subjects' ability to construct ad hoc scales in context, corresponding to the ability to derive particularized scalar implicatures.

At the implicit level, the ability of subjects with ASD to understand indirect speech acts has yielded conflicting findings. While MacKay and Shaw (2005) reported that subjects with ASD have problems explaining why a character in a story performed an indirect request, Ozonoff and Miller (1996) found that when subjects with ASD are asked to choose the continuation of a story ending with an indirect request, they choose follow-ups that demonstrate non-literal interpretations more frequently than literal interpretations, even though their performance on this task is lower than that of controls. Kissine, de Brabanter, and Leybaert (2012) also reported that children with ASD comply with requests in naturalistic conversations equally often when they are conveyed literally and non-literally. The difference between these studies seems to be a matter of possessing pragmatic versus meta-pragmatic skills. While children with ASD use pragmatic skills in their reaction to indirect requests, they cannot perform a meta-pragmatic reasoning about the social reasons for using indirect requests. A clearer consensus was reached for the most complex forms of implicit enrichment such as irony (Happé, 1993; Martin & McDonald, 2004; Wang, Lee, Sigman & Dapretto, 2006) as well as other forms of jokes and humor (Baron-Cohen, 1997; Emerich, Creaghead, Grether, Murray & Grasha, 2003) that have universally been reported to be impaired in the ASD population.

In addition to the ability to enrich the linguistic meaning of utterances, pragmatic skills also encompass the ability to relate several utterances coherently in a text or a discourse. The ASD population is also impaired at the level of discourse. Subjects with ASD are less able than controls to arrange utterances coherently and to use context to make a global inference (Joliffe & Baron-Cohen, 2000) and their narratives are also less causally connected compared with controls (Diehl, Bennetto & Young, 2006). They are in addition less able to shift perspective and viewpoints in narrative tasks (García-Pérez, Hobson & Lee, 2008). The ability to take the listener's perspective into account is also crucial in determining the choice of referring expressions across several utterances (see Chapter 8, Section 8.1). Arnold, Bennetto, and Diehl (2009) reported that subjects with ASD use fewer pronouns to describe an entity previously mentioned several utterances earlier in discourse compared with controls, in other words they tend to overspecify their referring expressions by using full noun phrases even in situations where a pronoun would be informative enough. The difference between groups diminished however as children with ASD got older.

In the literature, the pragmatic impairments reported in this section have been in most cases related to ASD subjects' deficits in theory of mind abilities and to their weak central coherence (see Loukusa & Moilanen, 2009). In the next sections, we discuss how these two psychological theories can account for the social and communicative impairments evidenced in the ASD population.

9.2. The theory of mind deficit hypothesis

For all inferential models of communication, the ability to reason about a speaker's mental states is a crucial skill ensuring the success of verbal communication in a number of cases involving non-literal language uses and deception (Sperber, 1994). In this section, we first show the existence of a theory of mind deficit in the ASD population (Section 9.2.1) and argue that this deficit explains some of their linguistic and communicative impairments (Section 9.2.2).

9.2.1. Theory of mind impairments in ASD

One of the most influential accounts explaining ASD children's lack of communicative skills is the hypothesis of a deficit in theory of mind, or 'mindblindness' (Baron-Cohen, 1995). This hypothesis was assessed using the Sally-Ann version of the false-belief task (see Chapter 5, Section 5.1.1), specifically designed to be simple enough to be used with ASD children (Baron-Cohen, Leslie & Frith, 1985). Results indicated that many, but not all, ASD subjects fail at such tasks. According to Frith and Happé (1994), about 20% of ASD children are able to pass simple (first-order) false-belief tasks. More subtle forms of theory of mind impairments are, however, found even in subjects who pass first-order theory of mind tasks like the Sally-Ann task. For example, only 10% of ASD subjects pass advanced (second-order) versions of the task (Baron-Cohen, 1989) that require the ability to reason about the thoughts entertained by someone about somebody else's thoughts (Perner & Wimmer, 1985). The small portion of subjects who also pass these second-order theory of mind tests often fail other forms of advanced tests, such as the 'strange stories test' (Happé, 1994) requiring the subject to explain a situation of double bluff in which someone tells the truth in the hope that his enemy will be misled to believe that he is lying, or the 'reading the mind in the eyes test' (Baron-Cohen, Wheelwright, Hill, Raste & Plumb, 2001), consisting in asking subjects to identify emotions expressed by pairs of eyes and to select the appropriate adjective to describe this emotion from a list.

Some further confirmation that ASD subjects think differently than controls about social behaviors comes from a study testing their moral judgments of situations resulting from a false belief. Moran et al. (2011) tested whether adults with ASD showed sensitivity to a person's intention rather than the outcome of his actions when judging his moral behavior. For example, there is a crucial difference of intention between someone poisoning someone else by putting arsenic in his coffee while thinking that it is sugar and someone putting in arsenic knowing it is poison. They reported that contrary to controls, subjects with ASD fail to make a moral distinction between accidental harm (first case) and voluntary harm (second case). These results tend to indicate that subjects with ASD base their reasoning on facts, in this case the outcome of someone's actions, rather than his beliefs when determining moral responsibility, contrary to control subjects and typically developing children starting from the age of four (Baird & Astington, 2004; Shultz, Wright & Schleifer, 1986).

A recent set of experiments, discussed in Chapter 5 (Section 5.1.2.), revealed that typically developing children already have an implicit ability to reason about mental states between the ages of 12 to 18 months, as evidenced by their eye movements. One of the questions raised by these results is whether ASD subjects also have implicit theory of mind abilities that are obscured by the linguistic complexities of classical verbal theory of mind tasks. Senju, Southgate, White, and Frith (2009) measured the implicit theory of mind abilities of HFA adults by using the anticipatory looking task of Southgate, Senju, and Csibra (2007). Even though their HFA group performed on a par with control adults on explicit false belief tasks, HFA subjects' eye-movements did not provide any evidence that they represented the actor's false-belief, contrary to controls and typically developing two-year-olds. Schneider, Slaughter, Bayliss, and Dux (2013) used a repeated trial approach to test whether a learning process could improve ASD subjects' looking behavior over one hour of testing. They also reported that HFA subjects fail to implicitly track false beliefs and that this lack of effect did not evolve during the multiple trials of their experiment. HFA subjects in this experiment were unimpaired on explicit measures of false belief understanding. These results confirm that HFA subjects have impairments in theory of mind reasoning. They also tend to reinforce the hypothesis that ASD children who pass explicit theory of mind tests develop compensatory strategies that do not reflect generally unimpaired mindreading skills. Indeed, children with ASD who pass the false-belief test do so significantly later than typically developing children and always have a mental age of seven years or more (Happé, 1996). It seems therefore that children with ASD do not fail traditional false-belief tests because they are linguistically too complex but on the contrary, language seems to play an important role in the development of compensatory strategies that enable them to pass these tests, as verbal age is the strongest predictor of success at the task (Fisher, Happé & Dunn, 2005; Happé, 1995).

These results are in addition compatible with recent studies indicating that HFA subjects can take social cues into account when explicitly instructed to do so. For example, Wang, Lee, Sigman, and Dapretto (2007) instructed ASD subjects to "pay close attention to the face and voice" in a task of irony comprehension and found that this explicit instruction was enough to increase ASD subjects' performance. Based on these results, it has been argued that ASD subjects are not spontaneously inclined to focus their attention on social cues (e.g. Chevallier, Kohls, Troiani, Brodkin & Schultz, 2012). It could indeed be the case that ASD children develop explicit strategies helping them to compensate for their lack of implicit attunement toward social reasoning. In the next section, we discuss how this tendency is reflected in their lack of spontaneous use of pragmatic cues in verbal communication.

9.2.2. Language and communication deficits related to theory of mind

The hypothesis of a deficit in theory of mind has often been put forward to explain several language and communication deficits in the ASD population. For example, in the domain of word learning, ASD children's delay has been attributed to this deficit. Contrary to normally developing children, who are able to use the speaker's attention as a cue to assign a meaning to an unknown word by the age of 18 months (see Chapter 2, Section 2.2.1.), children with ASD form erroneous associations because they are not sensitive to such cues (Baron-Cohen, Baldwin & Crowson, 1997), and this disturbs their lexical acquisition. By contrast, Preissler and Carey (2005) found that children with ASD were able to use their prior knowledge to attribute meaning to an unknown word. In their experiment, children were presented with two pictures of objects, one familiar and the other unfamiliar. They were then asked to show the experimenter a 'blicket' (or another non-word). ASD children got 82% accuracy in the test trials. These contrasting results indicate that the problem stems specifically from ASD children's inability to use social cues rather than a more general cognitive deficit related to memory or attention.

The importance of joint attention even seems to go beyond the level of lexical acquisition. Bono, Daley, and Sigman (2004) found that the level and consistency of joint attention skills were correlated with the level of early receptive and expressive language abilities and to later language skills. McDuffie, Yoder, and Stone (2005) found that the only predictor of later language comprehension in preverbal children with ASD was the initiation of joint attention.

As far as pragmatic abilities are concerned, many difficulties encountered by subjects with ASD have been explained by their lack of theory of mind abilities. For example, pragmatic skills include the ability to manage conversations appropriately and this requires the ability to take the listener's perspective into account. Two studies have tried to exploit this relation in order to improve ASD subjects' abilities. In one of them, children with ASD have been explicitly taught techniques to pass the false-belief test in order to improve their conversational skills (Hadwin, Baron-Cohen, Howlin & Hill, 1997). In the other, they have been taught a certain number of conversational skills such as ways to initiate a conversation or to change a topic appropriately in order to improve their theory of mind skills (Chin & Bernard-Opitz, 2000). In both cases, the improvement of abilities in one domain resulting from this extensive training has led to no improvement in the other. These negative results do not necessarily imply that there is no link between these abilities. Indeed, in a longitudinal study, Hale and Tager-Flusberg (2005) compared ASD children's ability to produce relevant utterances given the discourse topic and their theory of mind skills. They reported that when measured at a given point in children's development, theory of mind abilities were the best predictor of interindividual variance in discourse skills and vice versa. However, children's abilities in one domain did not predict their development in the other domain. The correlation between these two domains is therefore genuine but ASD children's progression in one of them may reflect the development of compensatory strategies that are not carried over to other domains.

From a cognitive point of view, the relation between pragmatics and theory of mind has mainly been illustrated at the level of nonliteral language uses. In a seminal paper, Happé (1993) has studied the ability of ASD children to understand metaphors and irony, and its relation with their theory of mind abilities. She found that only ASD children who pass first-order theory of mind tests can understand metaphors and only those who pass second-order tests understand irony. There have been some criticisms (reviewed in Chapter 5, Section 5.2.1) concerning the relation between metaphors and first-order theory of mind abilities. As discussed in Chapter 6 (Section 6.1), metaphors do not require a distinct interpretation procedure compared with other utterances. The difficulty of understanding them comes from the necessity to access relevant conceptual properties of the lexically encoded concept and suppress irrelevant ones in order to build the appropriate ad hoc concept. Following this account, the inability of many ASD children to understand metaphors might have another cause than their lack of mindreading skills. Indeed, Norbury (2005a) reported that semantic knowledge, and not theory of mind abilities, is the best predictor of performance on a task of metaphor understanding. In addition, in this study, all children suffering from language impairment, with or without autistic features, had trouble understanding metaphors. The case of metaphors illustrates an important fact about pragmatic skills in autism. They imply that some of their difficulties with language use may result from impairments in the structural domains of language such as semantics. We will come back to this issue in the next section.

Contrary to metaphors, the relationship between irony and second-order theory of mind abilities has proved to be very robust. Martin and McDonald (2004) found that ASD subjects often fail to understand irony and tend to believe that the speaker producing an ironic remark is lying. The authors also tested the role of weak central coherence (see Section 9.3) and advanced theory of mind abilities for the understanding of irony and found that only theory of mind abilities are involved in the comprehension of irony. This correlation has also been reported for subjects suffering from schizophrenia (Langdon, Davies & Coltheart, 2002). In addition to ironic jokes, ASD children are also impaired in the production and comprehension of teasing behaviors, and this impairment is also partially explained by their theory of mind deficits (Heerey, Capps, Keltner & Kring, 2005).

A correlation between pragmatics and theory of mind abilities was also established in a study assessing ASD children's ability to detect violations of Grice's maxims of conversation (see Chapter 1, Section 1.1.2.). Surian (1996) found that ASD children performed at chance level on this task, contrary to typically developing and children suffering from SLI. Moreover, the performance of ASD children was related to their theory of mind abilities.

To summarize, ASD subjects lack theory of mind abilities, but a portion of them develop compensatory strategies enabling them to pass explicit theory of mind tasks late during childhood. The development of these compensatory strategies seems to be strongly related to the development of linguistic skills, as verbal IQ is an important predictor of success at theory of mind tasks. Language skills also seem to be an important factor accounting for ASD subjects' development of pragmatic skills, as illustrated in the case of metaphor comprehension. In their study of scalar implicatures, Chevallier et al. (2010) also reported that higher verbal IQ is associated with pragmatically enriched interpretations of scalar words such as 'some' in the ASD population but not in their control group.

9.3. The weak central coherence hypothesis

In addition to the ability to reason about other people's mental states, another essential ingredient for pragmatic competencies is the ability to integrate contextual information from various sources as premises to inferential processes. The psychological theory of 'weak-central coherence' (Frith, 2003; Happé, 1999) seeks to explain part of the communicative impairments of the ASD population by their inability to integrate contextual information. More specifically, the main tenet of weak central coherence theory is that autism is characterized by a specific inability to integrate information across various levels. In normal individuals, one of the main characteristics of information processing is a tendency to put together various kinds of information in order to construct a global meaning in a given context, a tendency that Frith calls 'central coherence'. For example, people tend to remember the gist of a joke but not the exact words used to tell it. This tendency to deal with information at a global rather than a local level can also be observed in people's difficulty in placing an isolated detail of a jigsaw puzzle in the global image. In sum, people find it easier to remember information when it is organized than when it is presented as a collection of unrelated items. According to Frith, this universal human tendency is still found in people suffering from various mental handicaps but is missing in people with ASD. As Happé (1999) observed, weak central coherence in autism is best thought of as a cognitive style rather than a cognitive deficit. In fact, one of the main advantages of this theory is that it can explain both the deficits and the specific talents of autism. For example, subjects with ASD have a significantly better than average memory when they have to remember a random list of items. Similarly, they get excellent results at tests involving jigsaw puzzles, even when the image is presented upside down.

Various experimental studies have related ASD subjects' communication deficits with their weak central coherence. For example, a series of experiments conducted by Jolliffe and Baron-Cohen (1999) shed light on this relationship. In a first experiment, the authors showed the link between weak central coherence and the ability to disambiguate words that are homographs but not homophones like 'tear' in context. When control subjects have to read a sentence containing a homograph they automatically adapt their pronunciation depending on the most likely meaning in context. On the other hand, ASD subjects systematically choose the most frequent pronunciation of the word, even when the context makes it clear that the other one is appropriate. In a second experiment, Jolliffe and Baron-Cohen gave ASD subjects a scenario that required the hearer to make an inference in order for the story to become coherent, as in (1). Again, subjects with ASD were unable to make this inference (i.e. 'the bath had overflowed').

(1) George left his bath water running. George cleared up the mess in the bathroom.

In a third experiment, ASD subjects had to use context in order to interpret the meaning of utterances that contained a lexical ambiguity and in (2) where 'drew' can mean either 'make a drawing of' or 'take out'. Once again, ASD subjects systematically chose the most frequent meaning, even when the context made it clear that it was inadequate, as in (3). All the control subjects naturally chose the most plausible meaning in context.

(2) He drew a gun.
(3) John went to an art class. He drew a gun.

ASD subjects' inability to use context and establish global coherence appears to be dissociated from their theory of mind abilities. For example, all subjects in Jolliffe and Baron-Cohen's experiments passed advanced theory of mind tasks, indicating that weak central coherence and mindblindness are two distinct cognitive deficits in autism.

The hypothesis of weak central coherence has, however, not been confirmed by all experimental works. While some experiments have replicated the inability of ASD subjects to disambiguate homographs in context (e.g. Hala, Pexman, & Glenwright, 2007; Happé, 1997), subjects with ASD have also been found to be able to integrate contextual information in some cases. For example, Hala et al. (2007) reported that ASD subjects are sensitive to semantic priming. Lopez and Leekam (2003) found that the inability of ASD subjects to integrate context is limited to cases of complex verbal stimuli, but is not found in non-verbal tasks or simple verbal tasks involving identifying words or semantic category. These findings imply that ASD subjects' inability to integrate context in some cases might be to due limitations of linguistic skills rather than a cognitive style biased toward local coherence.

Further doubts about the validity of the weak central coherence hypothesis were cast in a study by Norbury (2005b), who reported that, contrary to the findings of Jolliffe and Baron-Cohen, ASD subjects respond more accurately and quickly to lexical disambiguation tasks in a context biasing the interpretation toward one of the possible meanings than in a neutral context, indicating that ASD children are using context when disambiguating words. However, in this experiment, children who had a form of language impairment, independently of autistic features, did not use context as efficiently as other subjects, indicating that linguistic skills are related to the ability to use (linguistic) contextual information. Brock, Norbury, Einav, and Nation (2008) provided some further indications, by analyzing eye-movements, that ASD subjects are able to use context. In their experiment, subjects had to perform a task involving the monitoring of spoken sentences for words corresponding to objects. In their analysis of eye-movements, Brocks et al. reported that subjects with ASD were less influenced by a phonological competitor when the object was semantically incongruous with the preceding verb, indicating that they used contextual information provided by previous linguistic elements in the sentence. This effect was, however, reduced in subjects with poor language skills. It appears therefore that the inability to use preceding linguistic context during a disambiguation task is related to language difficulties rather than a generalized cognitive deficit in the integration of context.

The role of linguistic skills for the integration of context was also evidenced in the case of idioms. In a set of experiments, Norbury (2004) found that all children, including those diagnosed with ASD, understand idioms better in context, contrary to what is predicted by the weak central coherence hypothesis. However, children with language deficits, with and without autistic features, did not benefit from context as much as the other children. This result is corroborated by Cain and Towse (2008), who reported impairments in idiom comprehension in children with poor language comprehension skills who do not suffer from autism. These results thus open the possibility that some pragmatic impairments in ASD may be secondary disorders resulting from linguistic impairments rather than primary disorders (Cummings, 2009).

To summarize, it appears that ASD subjects do not suffer from a generalized inability to integrate contextual information, contrary to the predictions of weak central coherence theory. Taken together, the experiments summarized in this section indicate ASD children can integrate context in several situations, when the task is not linguistically too complex. On the other hand, language impairments have a negative effect on the ability to integrate information from the linguistic context and result in inadequate word sense disambiguation and misunderstanding of some nonliteral language uses like idioms (see also Gernbacher & Pripas-Kapit, 2012).

9.4. Synthesis

In this chapter, we described the pragmatic deficits of children suffering from autistic spectrum disorders. We discussed two psychological theories of autism, each related to one aspect of pragmatic competencies, namely the ability to reason about mental states and to integrate contextual information. We concluded that while ASD subjects do indeed lack implicit theory of mind skills leading to some deficits in verbal communication, they are not uniformly impaired in the integration of contextual information. More generally, we argued that part of the communicative impairments of the ASD population might be due to linguistic rather than pragmatic deficits. Future work should seek to clarify further the exact nature and extent of these linguistic impairments and their relation with pragmatic competencies.

Note

1 According to the American Psychiatric Association (2000), a child presents a language delay when isolated words are not produced by the age of two and sentences are not produced by the age of three.

References

American Psychiatric Association. (2000). *Diagnostic and Statistical Manual of Mental Disorders, text revision DSM IV-TR*. 4th ed. Washington, DC: American Psychiatric Association.

American Psychiatric Association. (2013). *Diagnostic and Statistical Manual of Mental Disorders DSM-V*. 5th ed. Washington, DC: American Psychiatric Association.

Arnold, J., Bennetto, L., & Diehl, J. (2009). Reference production in young speakers with and without autism: Effects of discourse status and processing constraints. *Cognition, 110*(2), 131–146.

Attwood, T. (2006). *The Complete Guide to Asperger's Syndrome.* London: Jessica Kingsley Publishing.

Baird, J. & Astington, J. (2004). The role of mental state understanding in the development of moral cognition and moral action. *New Directions for Child and Adolescent Development, 103,* 37–49.

Baltaxe, C. (1977). Pragmatic deficits in the language of autistic adolescents. *Journal of Paediatric Psychology, 2,* 176–180.

Baron-Cohen, S. (1989). The autistic child's theory of mind: A case of specific developmental delay. *Journal of Child Psychology and Psychiatry, 30,* 285–297.

Baron-Cohen, S. (1995). *Mindblindness: An Essay on Autism and Theory of Mind.* Cambridge, MA: The MIT Press.

Baron-Cohen, S. (1997). Hey! It was just a joke! understanding propositions and propositional attitudes by normally developing children, and children with autism. *Israel Journal of Psychiatry, 37,* 174–178.

Baron-Cohen, S., Baldwin, D., & Crowson, M. (1997). Do children with autism use the speaker's direction of gaze (SDG) strategy to crack the code of language? *Child Development, 68,* 48–57.

Baron-Cohen, S., Leslie, A., & Frith, U. (1985). Does the autistic child have a "theory of mind"? *Cognition, 21,* 37–46.

Baron-Cohen, S., Wheelwright, S., Hill, J., Raste, Y., & Plumb, I. (2001). The "Reading the Mind in the Eyes" test revised version: A study with normal adults, and adults with Asperger syndrome or high-functioning autism. *The Journal of Child Psychology and Psychiatry and Allied Disciplines, 42*(2), 241–251.

Bettelheim, B. (1967). *The Empty Fortress: Infantile Autism and the Birth of the Self.* New York: The Free Press.

Bono, M., Daley, T., & Sigman, M. (2004). Relations among joint attention, amount of intervention and language gain in autism. *Journal of Autism and Developmental Disorders, 34*(5), 495–505.

Brock, J., Norbury, C., Einav, S., & Nation, K. (2008). Do individuals with autism process words in context? Evidence from language-mediated eye-movements. *Cognition, 108,* 896–904.

Cain, K. & Towse, A. (2008). To get hold of the wrong end of the stick: Reasons for poor idiom understanding in children with reading comprehension difficulties. *Journal of Speech Language and Hearing Research, 51,* 1538–1549.

Chevallier, C., Wilson, D., Happé, F., & Noveck, I. (2010). Scalar inferences in autistic spectrum disorders. *Journal of Autism and Developmental Disorders, 40,* 1104–1117.

Chevallier, C., Kohls, G., Troiani, V., Brodkin, E., & Schultz, R. (2012). The social motivation theory of autism. *Trends in Cognitive Sciences, 16*(4), 231–239.

Chin, Y. & Bernard-Opitz, V. (2000). Teaching conversational skills to children with autism: Effect on the development of a theory of mind. *Journal of Autism and Developmental Disorders, 30*(6), 569–583.

Cummings, L. (2009). *Clinical Pragmatics.* Cambridge: Cambridge University Press.

de Villiers, J., Stainton, R., & Szatmari, P. (2007). Pragmatic abilities in autism spectrum disorder: A case study in philosophy and the empirical. *Midwest Studies in Philosophy, 31,* 292–317.

Diehl, J., Bennetto, L., & Young, E.C. (2006). Story recall and narrative coherence of high-functioning children with autism spectrum disorders. *Journal of Abnormal Child Psychology, 34,* 87–102.

Durrleman S. & Zufferey, S. (2013). Investigating complex syntax in autism. In Stavrakaki, S. Konstantinopoulou, P., & Lalioti, M. (eds). *Advances in Language Acquisition* (pp. 405–415). Cambridge: Cambridge Scholar Publishing.

Eigsti, I.-M., Bennetto, L., & Dadlani, M. (2006). Beyond pragmatics: Morphosyntactic development in autism. *Journal of Autism and Developmental Disorders, 37*, 1007–1023.

Emerich, D.M., Creaghead, N.A., Grether, S., Murray, D., & Grasha, C. (2003). The comprehension of humorous materials by adolescents with high-functioning autism and Asperger's syndrome. *Journal of Autism and Developmental Disorders, 33*, 253–257.

Fisher, N., Happé, F., & Dunn, J. (2005). The relationship between vocabulary, grammar, and false belief task performance in children with autistic spectrum disorders and children with moderate learning difficulties. *Journal of Child Psychology and Psychiatry, 46*(4), 409–419.

Frith, U. (2003). *Autism: Explaining the enigma*. 2nd Edition. Oxford: Blackwell.

Frith, U. & Happé, F. (1994). Autism: beyond "theory of mind". *Cognition 50*, 115–132.

García-Pérez, R., Hobson, R., & Lee, A. (2008). Narrative role-taking in autism. *Journal of Autism and Developmental Disorders, 38*, 156–168.

Gernbacher, M. & Pripas-Kapit, S. (2012). Who's missing the point? A commentary on claim that autistic persons have a specific deficit in figurative language comprehension. *Metaphor and Symbol, 27*, 93–105.

Gold, R. & Faust, M. (2010). Right hemisphere dysfunction and metaphor comprehension in young adults with Asperger syndrome. *Journal of Autism and Developmental Disorders, 40*, 800–811.

Gotham, K., Bishop, S., & Lord, C. (2010). Diagnosis of autism spectrum disorders. In D. Amaral, G. Dawson, & D. Geshwind (eds), *Autism Spectrum Disorders* (pp. 30–43). New York: Oxford University Press.

Hadwin, J., Baron-Cohen, S., Howlin, P., & Hill, K. (1997). Does teaching theory of mind have an effect on the ability to develop conversation in children with autism? *Journal of Autism and Developmental Disorders, 27*(5), 519–537.

Hala, S., Pexman, P., & Glenwright, M. (2007). Priming the meaning of homographs in typically developing children and children with autism. *Journal of Autism and Developmental Disorders, 37*, 329–340.

Hale, C. & Tager-Flusberg, H. (2005). Social communication in children with autism: The relationship between theory of mind and discourse development. *Autism, 9*, 157–178.

Happé, F. (1993). Communicative competence and theory of mind in autism: A test of relevance theory. *Cognition, 48*, 101–109.

Happé, F. (1994). An advanced test of theory of mind: Understanding of story characters' thoughts and feelings by able autistic, mentally handicapped, and normal children and adults. *Journal of Autism and Developmental Disorders, 24*(2), 129–154.

Happé, F. (1995). The role of age and verbal ability in the theory of mind task performance of subjects with autism. *Child Development, 66*, 843–855.

Happé, F. (1996). *Autism: An Introduction to Psychological Theory*. Cambridge, MA: Harvard University Press.

Happé, F. (1997). Central coherence and theory of mind in autism: Reading homographs in context. *British Journal of Developmental Psychology, 15*, 1–12.

Happé, F. (1999). Autism: Cognitive deficit or cognitive style? *Trends in Cognitive Sciences, 3*, 216–222.

Heerey, E., Capps, L., Keltner, D., & Kring, A. (2005). Understanding teasing: Lessons from children with autism. *Journal of Abnormal Child Psychology, 33*(1), 55–68.

Hobson, R., Lee, A., & Hobson, J. (2010). Personal pronouns and communicative engagement in autism. *Journal of Autism and Developmental Disorders, 40*, 653–664.

Howlin, P. (2003). Outcome in high-functioning adults with autism with and without language delays: Implications for the differentiation between autism and Asperger syndrome. *Journal of Autism and Developmental Disorders, 33*(1), 3–13.

Hus, V., Taylor, A., & Lord, C. (2011). Telescoping of caregiver report on the autism diagnostic interview – Revised. *Journal of Child Psychology and Psychiatry, 52*, 753–760.

Jolliffe, T. & Baron-Cohen, S. (1999). A test of central coherence theory: Linguistic processing in high-functioning adults with autism or Asperger syndrome: Is local coherence impaired? *Cognition, 71*(2), 149–185.

Jolliffe, T. & Baron-Cohen, S. (2000). Linguistic processing in high-functioning adults with autism or Asperger's syndrome: Is global coherence impaired? *Psychological Medicine, 30*, 1169–1187.

Kanner, L. (1943). Autistic disturbances of affective contact. *Nervous Child, 2*, 217–250.

Kelley, E., Paul, J., Fein, D., & Naigles, L. (2006). Residual language deficits in children with a history of autism. *Journal of Autism and Developmental Disorders, 36*, 807–828.

Kerbel, D. & Grunwell, P. (1998). A study of idiom comprehension in children with semantic-pragmatic difficulties. Part II: Between-groups results and discussion. *International Journal of Language and Communication Disorders, 33*, 23–44.

Kissine, M., de Brabanter, P., & Leybaert, J. (2012). Compliance with requests by children with autism: The impact of sentence type. *Autism, 16*(5), 523–531.

Kjelgaard, M.M. & Tager-Flusberg, H. (2001). An investigation of language impairment in autism: Implications for genetic sub-groups. *Language and Cognitive Processes, 16*, 287–308.

Langdon, R., Davies, M., & Coltheart, M. (2002). Understanding minds and understanding communicated meanings in schizophrenia. *Mind and Language, 17*, 68–104.

Leonard, L. (1998). *Children with Specific Language Impairment*. Cambridge, MA: MIT Press.

Lopez, B. & Leekam, S. R. (2003). Do children with autism fail to process information in context? *Journal of Child Psychology and Psychiatry, 2*, 285–300.

Loukusa, S. & Moilanen, M. (2009). Pragmatic inference abilities in individuals with Asperger syndrome or high-functioning autism: A review. *Research in Autistic Spectrum Disorders, 3*, 890–904.

Martin, I. & McDonald, S. (2004). An exploration of causes of non-literal language problems in individuals with Asperger syndrome. *Journal of Autism and Developmental Disorders, 34*, 311–328.

MacKay, G. & Shaw, A. (2004). A comparative study of figurative language in children with autistic spectrum disorders. *Child Language, Teaching and Therapy, 20*, 13–32.

McCann, J., Peppé, S., Gibbon, F., O'Hare, A., & Rutherford, M. (2007). Prosody and its relationship to language in school age children with autism. *International Journal of Language and Communication Disorders, 42*(6), 682–702.

McDuffie, A., Yoder, P., & Stone, M. (2005). Prelinguistic predictors of vocabulary in young children with autistic spectrum disorders. *Journal of Speech, Language and Hearing Research, 48*, 1080–1097.

Moran, J., Young, L., Saxe, R., Lee, S., O-Young, D., Mavros, P., & Gabrieli, J. (2011). Impaired theory of mind for moral judgments in high-functioning autism. *Proceedings of the National Academy of Sciences of the United States of America, 108*(7), 2688–2692.

Norbury, C. (2004). Factors supporting idiom comprehension in children with communication disorders. *Journal of Speech, Language, and Hearing Research, 47*, 1179–1193.

Norbury, C. (2005a). The relationship between theory of mind and metaphor: Evidence from children with language impairment and autistic spectrum disorders. *British Journal of Developmental Psychology, 23*, 383–399.

Norbury, C. (2005b). Barking up the wrong tree? Lexical ambiguity resolution in children with language impairments and autistic spectrum disorders. *Journal of Experimental Child Psychology, 90*, 142–171.

Noveck, I. & Sperber, D. (2007). The why and how of experimental pragmatics. In N. Burton Roberts (ed), *Pragmatics* (pp. 184–212). Basingstoke: Palgrave.

Ozonoff, S. & Miller, J. (1996). An exploration of right-hemisphere contributions to pragmatic impairments of autism. *Brain & Language, 52*, 411–434.

Paul, R., Augustyn, A., Klin, A., & Volkmar, F. (2005). Perception and production of prosody by speakers with autism spectrum disorders. *Journal of Autism and Developmental Disorders, 35*(2), 205–220.

Perner, J. & Wimmer, H. (1985). "John thinks that Mary thinks that ...": Attribution of second-order beliefs by 5-to 10-year old children. *Journal of Experimental Child Psychology, 39*, 437–471.

Perovic, A., Nadya M., & Wexler, K. (2013). Comprehension of reflexive and personal pronouns in children with autism: A syntactic or pragmatic deficit? *Applied Psycholinguistics, 13*(4), 813–835.

Pijnacker, J., Hagoort, P., Buitelaar, J., Teunisse, J.-P., & Geurts, B. (2009). Pragmatic inferences in high-functioning adults with autism and Asperger syndrome. *Journal of Autism and Developmental Disorders, 39*, 607–618.

Phillips, C. (2005). Electrophysiology in the study of developmental language impairments: Prospects and challenges for a top-down approach. *Applied Psycholinguistics, 26*(1), 79–96.

Preissler, M. & Carey, S. (2005). The role of inferences about referential intent in word learning: Evidence from autism. *Cognition, 97*, B13–23.

Rapin, I. & Dunn, M. (2003). Update on the language disorders of individuals on the autistic spectrum. *Brain and Development, 25*, 166–172.

Rice, M., Wexler, K., & Hershberger, S. (1998). Tense over time: The longitudinal course of tense acquisition in children with specific language impairment. *Journal of Speech, Language, and Hearing Research, 41*(6), 1412–1431.

Roberts, J., Mabel, A., Rice, L., & Tager-Flusberg, H. (2004). Tense marking in children with autism. *Applied Psycholinguistics, 25*, 429–448.

Rundblad, G. & Annaz, D. (2010). The atypical development of metaphor and metonymy comprehension in children with autism. *Autism, 14*, 29–46.

Saxe, R. & Baron-Cohen, S. (2006). Editorial: The neuroscience of theory of mind. *Social Neuroscience, 1*(3–4), i-ix.

Schneider, D., Slaugher, V., Bayliss, A., & Dux, P. (2013). A temporally sustained implicit theory of mind deficit in autism spectrum disorders. *Cognition, 129*, 410–417.

Senju, A., Southgate, V., White, S., & Frith, U. (2009). Mindblind eyes: An absence of spontaneous theory of mind in Asperger syndrome. *Science, 325*(5942), 883–885.

Sheinkopf, S., Mundy, P., Oller, D., & Steffens, M. (2000). Vocal atypicalities of preverbal autistic children. *Journal of Autism and Developmental Disorders, 30*(4), 345–354.

Shultz, T., Wright, K., & Schleifer, M. (1986) Assignment of moral responsibility and punishment. *Child Development, 57*, 177–184.

Southgate, V., Senju, A., & Csibra, G. (2007). Action anticipation through attribution of false belief by 2-years-olds. *Psychological Science, 18*(7), 587–592.

Sperber, D. (1994). Understanding verbal understanding. In J. Khalfa (ed), *What is Intelligence?* (pp. 179–198). Cambridge: Cambridge University Press.

Surian, L. (1996). Are children with autism deaf to gricean maxims? *Cognitive Neuropsychiatry, 1*, 55–72.

Tager-Flusberg, H. (2001). Understanding the language and communicative impairments in autism. *International Review of Research in Mental Retardation, 23*, 185–205.

Volden, J. (2004). Conversational repair in speakers with autistic spectrum disorder. *International Journal of Language and Communication Disorders, 39*(2), 171–189.

Wang, A., Lee, S., Sigman, M., & Dapretto, M. (2006). Neural basis of irony comprehension in children with autism: The role of prosody and context. *Brain, 129*, 932–943.

Wang, A., Lee, S., Sigman, M., & Dapretto, M. (2007). Reading affect in the face and voice: neural correlates of interpreting communicative intent in children and adolescents with autism spectrum disorders. *Archives of General Psychiatry, 64*(6), 698–708.

Wetherby, A. & Prutting, C. (1984). Profiles of communicative and cognitive-social abilities in autistic children. *Journal of Speech and Hearing Research, 27*, 364–377.

Whitehouse, A., Barry, J., & Bishop, D. (2008). Further defining the language impairment of autism: Is there a specific language impairment subtype? *Journal of Communication Disorders, 41*, 319–336.

10

PRAGMATICS AND SECOND LANGUAGE ACQUISITION

In this chapter, we discuss the development of pragmatic competencies in the course of second language acquisition. Following common usage in the literature, we refer to any language that is not a speaker's mother tongue as 'second language', even when the person speaks several other non-native languages, and independently of the context in which the language is acquired. In the first part of the chapter, we review the development of various cognitive and social pragmatic competencies in a second language. We argue that even though the cognitive inferential mechanisms underlying pragmatic competencies are universal, learners still sometimes have difficulties in drawing the appropriate inferences, because of cultural differences between their first and their second languages and of limitations in linguistic proficiency. In the second part of the chapter, we discuss research questions that are specific to second language acquisition, such as the notion of pragmatic transfer and the role of explicit teaching for the development of pragmatic competencies in a second language.

10.1. The development of pragmatic competencies in a second language

It is generally assumed in pragmatics that the cognitive skills involved in pragmatic enrichment, such as the ability to derive implicatures and reasoning about the mental states, are universal. Foster-Cohen (2000: 89) stated for example that "the pragmatics of the comprehension process in L2 learners works in exactly the same way as for native speakers." Indeed, we reported evidence in Chapter 5 that theory of mind abilities develop at the same pace in children from different cultures. In Chapter 7, we also reported evidence that children acquiring different languages present a similar ability to derive scalar implicatures. The existence of such universals does not mean, however, that second language learners may not experience difficulties in handling cognitive aspects of pragmatic competencies. In this section, we start by reviewing the acquisition of cognitive pragmatic competencies in a second language such as the ability to derive implicatures (Section 10.1.1), understand figurative language (Section 10.1.2), and handle cohesive ties such as referring expressions and discourse connectives (Section 10.1.3). We then turn to the acquisition of social and cultural aspects of pragmatic competencies, such as the use of discourse markers to regulate interpersonal relations and the role of culture on the mode of realization of speech acts (Section 10.1.4). We conclude that difficulties for second language learners exist in all these domains and are caused by the necessity to integrate culture-specific information as input for inferential reasoning, and in some cases to limitations in linguistic proficiency.

10.1.1. Understanding implicatures in a second language

A central aspect of pragmatic enrichment from a cognitive perspective is the derivation of conversational implicatures. While the cognitive faculty of drawing inferences is universal, the question remains whether Grice's maxims of conversation and the implicatures that are associated with them are universal too. In a famous study of Malagasian society of Madagascar, Keenan (1976) reported that the quantity maxim was not used in a similar manner as in the Western world, as Malagasian speakers are expected to provide less information than is required by their addressee. This ethnographic study thus provided indications that the application of some maxims may not be universal.

Another way to test the universality of Gricean maxims is to assess the way native and non-native speakers coming from different cultures use them to derive conversational implicatures. Bouton (1988) tested the ability of advanced learners coming from different cultural backgrounds as well as native English speakers to derive various types of conversational implicatures, such as indirect criticism, relevance implicatures, and irony. Results indicate that learners often fail to derive the same implicatures as native speakers, and that learners from different cultural backgrounds also differ, confirming the influence of cultural assumptions for the derivation of implicatures. In a follow-up study, Bouton (1994a) tested a sub-group of the same learners again after four-and-a-half years of residence in the United States. Significant improvements were observed in the derivation of implicatures, with learners reaching an almost native-like competence in many cases and no specific type of implicature remaining systematically problematic. Bouton (1994a: 167) noted that "each item missed after 4½ years was simply linked to a specific culture point with which the subjects were not yet familiar." Bouton (1994a) also tested advanced learners twice within a 17-months interval and found that most of the implicatures that were problematic in the first testing session remained so in the second one. These results indicate that learners do improve in their ability to derive implicatures but that this improvement spans over many years.

The role of culture as an explanatory factor for learners' difficulties to derive some implicatures is also corroborated by studies focusing on implicatures that are shared across cultures. In a study focusing on generalized scalar implicatures, Slabakova (2010) tested the interpretation of scalar words such as 'some' by intermediate and advanced Korean learners of English, as well as native Korean and English speakers. She reported first that both groups of native speakers do not differ in their interpretation of scalar words, confirming that the scalar words tested function in a similar manner across the two languages. Second, no differences were found between the two groups of learners, indicating that scalar interpretations are available as soon as the words that trigger them are acquired. Crucially, results also indicate that learners do not have more difficulties deriving a pragmatically enriched meaning for scalar words than native speakers. In fact, Korean learners of English produced significantly more pragmatic interpretations of 'some' than native English and Korean speakers performing the task in their first language. These results provide some indications that scalar implicatures are not effortful to process (see Chapter 7, Section 7.1.2). Otherwise learners, who have limited processing resources compared with native speakers, should derive them less often.

Taken together, these results tend to indicate that the difficulties of implicatures are mostly related to cultural rather than cognitive difficulties. For this reason, while some types of implicatures such as generalized implicatures triggered by scalar words are easy even for learners with an intermediate level of proficiency, others such as relevance implicatures and irony require a long period of exposure before learners grasp them. In Section 10.2.2, we discuss whether explicit teaching can speed up this process.

Indirect speech acts represent yet another form of pragmatic enrichment by implicature. In Chapter 3, we concluded that children's ability to produce and understand them depended on the difficulty of the linguistic formulation and the complexity of the inferential process involved. One question for second language research is whether similar factors account for learners' difficulty to understand indirect speech acts. Contrary to children acquiring their first language, second language learners already possess a fully-fledged ability to derive implicatures in their first language that they can carry over to their second language, as long as deriving these implicatures does not require the use of cultural background knowledge that they ignore. By contrast, the limited linguistic abilities of learners before they reach a high fluency could prevent them from understanding some indirect formulations that are linguistically complex. Foster-Cohen (2000) also argued that lack of linguistic knowledge may lead learners to derive a very incomplete or even faulty logical form as a starting point for pragmatic processes, which in turn is likely to lead to a different utterance interpretation compared with native speakers. In Chapter 3, we reported that similar aspects of syntactic complexity affect children's ability to understand indirect speech acts in their first language. The role of linguistic complexity for learners' understanding of indirect speech acts received some confirmation in a study by Carrell (1981), who compared the ability of learners from four proficiency levels—ranging from low intermediate to advanced—to understand various forms of indirect requests. Carrell included 10 different formulations for the same speech act, consisting in requesting the hearer to color or not to color a circle blue. The formulations involved several degrees of indirectness and also several levels of syntactic complexity. Results indicate that differences between groups of learners were not related to the degree of indirectness, and therefore to the complexity of the inferential reasoning involved. While learners from all levels had no difficulty understanding indirect formulations such as (1), a difference between groups was observed for requests formulated in syntactically more complex ways, especially those involving interrogative (2), and negative formulations (3).

(1) I'll be very happy if you make the circle blue.
(2) Why color the circle blue?
(3) I'll be very happy unless you make the circle blue.

The role of language proficiency for learners' ability to understand implicatures was replicated in several other studies (but see Bouton, 1988). For instance, Roever (2005) reported a strong relationship between learners' ability to understand implicatures and their overall L2 proficiency, independently of the number of years of residence in the country. Taguchi, Li, and Liu (2013) reported that the level of proficiency affects learners' accuracy in interpreting implicated meaning as well as the speed at which they access this meaning.

Another important issue for the study of indirect speech acts, discussed in Chapter 3 (Section 3.1.2), is the hypothesis that some conventionalized forms frequently used to convey indirect speech acts may involve short-circuited implicatures, rendering them easier to process in communication. A question for second language research is whether differences also exist between the ability to understand conventional and unconventional forms to convey indirect speech acts. Taguchi et al. (2013) compared the ability of second language learners of Chinese to understand conventional and non-conventional implicatures used for conveying indirect refusals and found that conventional refusals were easier than non-conventional ones to understand. They noted that this result may be due to the fact that the conventional formulations used to indirectly make a refusal, such as the use of a rhetorical question, also exist in English, contrary to the unconventional refusals. Thus, learners may have been helped because of positive transfer (see Section 10.2.1) from their first language. This study does not therefore provide indications about the role of conventionalization in a second language when no similar forms exist in the learners' first language.

In conclusion, adult learners already possess the cognitive ability to draw inferences, and this ability enables them to understand implicit meaning in a second language, as long as the complexity of the linguistic formulation or the need to integrate culture-specific premises do not prevent them to do so. Foster-Cohen

(2000, 2004) argued more specifically that lack of linguistic knowledge leads to an incomplete or faulty logical form used as input to inferential processing and lack of cultural knowledge affects the cognitive context that is brought to bear during the inferential processes of utterance interpretation. We will discuss in Section 10.1.4 how cultural differences sometimes also prevent learners from understanding the sociocultural contexts in which speech acts are used, even when they understand their illocutionary force.

10.1.2. Understanding figurative language in a second language

Even though metaphors and irony both represent cases of figurative language uses, they involve different interpretation procedures, as argued in Chapter 6. In this section, we review the ability of learners to understand both figures of speech in turn.

We discussed in Chapter 6 two theories accounting for the role of metaphors in communication and cognition, namely cognitive linguistics and relevance theory. Both accounts predict some universals in the processes of metaphor formation and comprehension. First, according to cognitive linguistics, many basic level conceptual metaphors rely on bodily experience and should therefore be universal. Second, according to relevance theory, metaphors correspond to cases of ad hoc concepts, derived by inference based on salient properties of lexically encoded concepts, and such a derivation procedure is expected to be universal across languages and cultures. Yet, even though cross-linguistic research has confirmed the existence of many shared conceptual metaphors across cultures, differences are found as well, due to the weight attributed to source domain entities and events in a given culture and to the attitude that speakers hold toward the vehicle of a metaphor across cultures (e.g. Deignan, 2003; Deignan & Potter, 2004; Kövecses, 2003; Littlemore & Low, 2006).

Cross-cultural differences also affect the derivation procedure of metaphors, because the salience of conceptual features on which the ad hoc concept is built depends on cultural connotations. In a study assessing the role of conceptual metaphors for second language learner's ability to understand metaphors, Charteris-Black (2002) tested whether the difficulties of Malay-speaking learners of English to understand metaphors were related to differences of conceptual metaphors between Malay and English. Results indicate that metaphors relying on shared conceptual metaphors across the two languages are the easiest to understand. However, when similar figurative forms are used to express different conceptual metaphors across languages, or when metaphors rely on culture-specific forms, learners understand them less well. Charteris-Black also reported that when learners are processing unfamiliar figurative language in their second language, they resort to the conceptual basis provided by their first language. Thus, cultural background seems to be indeed an important factor for metaphor processing. Littlemore (2003) further assessed the effect of cultural background for Bangladeshi students' understanding of the metaphors used by a lecturer during a university course in English. She asked 18 students to explain the meaning of seven metaphors in context and to indicate how they perceived that the metaphor reflected the teacher's opinion on the subject, and also to provide their own opinion. Littlemore hypothesized that cultural differences between the Bengali and the British cultures, for example, in terms of power distance and uncertainty avoidance, would prevent students from understanding the meaning of some metaphors as well as the attitude the teacher conveyed by using them. Results confirm that students are indeed more likely to interpret metaphors in a way that is compatible with their own cultural values. Even when they correctly understand the meaning of a metaphor, they tend to relate it to their own rather than the teachers' cultural values. These difficulties disappeared, however, when the context made the intended meaning clear. Thus, it seems that learners are not conditioned by the cultural values of their society and can use context to override some of their cultural biases when they interpret non-literal language uses in a second language.

In addition to an understanding of cultural values, deriving metaphorical meaning also requires the possession of conceptual knowledge in order to be able to select relevant features for the formation of ad hoc concepts. Understanding metaphors in a second language is therefore also likely to depend on linguistic proficiency, and more specifically on the general level of language comprehension. The existence of such a relation between understating figurative meaning and understanding language has already been emphasized in Chapter 9 (Section 9.2.2), in the case of atypical pragmatic development. Indeed, several studies have demonstrated that the ability to understand metaphors and idioms is highly dependent on language comprehension skills (Cain, Oakhill & Lemmon, 2005; Cain & Towse, 2008; Norbury, 2004). In the field of second language acquisition, Doroodi and Hashemian (2011) reported that students with higher levels of reading comprehension skills are better able to understand idioms than less proficient students.

In addition to linguistic and cultural knowledge, another explanation for learners' ability to understand metaphors is that it could be related to their inclination to interpret metaphorical meaning in their first language. More specifically, some people who are prone to understand meaning in a metaphorical manner in their mother tongues may carry this advantage over to their second language, despite linguistic limitations. Littlemore (2010) reported that metaphorical competencies in first and second languages are indeed interrelated. She tested four aspects of metaphoric competence, such as metaphorical fluency (i.e. the number of associations triggered by a metaphor) and speed of access to metaphorical meaning. In her experiments, advanced learners scored lower in their second than in their first language only in the domain of metaphor fluency. Littlemore argued that this limitation can be attributed to the greater difficulty of linguistically formulating metaphorical associations in a second language, in other words to linguistic rather than cognitive limitations, as the speed of access to metaphorical meaning was not lower in learners compared with native speakers.

Similarly to metaphors, the comprehension of irony by second language learners is also dependent on the general level of proficiency (Shively, Menke &

Manzón-Omundson, 2008). Contrary to metaphors, however, understanding irony does not require building an ad hoc concept, but to understand the higher-order intention conveyed by the speaker. Building this metarepresentation is associated with advanced theory of mind abilities, representing a universal in human cognition (see Chapter 6, Section 6.2.1). It is therefore expected that second language learners should not be generally impaired with pragmatic skills related to theory of mind abilities. However, some forms of irony also rely on an allusion to cultural facts or norms (e.g. Wilson & Sperber, 1992). In such cases, cultural knowledge is required in addition to linguistic and mindreading skills in order to understand irony. It is expected that understanding such forms of irony could be problematic for second language learners who have not yet acquired the relevant aspects of the target culture. Bouton (1994a) provided some indications that understanding irony is indeed problematic because of lack of cultural knowledge. He observed that even after 17 months of residence in the United States, learners still had problems understanding Bill's remark in (4) as ironic:

(4) Context: Bill and Peter have been good friends since they were children. They roomed together at college and traveled Europe together after graduation. Now friends have told Bill that they saw Peter dancing with Bill's wife while he was away.
Bill: Peter knows how to be a really good friend.

About half of the learners thought that Bill's remark implied that he thought that Peter was a good friend and could be trusted. As Bouton (1994a: 163) noted, this interpretation reflects totally different attitudes toward marriage, friendship, and what the fact of dancing with someone implies, than the American ones.

In sum, even though metaphors and irony rely on distinct cognitive faculties, the problems encountered by second language learners to understand them are related to the same factors as those involved in other forms of pragmatic enrichment: limitations in linguistic proficiency and ignorance of the relevant cultural assumptions. The cognitive abilities involved for understanding figurative language (lexical adjustment and theory of mind abilities) are universal and carried over from the learners' first to their second languages.

10.1.3. Discourse pragmatic competencies in a second language

We discussed in Chapter 8 two discursive phenomena, namely the use of referential expressions and discourse connectives. In this section, we report learners' ability to deal with both discursive phenomena.

A crucial component of effective referential communication lies in the use of referring expressions reflecting an appropriate degree of accessibility for the audience (see Chapter 8, Section 8.1). While linguistic indications of accessibility exist in many languages, considerable cross-linguistic variations are observed in the form and distribution of referring expressions (see Chapter 4, Section 4.2.1). For this reason, it is expected that learners coming from a first language that has different means to express the accessibility of referents than the target second language may experience problems during the acquisition process. In order to assess the role of learners' first language, Crosthwaite (2013) compared the productions of referring expressions in English by learners ranging from beginner to advanced levels, with Korean and Mandarin mother tongue. Results from this corpus study indicate that at lower levels of proficiency, learners from both mother tongues fail to incorporate syntactic markings of reference, but gradually incorporate them when they reach higher levels of linguistic proficiency. In addition, a significant difference emerged between the two groups of learners, with Korean-speaking learners producing more errors at all levels of language learning than Mandarin-speaking learners. Crosthwaite related this effect to the nature of reference marking in the learners' first languages. More specifically, Mandarin learners may have an advantage over Korean learners because in Mandarin, numerals and demonstratives have a potential for grammaticalization resembling the English reference system. In other words, these learners may use positive transfer (see Section 10.2.1), thus increasing their ability to use accessibility markers in English. These results reflect the fact that using referring expressions requires linguistic proficiency but also a pragmatic awareness of the procedural instructions of accessibility that they encode. Developing this awareness is difficult for learners coming from languages where similar procedural markers do not exist.

Discourse connectives represent yet another type of discourse relational devices that learners must acquire in order to produce cohesive texts and discourses. Even though many languages possess a set of discourse connectives (Dixon & Aikenvald, 2009) in most cases no one-to-one mappings between connectives can be established, even between typologically related languages (Degand, 2004; Zufferey & Cartoni, 2012). For this reason, discourse connectives are difficult lexical items to master in a second language, and numerous studies report that production errors remain even in learners with a high level of proficiency (Altenberg & Tapper, 1998; Crewe, 1990; Field & Yip, 1992; Granger & Tyson, 1996; Müller, 2005; Tapper, 2005). In these studies, learners have been found to be overusing some connectives while underusing others compared with their average frequency in the productions of native speakers, as well as misusing some of them. The causes for these misuses include first language transfer (see Section 10.2.1) and limitations in second language proficiency. Some studies have also revealed that these difficulties might result from an inability to use connectives already in learners' first language. For example, Nelson and Huang (2002) investigated the overuse and underuse of connectives in English by comparing essays written by non-native speakers in Hong-Kong and native speakers in Great Britain and found that both populations tend to overuse connectives compared with professional academic writing. In a nutshell, discourse connectives represent complex lexical items to master even in a first language and their complexity is confirmed by the difficulty of second language learners to grasp the full extent of the procedural instructions they encode.

10.1.4. Social and cultural aspects of pragmatic development in a second language

In order to become pragmatically proficient, learners must come to appreciate which speech acts are adequate in a given situation in addition to the ability to understand and produce them. We argued in Chapter 4 (Section 4.2.1) that the mode of realization of speech acts varies across languages and cultures. We discussed, for example, the continuum of indirectness going from West to East, with English and German speakers favoring the communication of requests by conventional indirect means whereas Polish and, to an even greater extent, Russian speakers favor direct means and achieve politeness by the use of mitigators (Ogiermann, 2009). Blum-Kulka, House, and Kasper (1989) also reported many cross-cultural differences in the modes of performing speech acts such as requests and apologies across five different languages and cultures (Canadian French, Australian English, German Argentine Spanish, and Hebrew). It is therefore expected that second language learners will experience difficulties adapting to the mode of productions of speech acts in a second language with different communication norms, even when they possess the necessary linguistic competence to convey the intended act (Walters, 1980). Many studies have confirmed this difficulty.

Woodfield (2008) reported, for example, that Japanese learners use significantly more direct forms and less mitigators to express requests compared with native English speakers and German learners, a result that the author attributes to a lack of proficiency preventing them from using indirect formulations, as well as to false stereotyping, leading Japanese learners to exaggerate the use of direct forms perceived as being socially acceptable in the English-speaking culture.

Refusals constitute another face-threatening speech act with high potential for variations across cultures. In their analysis of refusals produced by Persian learners of English, native English speakers and native Persian speakers, Allami and Naeimi (2011) reported several cultural differences (see also Mirzaei, Roohani & Esmaeili, 2012). While speakers from both cultures frequently produced excuses and explanations as a motivation for refusal, English speakers were more direct whereas Persian speakers were more vague and implicit. In addition, while English speakers were insensitive to the power status of their addressee when formulating a refusal, Persian speakers showed great variations depending on the perceived status of their addressee. In a similar comparison of refusals among American English speakers and Chinese learners, Chang (2009) reported that American speakers use more direct refusals than Chinese learners, because of differences of communication styles between China and America. Chang also reported that some comments made by Chinese learners after refusing someone with a lower status rank, for example, urging a maid to be more careful in the future after refusing her offer to pay for a broken vase, were absent from the American data. Chang attributed this difference to the more hierarchical society of China, and its greater perception of power relations compared with American culture. In addition, some excuses typically provided by Chinese learners for refusing someone were also totally absent from the native speakers' repertoire, also reflecting differences of cultures. Similar examples of variations between native speakers and foreign language learners' mode of realization for speech acts abound in the early literature on second language pragmatic development (see Ellis, 1994 for a review).

We argued in Chapter 4 (Section 4.1.1) that discourse markers could also reflect interpersonal relations. The use of discourse markers has also been an object of enquiry in second language research, with results that are variable across markers and discourse functions. For example, while Buysse (2012) reported that all functions of 'so' are used by Dutch-speaking learners of English, Aijmer (2011) reported that the discourse marker 'well' is overused by Swedish-speaking learners as a fluency device but underused as marker of speaker's attitude. Differences between markers were also observed for the same learner. Polat (2011) studied the use of the three discourse markers 'you know', 'like', and 'well' in a developmental learner corpus of one Turkish-speaking adult learner of English over one year. She reports great fluctuations in the use of the three discourse markers. While 'you know' was used with a very high frequency at the beginning of the year and steadily declined later on, 'well' was never used with a discourse marker function. The discourse marker 'like' was not used at all at the beginning of the year, then heavily used some months later and used much less again at the end of the year. Taken together, these studies reveal that when learners incorporate lexical items functioning as discourse markers in their mental lexicon, they do not always use them with all the functions and in the same situations as native speakers. This reflects the fact that sociocultural norms of communication need to be learned as well as the lexical items themselves before these markers can be used with their target functions. The mastery of discourse markers in a second language also depends on the existence of markers with similar functions in the learners' first language, as we argue in Section 10.2.

10.2. First versus second language acquisition

A major difference between first and second language acquisition is that speakers acquiring a second language already possess a fully-fledged linguistic system in their mind. An important question for second language research is therefore to what extent the speakers' first language and also all the other languages they already know influence their acquisition of a second language, a phenomenon called 'language transfer' (Odlin, 1989). In this section, we start by discussing the notion of transfer and its manifestations in the domain of pragmatic competencies (Section 10.2.1). Then we examine what needs to be taught so that learners develop pragmatic competencies and also whether explicit teaching techniques can speed up the acquisition process compared to exposure alone (Section 10.2.2).

10.2.1. Pragmatic transfer

The manifestations of language transfer in the structural aspects of language acquisition have long been studied in second language research. More recently, researchers have also investigated the possibility that transfer also occurs for pragmatic competencies. Kasper (1992: 207) defined the notion of pragmatic transfer as "the influence exerted by learners' pragmatic knowledge of languages and cultures other than L2 on their comprehension, production and learning of L2 pragmatic information." Kasper noted that both the types of formulations used (called 'pragmalinguistic' knowledge) and cultural assumptions (called 'sociopragmatic' knowledge) can be the object of pragmatic transfer. In his definition of language transfer, Ellis (1994: 341) noted that "the study of transfer involves the study of errors (negative transfer), facilitation (positive transfer), avoidance of target language forms and their overuse." We argue in this section that pragmatic transfer can take all these different forms as well.

One of the best-known manifestations of pragmatic transfer is 'negative transfer', in other words interferences from the first language preventing learners from reaching native-like competencies. Examples of negative transfer have been found in many areas of pragmatic competencies. For example, in the case of discourse connectives, Zufferey, Mak, Degand, and Sanders (submitted) found that advanced learners were unable to identify misuses of English connectives in a grammaticality judgment task only when these misuses corresponded to a licensed use in their first language. On the production side, negative transfer also affects learners' uses of discourse markers and connectives. For example, the use of 'comme' by English-speaking learners of French mimics the uses of the discourse marker 'like' in English (Sankoff et al., 1997). Liu (2013) also reported several transfer effects in Chinese learners' use of English discourse markers. These learners use markers in syntactic positions and with discourse functions that are absent from the speech of native English speakers but that correspond to possible uses in Chinese. For example, they use the marker 'ah' in clause medial position to introduce self-corrections, a usage that is absent from native speakers' speech but corresponds to a possible use of the Chinese marker 'a'. Another example of negative transfer in the domain of speech acts concerns the expression of gratitude by Chinese learners of English, which may take inappropriate forms such as 'I am sorry' because in Chinese, the target gratitude marker 'thank you' would be considered as insufficiently sincere and is therefore not used in such situations (Richards & Sukwiwat, 1983).

Weizman (1993) noted that 'positive transfer' exists in pragmatics as well, when some forms and functions found in the first language have equivalents in the second language and therefore help the learners from such languages to use them appropriately. Weizman gives the example of hints, a form of indirect speech act that is used for indirect requests in many different languages, with the consequence that the learners of English and Hebrew she examined used these forms of requests correctly in their second language. Taguchi et al. (2013) noted that the ability of English learners of Chinese to understand some conventional forms of indirect refusals could be due to the existence of similar strategies in English, leading to positive transfer. Kasper and Schmidt (1996: 155) noted, however, that "whereas learners may hesitate to transfer strategies that may be universal in some cases, a more common problem is that they assume universality (and transferability) when it is not present." Thus one aspect of learners' difficulties may result from their erroneous assumptions about the way communication works across cultures, leading to a lack of positive transfer as well as negative transfer effects.

Pragmatic transfer can also affect the propensity to use some forms and avoid others. Richards and Sukwiwat (1983) noted, for example, that Thai speakers learning English may find that this language lacks appropriate high honorifics, leading them to overuse honorifics and titles like 'sir' in English. Examples of overuse due to transfer were also often observed on the literature on discourse connectives. For instance, Granger and Tyson (1996) noted that French-speaking learners of English overuse corroborative connectives such as 'in fact', 'indeed', and 'actually' because of the frequent use of the connective 'en effet' in French. Conversely, Kasper (1992) noted an avoidance of the discourse marker 'I mean' by German-speaking learners even though an equivalent expression 'Ich meine' is also frequently used in German. Further investigation revealed that the learners wrongly perceived this usage as specific to German, and this false belief prevented them from using positive transfer.

For a long time, research on transfer effects mostly focused on the effects of learners' first language on their use and understanding of a second language. Recent research has shown, however, that transfer might be more accurately defined as a mutual process, in which the learning of a second language, when learners reach a high proficiency level, also influences the use of their first language (e.g. Pavlenko & Jarvis, 2002). In the case of pragmatic competencies, an example of mutual transfer was found in the use of requests. Blum-Kulka (1990) reported that a group of American immigrants to Israel produced requests that did not fully correspond either to English or Hebrew patterns. These speakers used a level of indirectness that was situated between the direct Hebrew and indirect American styles, corresponding to what she calls an 'intercultural style' (Blum-Kulka, 1991). A similar example of intercultural style was found in the formulation of requests by native Spanish speakers who spoke English fluently. Cenoz (2003) reported that these learners have a style of requesting that does not fully correspond to either English or Spanish standards.

An important question for studies of transfer is whether this phenomenon evolves as learners achieve greater proficiency. Studies investigating the relations between language proficiency and transfer have, however, yielded conflicting findings. On the one hand, some authors (Koike, 1996; Maeshiba, Yoshinaga, Kasper & Ross, 1996) report a negative correlation between language proficiency and the likelihood of transfer. In their experiments, advanced learners were better able than intermediate ones to identify contexts where an apology strategy could or could not be used, leading to a diminution of negative transfer. On the other hand, other authors (e.g. Takahashi & Beebe, 1987) argue that transfer strategies require the ability to analyze the components of complex speech acts, something that advanced learners are more likely to do than less proficient ones, leading to greater negative transfer when learners become more proficient. Conflicting results are also found in studies focusing on the same pragmatic phenomenon. For instance, Allami and Naeimi (2011) reported a positive correlation between Persian learners' level of English and their transfer of first language strategies of refusal. In contrast, Chang (2009) does not report a greater transfer in the formulations used to convey refusals as the proficiency of Chinese learners of English increases. The lack of consensual results on this question may indicate that transfer does not operate in the same way for all pragmatic phenomena and learners, and that other cognitive and cultural factors may be more important than linguistic proficiency to account for this phenomenon.

Methodological considerations are also important in the study of transfer effects, as several studies have found that transfer effects are not always replicated across different empirical methods, even when they involve the same learners. For example, Roberts, Gullberg, and Indefrey (2008) reported that German-speaking learners perform on a par with native Dutch speakers on the resolution of ambiguous subject pronouns in an off-line task, contrary to Turkish-speaking learners who reached a lower performance. The authors explain this effect by differences in the learners' first languages: German is a non-null subject language like Dutch, whereas Turkish is a null subject language. A similar transfer effect was, however, not found in an eye-tracking experiment, as both groups of learners performed lower than native speakers. The authors conclude that the processing limitations experienced by learners in an on-line task could override transfer effects. In contrast, Zufferey et al. (submitted) report that transfer is an important factor preventing advanced learners from identifying misuses of connectives in a grammaticality judgment task. In an eye-tracking experiment, the same learners did however show a native-like ability to implicitly detect misuses of connectives, and were immune to transfer effects. The authors conclude that advanced learners may go through a phase of implicit knowledge preceding the explicit ability to discriminate correct from incorrect uses of connectives, similar to the phase of implicit learning evidenced in several aspects of first language acquisition (Chapter 8, Section 8.1.3) and cognitive development (Chapter 5, Section 5.1.2). Thus the use of an on-line task produced opposite results in both studies: they hindered the ability of learners to resolve ambiguous pronouns while revealing their sensitivity to misuses of connectives. These two studies illustrate the fact that transfer effects as well as cognitive factors influencing pragmatic competencies differs across pragmatic phenomena.

In sum, one of the main characteristics of second language acquisition as opposed to first language acquisition is that learners already possess linguistic and cultural knowledge in at least one language and culture. Studying the influence of these pre-existing competencies is therefore crucial for understanding the way learners develop pragmatic competencies in a second language. Recent research has shown that transfer can take many different forms and affect both first and second language performance. These effects are sometimes variable across tasks and such variability should be taken into account before strong conclusions can be reached about native languages' influences on the use and understanding of a second language.

10.2.2. Teaching pragmatic competencies

Explicit teaching is involved in most cases of second language acquisition. In the case of pragmatic competencies, however, the usefulness of teaching is still often questioned on the grounds that second language learners bring with them a wealth of universal pragmatic knowledge that they can simply reuse in their second language by positive transfer. In addition, when pragmatic competencies are taught, such teaching is only included at very advanced stages, under the assumption that pragmatic competencies rest on full-fledged structural language skills. In this section, we question these assumptions and report evidence that teaching pragmatic skills can have a beneficial influence of learners' performance, even before learners reach high proficiency levels.

In a meta-analysis of studies involving language instruction, Norris and Ortega (2002) concluded that instruction is effective for second language acquisition and that explicit instruction leads to more robust improvements than implicit instruction. In the domain of pragmatic competencies, studies have demonstrated the benefits of teaching in many different areas as well. For example, Bouton (1994b) tested whether teaching learners how to interpret a range of implicatures could help them to improve their ability to interpret them faster than the four years that were necessary to see improvements when only natural immersion in American culture took place (see Section 10.1.1). He compared the performances of a group of students tested before and after explicit teaching over a six week period corresponding to about six hours of instructions, focusing on five types of implicatures (relevance, Pope Q, irony, indirect criticism, and sequence). Results indicate that six weeks of instructions were enough to get learners to perform on a par with students who had spent between 17 months to over four years on campus. However, significant differences emerged between different types of implicatures. For implicatures that involved highly routinized formulations and that were initially the hardest types for learners, such as the Pope Q implicatures (involving the use of a rhetorical question to answer another question by analogy), great improvement was observed. For particularized implicatures such as relevance implicatures, for which no systematic routine can be established, little progress was observed on those of the items that learners had difficulties to understand. These results indicate that teaching is effective to help learners to identify a pattern that can be generalized to new implicatures. When no such pattern exists and the interpretation of implicature is solely dependent on context, as it is the case with relevance implicatures, teaching is not effective because each occurrence requires new inferences that cannot be generalized to other implicatures. These findings were replicated with Japanese learners of English in Japan. Kubota (1995) reported that learners who received explicit instruction about implicatures and those who performed consciousness-raising tasks through group discussions significantly improved their ability to derive implicatures compared with a control group. Other examples of positive effects of teaching were reported in the domain of speech act uses (Billmyer, 1990; Olshtain & Cohen, 1990; Rose & Ng, 2001) and more specifically on the use of politeness mitigators for the production of face threatening acts (Fukuya & Clark, 2001; Takahashi, 2001). Progress was also observed in the domains of conversational management (Liddicoat & Crozet, 2001; Wildner-Bassett, 1986, 1994) and discourse marker usage (Yoshimi, 2001).

Despite explicit teaching and years of immersion, studies on the development of the structural components of a second language have long observed that some mistakes become fossilized, in other words they persist even at the ultimate stages of language development. In the domain of pragmatics, fossilization has not been thoroughly researched, possibly because non-native-like pragmatic behaviors are more difficult to identify than grammatical or phonological errors, and are sometimes assimilated with learners' personality traits. For example, inadequate requesting behaviors in fluent non-native speakers may be assimilated to rude personality instead of an inability to perform the speech act adequately. Some studies have, however, described forms of pragmatic fossilization. In one of them, Romero Trillo (2002) observed fossilization in the way proficient adult learners still failed to appropriately use discourse markers such as 'you know', 'you see', and 'I mean'. Another example reported by Takahashi (1996) concerned the perception of request strategies by Japanese learners of English, who even after seven to 10 years of instruction still failed to perceive the functional differences between the two languages. Scarcella (1983) also reported that highly proficient Spanish-speaking learners of English still fail to use conversational features adequately even after 12 to 17 years of residence in the United States starting before the age of seven. The mistakes made by these learners were recurrent and systematic, leading Scarcella to conclude that they had been transferred during earlier stages of language development and became fossilized. Further work is needed to explore the possibility that other components of pragmatic competencies can lead to fossilization.

So far, we reviewed evidence that teaching pragmatic skills leads to significant improvements in many areas of pragmatic competencies. An important practical issue from a pedagogical perspective is to identify the factors that influence the outcome of teaching. Kasper and Rose (2002) noted that a number of potentially important factors such as the nature of the target language and its relation with the learners' first language and the age of the learners have not been thoroughly investigated in the literature. Indeed, most studies focus on English as a second language and almost all of them focus on adults learning a language at the university level. In addition to teaching techniques, a range of environmental factors such as attitude and motivation may also explain the inter-individual variations in learners' successes in acquiring a second language (Kasper & Rose, 2002).

Finally, teaching pragmatic competencies raises the question of when learners are more likely to benefit from such instruction during the course of second language acquisition. Even though it is an open question whether all aspects of pragmatic competencies can be taught to beginning learners, studies have demonstrated that at least some pragmatic routines can be taught successfully at this level (Tateyama, 2001). Conversely, the study of Bouton described above indicates that even advanced learners can benefit from explicit teaching of pragmatic competencies. This issue brings into question the nature of the interrelations between pragmatic competencies and structural components of language, in other words how linguistically proficient learners need to be in order to develop and use pragmatic competencies. Research on the pragmatics/grammar interface in second language acquisition indicates that some pragmatic competencies are already put to use by learners in the absence of a correct grammar, due to positive transfer of pragmatic universals (Eisenstein & Bodman, 1986). For example, several studies report attempts to apologize or request by learners who lack the linguistic competence to formulate these speech acts in a grammatically correct manner. However, other studies also note that lack of grammatical knowledge hinders learners' ability to perform pragmatically adequate acts. For example, Salsbury and Bardovi-Harlig (2000) noted that a learner's limited knowledge of modal verbs prevented him from formulating disagreement in a polite manner. Other studies have also observed that highly proficient learners sometimes fail to use the grammatical structures that they know to perform the appropriate function, or to use them in a socially appropriate way (e.g. Beebe & Takahashi, 1989). In sum, structural components of language and pragmatics are not acquired in sequence but are in many ways interrelated. Learners bring pragmatic knowledge from their first language that they can put to use even when they lack the knowledge to express it correctly in a second language. Conversely, even when they reach high levels of proficiency, learners sometimes fail to grasp all the pragmatic functions associated with some words like modal verbs and discourse connectives in a second language, leading to inappropriate uses.

10.3. Synthesis

In this chapter, we surveyed the acquisition of pragmatic competencies in a second language. We argued that even though second language learners can use their universal cognitive abilities to enrich the linguistic meaning of utterances in a foreign language, they still experience difficulties in many areas of pragmatic competencies due to the necessity to integrate culture-specific knowledge as input to inferential processes. In addition, at lower levels of proficiency, lack of linguistic knowledge also prevents learners from making the correct form-function mappings. In the second part of the chapter, we presented evidence that transfer effects play an important role for second language learners' ability to understand and use pragmatic skills in a second language and that the development of pragmatic skills does benefit from explicit teaching strategies, especially when patterns can be generalized.

References

Aijmer, K. (2011). Well I'm not sure I think... The use of well by non-native speakers. *International Journal of Corpus Linguistics, 16*(2), 231–254.

Allami, H. & Naeimi, A. (2011). A cross-linguistic study of refusals: An analysis of competence development in Iranian EFL learners. *Journal of Pragmatics, 43*, 385–406.

Altenberg, B. & Tapper, T. (1998). The use of adverbial connectors in advanced Swedish learners' written English. In S. Granger (ed), *Learner English on Computer* (pp. 80–93). London: Addison-Wesley Longman.

Beebe, L. & Takahashi, T. (1989). Do you have a bag? Social status and patterned variation in second language acquisition. In S. Gass, C. Madden, D. Preston, & L. Selinker (eds), *Variation in Second Language Acquisition: Discourse and Pragmatics* (pp. 103–128). Clevedon: Multilingual Matters.

Billmyer, K. (1990). "I really like your lifestyle": ESL learners learning how to compliment. *Working Papers in Educational Linguistics, 6*(2), 31–48.

Blum-Kulka, S. (1990). You don't touch lettuce with your fingers: Parental politeness in family discourse. *Journal of Pragmatics, 14*, 259–288.

Blum-Kulka, S. (1991). Interlanguage pragmatics: The case of requests. In R. Phillipson, E. Kellerman, L. Selinker, M. Sharwood Smith, & M. Swain (eds), *Foreign/Second Language Pedagogy Research* (pp. 255–272). Clevedon: Multilingual Matters.

Blum-Kulka, S., House, J., & Kasper, G. (1989). *Cross-Cultural Pragmatics: Requests and Apologies*. Norwood, NJ: Ablex.

Bouton, L. (1988). A cross-cultural study of ability to interpret implicatures in English. *World Englishes, 7*, 183–196.

Bouton, L. (1994a). Conversational implicature in a second language: Learned slowly when not deliberately taught. *Journal of Pragmatics, 22*(2), 157–167.

Bouton, L. (1994b). Can NNS skill in interpreting implicature in American English be improved through explicit instruction? A pilot study. In L. Bouton, & Y. Kachru (eds), *Pragmatics and Language Learning* (pp. 89–109). Urbana-Champaign: University of Illinois.

Buysse, L. (2011). So as a multifunctional discourse marker in native and learner speech. *Journal of Pragmatics, 44*, 1764–1782.

Cain, K., Oakhill, J., & Lemmon, K. (2005). The relation between children's reading comprehension level and their comprehension of idioms. *Journal of Experimental Child Psychology, 90*, 65–87.

Cain, K. & Towse, A. (2008). To get hold of the wrong end of the stick: Reasons for poor idiom understanding in children with reading comprehension difficulties. *Journal of Speech Language and Hearing Research, 51*, 1538–1549.

Carrell, P. (1981). Relative difficulty of request forms in L1/L2 comprehension. In M. Hines & W. Rutherford (eds), *On TESOL'81* (pp. 141–152). Washington: TESOL.

Cenoz, J. (2003). The intercultural style hypothesis: L1 and L2 interaction in requesting behavior. In V. Cook (ed), *Effects of the Second Language on the First* (pp. 62–80). Clevedon: Multilingual Matters.

Chang, Y.-F. (2009). How to say no: An analysis of cross-cultural difference and pragmatic transfer. *Language Sciences, 31*, 477–493.

Charteris-Black, J. (2002). Second language figurative proficiency: A comparative study of Malay and English. *Applied Linguistics, 23*, 104–133.

Crewe, W. (1990). The illogic of logical connectives. *ELT Journal, 44*(4), 316–325.

Crosthwaite, P. (2013). An error analysis of L2 English discourse reference through learner corpora analysis. *Linguistic Research, 30*(2), 163–193.

Degand, L. (2004). Contrastive analyses, translation and speaker involvement: The case of *puisque* and *aangezien*. In Achard, M. & Kemmer, S. (eds), *Language, Culture and Mind* (pp. 251–270). Chicago: The University of Chicago Press.

Deignan, A. (2003). Metaphorical expressions and culture: An indirect link. *Metaphor and Symbol, 18*(4), 255–271.

Deignan, A. & Potter, L. (2004). A corpus study of metaphors and metonyms in English and Italian. *Journal of Pragmatics, 36*, 1231–1252.

Dixon, R.M. & Aikhenvald, A. (eds) (2009). *The Semantics of Clause Linking. A Cross-Linguistic Typology*. Oxford: Oxford University Press.

Doroodi, S. & Hashemian, M. (2011). The relationship between reading comprehension and figurative competence in L2 learners. *Theory and Practice in Language Studies, 1*(6), 711–717.

Eisenstein, M. & Bodman, J. W. (1986). 'I very appreciate': Expressions of gratitude by native and non-native speakers of American English. *Applied Linguistics, 7*, 167–185.

Ellis, R. (1994). *The Study of Second Language Acquisition*. Oxford: Oxford University Press.

Field, Y. & Yip, L. (1992). A comparison of internal cohesive conjunction in the English essay writing of Cantonese speakers and native speakers of English. *RELC Journal, 23*, 15–28.

Foster-Cohen, S. (2000). Review article. In D. Sperber, & D. Wilson (1986, 1995). *Relevance: Communication and Cognition. Second Language Research, 16*(1), 77–92.

Foster-Cohen, S. (2004). Relevance theory and second language learning/behavior. *Second Language Research, 20*(3), 189–192.

Fukuya, Y. & Clark, M. (2001). A comparison of input enhancement and explicit instruction of mitigators. In L. Bouton (ed), *Pragmatics and Language Learning* (pp. 111–130). Urbana Champaign, IL: University of Illinois.

Granger, S. & Tyson, S. (1996). Connector usage in English essay writing of native and non-native EFL speakers of English. *World Englishes, 15*, 19–29.

Kasper, G. (1992). Pragmatic transfer. *Second Language Research, 8*, 203–231.

Kasper, G. & Rose, K. (2002). *Pragmatic Development in a Second Language*. Oxford: Blackwell.

Kasper, G. & Schmidt, R. (1996). Developmental issues in interlanguage pragmatics. *Studies in Second Language Acquisition, 18*, 149–169.

Keenan, E. (1976). The universality of conversational postulates. *Language and Society, 5*, 67–79.

Koike, D. (1996). Transfer of pragmatic competence and suggestions in Spanish foreign language learning. In S. Gass & J. Neu (eds), *Speech Acts Across Cultures: Challenges to Communication in a Second Language* (pp. 257–281). New York: Mouton de Gruyter.

Kövecses, Z. (2003). Language, figurative thought and cross-cultural comparison. *Metaphor and Symbol, 18*(4), 311–320.

Kubota, M. (1995). Teachability of conversational implicature to Japanese EFL learners. *IRLT Bulletin, 9*, 35–67.

Liddicoat, A.J. & Crozet, C. (2001). Acquiring French interactional norms through instruction. In K.R. Rose, & G. Kasper (eds), *Pragmatics in Language Teaching* (pp. 125–144). Cambridge: Cambridge University Press.

Littlemore, J. (2003). The effect of cultural background on metaphor interpretation. *Metaphor and Symbol, 18*(4), 273–288.

Littlemore, J. (2010). Metaphoric competence in the first and second language: Similarities and differences. In M. Pütz, & L. Sicola (eds), *Cognitive Processing in Second Language Acquisition: Inside the Learner's Mind* (pp. 293–316). Amsterdam: John Benjamins.

Littlemore, J. & Low, G. (2006). *Figurative Thinking and Foreign Language Learning*. New York: Palgrave Macmillan.

Liu, B. (2013). Effects of first language on the use of English discourse markers by L1 Chinese speakers of English. *Journal of Pragmatics, 45*, 149–172.

Maeshiba, N., Yoshinaga, N., Kasper, G., & Ross, S. (1996). Transfer and proficiency in interlanguage apologizing. In S. M. Gass, & J. Neu (eds), *Speech Acts Across Cultures: Challenges to Communication in a Second Language* (pp. 155–187). New York: Mouton de Gruyter.

Mirzaei, A., Roohani, A., & Esmaeili, M. (2012). Exploring pragmalinguistic and sociopragmatic variability in speech act production of L2 learners and native speakers. *The Journal of Teaching Language Skills, 4*(3), 79–102.

Müller, S. (2005). *Discourse Markers in Native and Non-native English Discourse*. Amsterdam: John Benjamins.

Norbury, C. (2004). Factors supporting idiom comprehension in children with communication disorders. *Journal of Speech, Language, and Hearing Research, 47*, 1179–1193.

Norris, J. & Ortega, L. (2000). Effectiveness of L2 instruction: A research synthesis and quantitative meta-analysis. *Language Learning, 50*, 417–528.

Odlin, T. (1989). *Language Transfer*. Cambridge: Cambridge University Press.

Ogiermann, E. (2009). Politeness and in-directness across cultures: A comparison of English, German, Polish and Swedish requests. *Journal of Politeness Research, 5*, 189–216.

Olshtain, E. & Cohen, A. (1990). The learning of complex speech act behavior. *TESL Canada Journal, 7*, 45–65.

Pavlenko, A. & Jarvis, S. (2002). Bidirectional transfer. *Applied Linguistics, 23*(2), 190–214.

Polat, B. (2011). Investigating acquisition of discourse markers though a development learner corpus. *Journal of Pragmatics, 43*, 3745–3756.

Richards, J. & Sukwiwat, M. (1983). Language transfer and conversational competence. *Applied Linguistics, 4*(2), 113–125.

Roberts, L., Gullberg, M., & Indefrey, P. (2008). Online pronoun resolution in L2 discourse. L1 influence and general learner effects. *Studies in Second Language Acquisition, 30*, 333–357.

Roever, C. (2005). *Testing ESL Pragmatics*. Frankfurt: Peter Lang.

Romero Trillo, J. (2002). The pragmatic fossilization of discourse markers in non-native speakers of English. *Journal of Pragmatics, 34*, 769–784.

Rose, K. & Ng, C. (2001). Inductive and deductive teaching of compliments and compliment responses. In K. Rose, & G. Kasper (eds), *Pragmatics in Language Teaching* (pp. 145–170). Cambridge: Cambridge University Press.

Salsbury, T. & Bardovi-Harlig, K. (2000). "I know what you mean, but I don't think so": Disagreement in L2 English. In L. Bouton (ed), *Pragmatics and Language Learning* (pp. 1–25). Urbana-Champaign, IL: University of Illinois.

Sankoff, G., Thibault, P., Nagy, N., Blondeau, H., Fonollosa, M.-O., & Gagnon, L., (1997). Variation in the use of discourse markers in a language contact situation. *Language Variation and Change, 9*, 191–217.

Scarcella, R. (1983). Discourse accent in second language performance. In S. Gass & L. Selinker (eds), *Language Transfer in Language Learning*, (pp. 306–326). Rowley: Newbury House.

Shively, R., Menke, M., & Manzón-Omundson, S. (2008). Perception of irony by L2 learners of Spanish. *Issues in Applied Linguistics, 16*(2), 101–132.

Slabakova, R. (2010). Scalar implicatures in second language acquisition. *Lingua, 120*(10), 2444–2462.

Taguchi, N., Li, S., & Liu, Y. (2013). Comprehension of conversational implicature in L2 Chinese. *Pragmatics and Cognition, 21*(1), 139–157.

Takahashi, S. (1996). Pragmatic transferability. *Studies in Second Language Acquisition, 18*, 189–223.

Takahashi, S. (2001). The role of input enhancement in developing pragmatic competence. In K. Rose, & G. Kasper (eds), *Pragmatics in Language Teaching* (pp. 171–199). Cambridge: Cambridge University Press.

Takahashi, T. & Beebe, L. (1987). The development of pragmatic competence by Japanese learners of English. *JALT Journal, 8*, 131–155.

Tapper, M. (2005). Connectives in advanced Swedish EFL learners' written English: Preliminary results. *The Department of English: Working Papers in English Linguistics, 5*, 115–144.

Tateyama, Y. (2001). Explicit and implicit teaching of pragmatic routines: Japanese *sumimasen*. In K. Rose, & G. Kasper (eds), *Pragmatics in Language Teaching* (pp. 200–222). Cambridge: Cambridge University Press.

Walters, J. (1980). Grammar, meaning, and sociological appropriateness in second language acquisition. *Canadian Journal of Psychology, 34*, 337–345.

Weizman, E. (1993). Interlanguage requestive hints. In G. Kasper, & S. Blum-Kulka (eds) *Interlanguage Pragmatics* (pp. 123–137). Oxford: Oxford University Press.

Wildner-Bassett, M. (1986). Teaching and learning 'polite noises': Improving pragmatic aspects of advanced adult learners' interlanguage. In G. Kasper (ed), *Learning, Teaching, and Communication in the Foreign Language Classroom* (pp. 163–177). Aarhus: Aarhus University Press.

Wildner-Bassett, M. (1994). Intercultural pragmatics and proficiency: 'Polite' noises for cultural awareness. *International Review of Applied Linguistics in Language Teaching, 32*, 3–17.

Wilson, D. & Sperber, D. (1992). On verbal irony. *Lingua, 87*, 53–76.

Woodfield, H. (2008). Interlanguage requests: A contrastive study. In M. Putz & J.N. Aerselaer (eds), *Developing Contrastive Pragmatics and Cross-Cultural Perspectives* (pp. 231–264). Berlin: Mouton de Gruyter.

Yoshimi, D. (2001). Explicit instruction and JFL learners' use of interactional discourse markers. In K. Rose & G. Kasper (eds), *Pragmatics in Language Teaching* (pp. 223–244). Cambridge: Cambridge University Press.

Zufferey, S. & Cartoni, B. (2012). English and French causal connectives in contrast. *Languages in Contrast, 12*(2), 232–250.

Zufferey, S., Mak, W., Degand, L., & Sanders, T. (submitted). Advanced learners' comprehension of discourse connectives: The role of L1 transfer across on-line and off-line tasks *Second Language Research.*

CONCLUSION

Throughout the book, we reviewed the acquisition of a range of pragmatic competencies. The general picture resulting from this overview is that the acquisition of pragmatic competencies spans over a very long period of time, starting before language production begins and continuing until late during childhood, in the following sequence. Before language production begins, children already display pragmatic competencies evidenced by their eye-movements and their pointing behaviors. For example, through their pointing behaviors, children show sensitivity to the informational needs of their addressee based on contextual information. Young children also possess implicit theory of mind abilities already around their first birthday. Between the age of two to three, children produce and understand both direct and indirect forms used to convey basic speech acts such as requests. Between the ages of three to four, they become able to modulate the use of referring expressions depending on the accessibility of the referent for their addressee. By the age of four, children understand metaphorical meaning in context, and a majority of them also become able to derive scalar implicatures related to words such as 'some' and 'or' as evidenced in simple experimental settings. By the age of six, children understand irony when contextual and prosodic cues are salient. From the age of eight, children are able to use the procedural instructions of commonly used connectives such as 'because' and 'but' for sentence processing. By the age of 10, children come to grasp the felicity conditions underlying complex speech acts like promises.

It is widely assumed in the literature that pragmatic competencies are acquired late, and that their acquisition begins only when structural language competencies are already in place. For example, Papafragou and Skordos (to appear) note that for this reason "many researchers thought it safe to assume that theories of lexical and grammatical development can be advanced without considering the development of the pragmatic component." We demonstrated, however, that even though the acquisition of pragmatic competencies continues until late childhood, the assumption that young children lack them completely must be radically changed. Indeed, the basic cognitive faculties underlying pragmatic competencies, namely inferential reasoning, mental state attribution and integration of contextual information are operational even before children start producing their first words. Origgi and Sperber (2000) argued that in phylogeny, inferential communication appeared before language and enabled the development of communication by means of a linguistic system. The picture resulting from the acquisition of pragmatic competencies suggests that a similar sequence could be observed in ontogeny, with children's ability to engage in inferential communication preceding their mastery of a linguistic code and to some extent enabling its development. We argued for instance in Chapter 2 that children's early theory of mind abilities guide them in the process of word learning and that once language starts to develop, a mutual bootstrapping takes place (de Villiers, 2007).

Why then, if the basic cognitive ingredients underlying pragmatic competencies are operational when language production begins, do children fail to become pragmatically proficient earlier? Part of the answer to this question lies in the fact that deriving pragmatic inferences for verbal communication requires the possession of complex linguistic and conceptual knowledge in addition to pragmatic competencies, and this hinders young children's ability to engage in inferential communication. For example, in Chapter 3, we reported that children's ability to understand and produce indirect speech acts depended on the complexity of the linguistic structure rather than the degree of indirectness, as children produce indirect speech acts already at the telegraphic stage of language development (Ervin-Tripp, 1977). We also argued that the complexity of some indirect speech acts depended on the type of conceptual knowledge that had to be integrated as premises to the inferential reasoning. The possession of conceptual knowledge is also essential for understanding metaphorical meaning and pragmatically enriching the meaning of scalar words. We argued in Chapter 6 that metaphor understanding was strongly dependent on the correct selection of salient conceptual features and the suppression of irrelevant ones. In Chapter 7, we reported that an important factor preventing young children from deriving scalar implicatures was their lack of semantic and conceptual knowledge about the way words are related on a scale. Thus, it should not come as a surprise that the acquisition of pragmatic competencies taking language as input data must wait until the required linguistic and conceptual competencies become operational. However, contrary to what was often argued, this does not mean that young children lack the basic competencies to engage in inferential communication, as the recent body of literature of early theory of mind abilities has revealed.

In addition to linguistic and conceptual development, specific factors must be called upon to explain the rather late acquisition of some pragmatic competencies. In the case of irony, children's comprehension rests on the possession of advanced theory of mind abilities, which become operational only around the age of five or six. Social reasoning is also involved for the understanding of speech acts like promises. In this particular case, mastery is achieved only around the age of 10 because in addition to developing advanced theory of mind abilities, children also need to learn a set of cultural and social rules. Finally, in addition to linguistic and conceptual limitations, it is likely that young children's pragmatic skills are also limited by lack of processing resources in working memory. Indeed, limitations in working memory have been argued to affect computations at the syntax/pragmatics interface for adults (see Reinhart, 2006 for a discussion) and it is likely that these limitations affect children even more due to their more limited resources. Limitations in working memory have been recently called upon to explain the delay between the development of implicit and explicit theory of mind abilities (see Carruthers, 2013 for a discussion). The role of working memory limitations for the development of pragmatic competencies remains, however, to a large extent an underexplored question that future work in the field will need to address.

From a methodological perspective, the study of pragmatic competencies lacked until recently the appropriate tools to assess children's development. Many early studies involved a form of metalinguistic judgment that artificially delayed the age of success and even provided an inaccurate picture of the sequence of acquisition between several pragmatic competencies (Bernicot, Laval & Chaminaud, 2007). In recent experimental designs, care is taken to present children with plausible tasks in context, for example, the derivation of communicated rather than potential implicatures (Papafragou & Tantalou, 2004); children are required to act rather than provide metalinguistic judgments (Pouscoulous, Noveck, Politzer & Bastide, 2007); and comprehension is assessed with online measures of eye-movements during utterance interpretation (Huang & Snedeker, 2009). These new research paradigms remain to be applied to a wider range of pragmatic phenomena in order to reassess children's developing pragmatic competencies, while avoiding the confounds of earlier methods. Given the active trend of research in developmental pragmatics during the past decade, it is expected that many advances will be made in the near future and it is likely that future research will further reveal the wealth of pragmatic competencies already possessed by young children, paving the way for the integration of pragmatic competencies in the study of children's early linguistic and cognitive development.

References

Bernicot, J., Laval, V., & Chaminaud, S. (2007). Nonliteral language forms in children: In what order are they acquired in pragmatics and metapragmatics? *Journal of Pragmatics*, *39*, 2115–2132.

Carruthers, P. (2013). Mindreading in infancy. *Mind & Language*, *28*(2), 141–172.

de Villiers, J. (2007). The interface of language and theory of mind. *Lingua*, *117*, 1858–1878.

Ervin-Tripp, S. (1977). Wait for me, roller skate! In S. Ervin-Tripp & C. Mitchell-Kernan (eds), *Child Discourse* (pp. 165–188). New York: Academic Press.

Huang, Y.T. & Snedeker, J. (2009). Online interpretation of scalar quantifiers: Insight into the semantic-pragmatics interface. *Cognitive Psychology*, *58*, 376–415.

Origgi, G. & Sperber, D. (2000). Evolution, communication and the proper function of language. In P. Carruthers, & A. Chamberlain (eds), *Evolution and the Human Mind: Language, Modularity and Social Cognition* (pp. 140–169). Cambridge: Cambridge University Press.

Papafragou, A. & Skordos, D. (to appear). Implicature. In J. Lidz, W. Snyder, & J. Pater (eds), *The Oxford Handbook of Developmental Linguistics*. Oxford: Oxford University Press.

Papafragou, A. & Tantalou, N. (2004). Children's computation of implicatures. *Language Acquisition*, *12*(1), 71–82.

Pouscoulous, N., Noveck, I., Politzer, G., & Bastide, A. (2007). A developmental investigation of processing costs in implicature production. *Language Acquisition*, *14*, 347–376.

Reinhart, T. (2006). *Interface Strategies. Optimal and Costly Computations*. Boston: The MIT Press.

INDEX

UNIVERSITIES AT MEDWAY LIBRARY